365 DAYS OF POWER

*Personalized Prayers and Confessions
To Build Your Faith and Strengthen Your Spirit*

By Rick Renner

Harrison House
Tulsa, Oklahoma

All Scripture quotations are taken from the *King James Version* of the Bible.

11 10 09   14 13 12 11

365 Days of Power:
Personalized Prayers and Confessions To
Build Your Faith and Strengthen Your Spirit
ISBN 13: 978-1-57794-719-6
ISBN 10: 1-57794-719-3
Copyright © 2004 by Rick Renner
P.O. Box 1709
Tulsa, OK 74101-1709

Published by Harrison House, Inc.
P.O. Box 35035
Tulsa, OK 74153

Introduction

365 Days of Power is a powerful collection of prayers and confessions that are designed to help you grow strong in your walk with God. Each devotional prayer and correlated confession is based on a powerful Scripture and an in-depth Greek word study taken from Rick Renner's 1,100-page devotional, *Sparkling Gems From the Greek*. This smaller version, containing all the original prayers and confessions, is designed to make it easy for you to read and apply these "gems" of God's truth on a daily basis.

When you pray and confess the Word over your life every day, you will strengthen your inner man and grow in faith and confidence. Never underestimate the power of God's Word. It is full of life and will minister healing and strength to you in every area!

God's Peace for Your Heart

My Prayer for Today

Lord, I don't want to let my emotions get the best of me today, so I ask that Your peace would rise up like a mighty umpire and referee in my heart, mind, and emotions. Help me recognize those moments when unhelpful emotions try to sneak up on me. I ask You to teach me how to put those emotions aside and release Your supernatural peace that is resident in my heart—the peace that is always ready at every moment to moderate every thought and emotion that tries to pass into my life. I pray this in Jesus' name!

And let the peace of God rule in your hearts, to the which also ye are called in one body; and be ye thankful.

Colossians 3:15

My Confession for Today

I confess that God's supernatural peace dominates me. When I am tempted to get upset and my emotions try to take control of me, I put these emotions aside and allow the Spirit of God to release a supernatural, dominating, moderating peace to rule my heart, mind, and emotions. I declare this by faith in Jesus' name!

Strength To Make It Through Your Day

For I know that this shall turn to my salvation through your prayer, and the supply of the Spirit of Jesus Christ.

Philippians 1:19

My Prayer for Today

Lord, I realize I don't have enough strength by myself to do what You have asked me to do. Today I'm asking You to donate a new supply of Your Spirit into my life. Right now, I open my heart and ask You to fill every nook and cranny of my life with the power of the Holy Spirit so I can get back on my feet again and fulfill what You have told me to do. I pray this in Jesus' name!

My Confession for Today

I declare by faith that I am refilled and recharged with the Spirit of God. There is no lack of strength in me because Jesus continuously provides a huge supply of the Spirit in my life that empowers me to achieve everything I need to do. There is no excuse for me to fail or to stop short of the goals God has given me for my life, because in the Spirit of God there is enough supernatural strength and power to energize me to finish my divine assignment. I declare this by faith in Jesus' name!

Recalling God's Deliverance in Your Life

My Prayer for Today

Lord, You have always been faithful. I thank You that even in my present situation, You are going to be faithful again. Please help me recall all the times in the past when You delivered and rescued me from other situations that also looked hopeless. Thank You for helping me keep those awesome experiences alive and fresh in my mind and heart. I thank You for always being faithful to me! I pray this in Jesus' name!

Wherefore I put thee in remembrance that thou stir up the gift of God, which is in thee by the putting on of my hands.

2 Timothy 1:6

My Confession for Today

I confess that God has never failed me or let me down. He has always delivered me from difficult times, and He will rescue and deliver me now as well. Today I will dwell on those past moments when God did for me what everyone thought was impossible. Just as He intervened on my behalf in the past, He will intervene on my behalf again! I will not succumb to fear, doubt, or failure. With God's help, I will conquer what the enemy meant for my downfall and defeat. I declare this by faith in Jesus' name!

Faithful in Prayer

Praying always with all prayer and supplication in the Spirit, and watching thereunto with all perseverance and supplication for all saints.

Ephesians 6:18

My Prayer for Today

Lord, I ask You to help me become consistent in prayer. I admit that other things have distracted me from being in Your Presence, but I ask You to forgive me for this and to give me the strength to say no to those things that keep pulling me away from time in prayer. Thank You for helping me to make this a high priority in my life. I know that with Your help, I can learn to discipline myself to pray. Thank You for helping me get started on the right path today! I pray this in Jesus' name!

My Confession for Today

With God's help, I have the power to say no to the distractions that keep trying to steal my time with God. Prayer is a top priority in my life; therefore, I am consistent and habitual in my prayer time. Nothing is a higher priority than the time I spend every day with God. From this moment onward, I will be as faithful as can be when it comes to this issue of prayer. I declare this by faith in Jesus' name!

Do Not Grieve the Holy Spirit

My Prayer for Today

Lord, I ask You to forgive me for allowing attitudes and actions in my life that are dishonoring to You. I want to please You more than ever before, so I ask You to help me recognize those negative things in my life that cause You pain. Help me to permanently walk free of them. From the depths of my heart, I thank You for all You have done inside me. Starting right now, I want to live every moment of my life with the intent to please You and to never cause You grief again. I pray this in Jesus' name!

And grieve not the Holy Spirit of God, whereby ye are sealed unto the day of redemption.

Ephesians 4:30

My Confession for Today

Starting today, I make the choice to walk away from everything in my life that is displeasing and desecrating to the Holy Spirit's Presence within me. I walk away from every negative thought, word, and deed that has tried to operate in me and that is dishonoring to Him. I turn the other direction to walk a new walk and talk a new talk that shows respect and love for the Spirit of God who dwells inside me. I declare this by faith in Jesus' name!

Free From Wrong Attitudes

Wherefore lay apart all filthiness and superfluity of naughtiness, and receive with meekness the engrafted word, which is able to save your souls.

James 1:21

My Prayer for Today

Lord, help me step out of the sins and bad attitudes that have held me captive for so long. Help me know the right steps to take to remove these destructive and unworthy things from my life. You want me to be free, and I desire to be free. With Your help, I know I can be permanently set free from these negative things, stepping out of them and pushing them so far away that I will never pick them up again! I pray this in Jesus' name!

My Confession for Today

The Word of God reveals those areas in my life that are unclean and that need to change. Rather than act like a victim who cannot do anything about myself or my circumstance, today I start the process of acknowledging my sin and removing these attitudes, actions, and sins that are unworthy of who I am today in Christ. I can be free, and I will be free. I will be ALL that God intended for me to be! I declare this by faith in Jesus' name!

Putting God's Word Into Practice

My Prayer for Today

Lord, I ask You to help me become a doer of the Word and not a hearer only. Forgive me for the times I've heard the Word of God preached in power and even said "Amen" to the message, yet failed to walk out the truth I heard or to make it a part of my life. Starting today, I make the decision to be a doer of the Word of God. Holy Spirit, give me the strength and divine energy I need to take the Word I hear or read and put it into practice in my life. I pray this in Jesus' name!

> *But be ye doers of the word, and not hearers only, deceiving your own selves.*
>
> *James 1:22*

My Confession for Today

I declare that I am a doer of the Word of God. I am among those who hear the Word and immediately apply it to their lives. I experience the power of God's Spirit in my life because of my obedience to walk in what God has revealed to me. I declare this by faith in Jesus' name!

Speak the Truth in Love

*And others save
with fear....*

Jude 1:23

My Prayer for Today

Lord, help me know exactly what to say and what to do when I see fellow brothers or sisters who are headed in a wrong spiritual direction. Give me Your heart, Your wisdom, and Your boldness to speak the words I need to speak. Help me love them enough to speak the truth to them. I realize the consequences of sin are great, so please help me do everything within my ability to see them rescued as soon as possible. I pray this in Jesus' name!

My Confession for Today

I confess that I am moved to action when I see fellow believers caught in sin. I pray and believe for their deliverance. I go to them in love to express my concerns to them. I love them enough to speak the truth. I act fast on their behalf and do what I can to save them. I declare this by faith in Jesus' name!

Thankful for Good Friends

My Prayer for Today

Lord, You have blessed me with the most wonderful friends—and today I want to thank You for putting such great people in my life. Long-term, real friends are such a treasure, so I want to start this day by thanking You for these gifts of precious relationships. Help me never lose sight of how much I need these people. Help me also to never fail to show them how much I love and appreciate them. I pray this in Jesus' name!

[I] cease not to give thanks for you, making mention of you in my prayers.

Ephesians 1:16

My Confession for Today

I am thankful for the relationships God has placed in my life. They are a blessing to me, and I am a blessing to them. God brought us together, and Satan will not tear us apart. I will learn to love them more dearly, forgive them more quickly, and show them the same patience I want them to show me. I am richly blessed with some of the best friends I could ever ask for! I declare this by faith in Jesus' name!

Learn To 'Follow the Leader'

For as many as are led by the Spirit of God, they are the sons of God.

Romans 8:14

My Prayer for Today

Lord, I want to learn how to follow the leading of the Holy Spirit. I know that You sent Him to be a Leader and a Guide for my life, so today I open my heart to Him. I ask You to help me learn to recognize the Holy Spirit's voice and to know what He is leading me to do. With all my heart, I request that You help me become sensitive to Him so that He can lead me in all the paths You have designed for my life. I pray this in Jesus' name!

My Confession for Today

I confess that I am spiritually sensitive and that the Holy Spirit is actively leading my life. I am His constant tag-along—watching what He's doing, where He's going, and how He's leading. I am so sensitive to the Holy Spirit's leading that I pick up every "nudge" He puts in my heart. He is my Leader, and I faithfully follow wherever He leads me to go. I declare this by faith in Jesus' name!

Walk as the New Creature You Are

My Prayer for Today

Lord, I thank You for washing me with the blood of Jesus and for making me brand new. Forgive me for clinging to my old ways of thinking and of doing things. Today I ask You to help me drop those old habits and attitudes and to never pick them up again. By myself, this would be almost impossible, but I know that by Your power, I can walk free. Right now, I release those old attitudes and habits that I've been carrying around with me for so long. I ask You to help me think and behave in a way that's consistent with the new creature in Jesus Christ You have made me to be. I pray this in Jesus' name!

*Therefore if any man be in Christ, he is a **new creature**: old things are passed away; behold, all things are become new.*

2 Corinthians 5:17

My Confession for Today

I declare by faith that I am free from wrong habits and attitudes from my past. I have laid them down, and I am free of them forever. Now I have the mind of Christ, the power of the Spirit, and the fruit of Jesus Christ working inside my life. I declare this by faith in Jesus' name!

You Are a Receptacle for the Power of God!

Finally, my brethren, be strong in the Lord and in the power of his might.

Ephesians 6:10

My Prayer for Today

Lord, it is clear that You want me to be filled with Your power and strength today, so I open my heart right now and ask You to fill me with Your Spirit. Thank You for creating me to be the receptacle for this wonderful power—and by faith, I receive a fresh infilling of Your Spirit right now! I pray this in Jesus' name!

My Confession for Today

I declare by faith that I am filled with the Spirit of God. I am specially made by God to be the container of the Holy Spirit. He lives in me, He fills me, and He empowers me to conquer every attack that the devil tries to bring against me. God knew I needed this power and therefore gave it to me. I boldly confess that I am filled with the supernatural, wonder-working, and dynamic power of the Holy Spirit! I declare this by faith in Jesus' name!

Fellowshipping With the Saints

My Prayer for Today

Lord, I ask You to help me push my flesh and my feelings aside when I am tempted to be down and depressed. Your Word promises that I'll be encouraged if I fellowship with the saints, so I ask You to help me shove my lying emotions out of the way, get out of my house, and stop focusing on my defeat. Give me the strength of will to go attach myself to a band of believers who will encourage me to stand up, stand tall, and fight like someone who has the armor and the power of God working in my life. I pray this in Jesus' name!

Not forsaking the assembling of ourselves together, as the manner of some is....

Hebrews 10:25

My Confession for Today

I declare that Satan does not have the power to keep me down and depressed! When life comes against me and the devil tries to tell me that I have no hope of ever getting out of my problems, I run to people of faith so I can get encouraged. I don't fall out of fellowship, and I don't stay away from church. I am faithful in my church attendance, and I receive encouragement every time I get in God's Presence and rub shoulders with the people of God. I declare this by faith in Jesus' name!

Live Life as an Encourager

And let us consider one another to provoke unto love and to good works. Not forsaking the assembling of ourselves together, as the manner of some is; but exhorting one another....

Hebrews 10:24,25

My Prayer for Today

Lord, today I want to be used by You to encourage someone. I ask You to lead me to those You want me to encourage. Show me what to say, how much to say, and when to say it. Teach me to recognize the needs in other people and not to focus only on my own needs. I pray this in Jesus' name!

My Confession for Today

I confess that I am going to be a major blessing in someone's life today. The Holy Spirit is going to open my eyes and show me exactly whom I am supposed to encourage. With the help of the Spirit, I will speak the right words at the right time, and I will say only as much as I need to say. When this day concludes, someone will thank God for the way I stepped into his or her life to be a source of encouragement. I declare this by faith in Jesus' name!

Get Creative in 'Doing the Word'

My Prayer for Today

Lord, I ask You to help me think of new ways to do the Word of God. You have all the fresh ideas I'll ever need, so I am looking to You to show me how to put the Word into practice in my life. You are full of creative power and fresh ideas, so please open my eyes and show me how I can serve, how I can bless someone else, or any other way I can become obedient to do the Word that has been revealed so powerfully in my life. I pray this in Jesus' name!

But be ye doers of the word, and not hearers only, deceiving your own selves.

James 1:22

My Confession for Today

I declare that I never run short of ideas on how to walk out the Word that has been preached to me. I do what I've heard; I obey what I've read; and I get better and better every day at finding ways to put into operation the Word that God has so graciously brought into my life. I declare this by faith in Jesus' name!

Pay Attention to Yourself

Take heed to thyself....

1 Timothy 4:16

My Prayer for Today

Lord, help me remember not to neglect my own spiritual life. My time with You is vital if I am to remain spiritually fresh and empowered to serve others. When life gets so busy that I think there is no time to spend with You, help me refocus and reschedule my life so that my relationship with You remains my greatest priority. And after I've been refreshed by Your Word and Your Presence, help me then to minister the fullness of Your Spirit and Your love to those around me. I pray this in Jesus' name!

My Confession for Today

I boldly proclaim by faith that my spiritual life is my number-one priority. I pay attention to my walk with God, and I do everything I can do to make sure my spiritual life is alive, growing, and constantly reaching out for more of the Lord. I am sensitive to God's Spirit. I am attuned to His Word. As a result of putting my own spiritual life first, I am filled with enough power and love to adequately serve the needs of those who are around me. I declare this by faith in Jesus' name!

Overcoming Obstacles in Your Life

My Prayer for Today

Lord, I've run into an impasse, and I don't know how to get past it by myself. I have done everything I know to do, but the problem continues to persist in my life. Today I am asking You for the strength I need to keep pushing forward and to overcome the obstacles that Satan has set in my path. I know that greater is He who is in me than he that is in the world, so today I fervently ask that the power of God residing within me be released to overcome each attack the devil has tried to bring against me. I pray this in Jesus' name!

Wherefore we would have come unto you, even I, Paul, once and again; but Satan hindered us.

1 Thessalonians 2:18

My Confession for Today

I know I am not the first to encounter difficulties. Therefore, I confess that with God's help, the devil's attack will cease and the way for me to move ahead will become clear. God is going to give me the exact wisdom I need to get where I need to go. I am not going to give in just because I've hit some kind of impasse. The devil has never had the last word on anything, and he isn't going to have the last word on this situation either! I declare this by faith in Jesus' name!

Turning Dead-End Situations Around

But we had the sentence of death in ourselves, that we should not trust in ourselves, but in God which raiseth the dead.

2 Corinthians 1:9

My Prayer for Today

Lord, I have found that in my own strength, I am no match for life's problems. I thank You for revealing this to me today. From this day forward, please help me turn to You immediately when I come up against a dead-end place in my life. I ask You, Lord, to help me fully surrender each of these areas to You so You can have full access to them and raise them, one by one, from the dead. Please show me Your life-giving power today. I pray this in Jesus' name!

My Confession for Today

I confess that God's resurrection power is released on my behalf to turn all dead-end situations in my life around! I do not trust in my own efforts or human thinking but in God and His life-giving power. I choose to partake of this power today by releasing every dead-end place to the Lord. I trust Him to perfect that which concerns me, and I look to see His power made manifest this day in my life. I declare this by faith in Jesus' name!

Soldiers in God's Army

My Prayer for Today

Lord, I ask You to help me see myself and other Christian brothers and sisters as soldiers in the army of God. Help me develop an attitude of determination that refuses to surrender to hardship or to throw in the towel in the face of difficulty. At the same time that this attitude is being developed inside me, use me to help fortify the same determined attitude in other Christian soldiers who face hostile forces that have come to steal their victory and joy. I pray this in Jesus' name!

Thou therefore endure hardness, as a good soldier of Jesus Christ... endure all things for the elect's sakes, that they may also obtain the salvation which is in Christ Jesus with eternal glory.

2 Timothy 2:3,10

My Confession for Today

I confess that regardless of how much resistance the devil is trying to bring against my life, I will never surrender to defeat. Others may give up, but not I! As long as I am alive, I will stay in the fight. I refuse to relinquish my stand of faith. I am an exceptionally fine soldier—-exactly the kind other Christian soldiers should be happy to associate with—- because I am committed and determined to fight until my victory is complete. I declare this by faith in Jesus' name!

You Are More Than a Conqueror

Nay, in all these things we are more than conquerors through him that loved us.

Romans 8:37

My Prayer for Today

Lord, I thank You for making me a phenomenal, walloping, conquering force! Because of what Jesus has done for me, I am no longer a struggling loser. Instead, I possess the power to be an enormous overcomer! Holy Spirit, I ask You to help me take my eyes off my past failures so I can focus on the power of the resurrection that lives inside me. I pray this in Jesus' name!

My Confession for Today

I boldly declare that in Jesus Christ, I am a conqueror who is utmost, paramount, foremost, first-rate, first-class, and top-notch; greater, higher, and better than; superior to; preeminent, dominant, incomparable; more than a match for; unsurpassed, unequaled, and unrivaled by any challenge that would ever try to come against me! I declare this by faith in Jesus' name!

Wisdom and Revelation for You

My Prayer for Today

Lord, I ask You to give me the insight and wisdom I need for this moment in my life. There is so much I need to know, but I am unable to figure it all out by myself. Today I ask that the Holy Spirit would take away the veil that has obscured my view. I ask that my eyes be opened to see exactly what I need to know. I ask You to give me a real revelation about my life, my situation, and the truth I need to know right now. I pray this in Jesus' name!

That the God of our Lord Jesus Christ, the Father of glory, may give unto you the spirit of wisdom and revelation in the knowledge of him.

Ephesians 1:17

My Confession for Today

I boldly declare that God gives me "a spirit of wisdom and revelation" regarding the truth I need in my life right now. God has all the answers I need—answers I will not find with my own natural reasoning. At the right moment, the Holy Spirit will remove the veil of ignorance that has blinded my view and help me see clearly the things I need to understand. I declare this by faith in Jesus' name!

Fervent in Prayer for Others

*And others save
with fear, pulling
them out of
the fire....*

Jude 1:23

My Prayer for Today

Lord, I ask You to give me Your heart for brothers and sisters who are living in sin. Forgive me for the times I have been insensitive to the dangerous nature of sin. Help me to be passionate and fervent in prayer for them and to keep praying for them until their deliverance is complete and they are fully restored. Help me consider the way I would want others to pray for me if I were in the same situation. I pray this in Jesus' name!

My Confession for Today

I confess that I will do everything within my power to snatch people from spiritually dangerous predicaments. Although they may not feel the heat of the fire at the moment or realize the seriousness of their spiritual condition, I will obey the Word of God and speak truthfully to them in order to seize their hearts and set them free. I believe that God will open a door and show me how and when I am to speak the truth. I declare this by faith in Jesus' name!

Filled With the Riches of God

My Prayer for Today

Lord, I ask You to help me become so full of the Word of God that my entire being is affected by its life-giving truth. As I dwell on Your Word and let it live inside me, my heart will be filled with joy, my mind will be flooded with wisdom and understanding, and my mouth will be filled with songs. Lord, I know that Your Word will take me to the richest spiritual place I've ever known in my life. So help me make Your Word feel at home in my heart so I can start living each day like I've struck it spiritually rich! I pray this in Jesus' name!

Let the word of Christ dwell in you richly....

Colossians 3:16

My Confession for Today

I confess that the Word of God enriches me with spiritual wisdom and insight. It puts victory in my heart and a song in my mouth! As I meditate on the Word, it enriches my life, and I always have something spiritually to donate, to bequeath, or to freely share with others. I am so filled with the riches of God's Word that I automatically find myself admonishing and encouraging other people in their faith. I declare this by faith in Jesus' name!

Victory Over the Challenges of Life

Wherefore seeing we also are compassed about with so great a cloud of witnesses, let us lay aside every weight, and the sin which doth so easily beset us, and let us run with patience the race that is set before us.

Hebrews 12:1

My Prayer for Today

Lord, Your Word says nothing is impossible to those who believe, so I am releasing my faith in Your promises. I fully believe that what You did for the faithful believers who came before me, You will also do for *me!* I pray this prayer in Jesus' name!

My Confession for Today

I confess that I have victory over the challenges I face in life! I know that many have faced the same battles I'm facing and victoriously won their fight. My battle isn't worse than the battles others have faced, so I boldly declare that I will be triumphant in my fight, just as they were triumphant in theirs! It is a fact that hard times will pass—-and when they do, I will see the Word of God bring me the victory that I declare and desire. It is not a matter of IF I will win, but only a question of WHEN I will win! I declare this by faith in Jesus' name!

Staying Untangled From the World

My Prayer for Today

Lord, I ask You to help me keep my heart free from the things of the world. You have called me to be a committed and focused Christian soldier. I cannot permit anything to ensnare and entrap me, thus distracting me from the good fight of faith You've called me to fight and win. You are the revealer of the secrets of men's hearts, so today I am looking to You to reveal to me any areas in my soul where I have allowed something to entrap me so greatly that it threatens to eliminate me from the fight. I pray this in Jesus' name!

No man that warreth entangleth himself with the affairs of this life; that he may please him who hath chosen him to be a soldier.

2 Timothy 2:4

My Confession for Today

I boldly declare that my heart and soul are free to follow Jesus Christ! My worldly possessions are in my hands, but they are not in my heart. I will remain free of materialism, worry, and other worldly concerns, and I will stay focused on the task Jesus Christ has assigned to me. I declare this by faith in Jesus' name!

Don't Throw in the Towel

But call to remembrance the former days, in which, after ye were illuminated, ye endured a great fight of afflictions....

Hebrews 10:32

My Prayer for Today

Lord, as I take a stand of faith in response to that word I have received from You for my life, I realize that Satan may try to use negative thoughts to war against my mind. Thank You for alerting me to the fact that the devil may even try to use people and circumstances to thwart Your plan for my life. But I also thank You that Satan cannot stop Your plan from coming to pass. With Your Spirit illuminating my mind, I know I will be able to discern the attacks of the enemy and successfully resist each and every attack. I pray this in Jesus' name!

My Confession for Today

I boldly declare that I won't back down! I won't surrender to Satan's vicious lies—his attacks against my body, his challenges to my finances, and his assaults against my relationships. Regardless of how much resistance he tries to bring against me, I will not back up on the word that God gave me. I will stand fast, holding tightly to what God has promised, and the devil will be the one to throw in the towel and surrender! I will resist him until he flees and leaves me. I declare this by faith in Jesus' name!

Change Your Environment

My Confession for Today

Lord, I want to stay in an environment that will keep my faith alive and strong. Help me recognize those relationships and places I should avoid to keep my faith from being negatively affected. As You show me places, people, and things I should avoid, give me the strength I need to do what is right—and give me the wisdom I need to know how to avoid those places and people. I pray this in Jesus' name!

Wherefore seeing we also are compassed about with so great a cloud of witnesses, let us lay aside every weight and the sin which doth so easily beset us....

Hebrews 12:1

My Prayer for Today

I confess that I will physically remove myself from unprofitable situations that are not positive for my faith. I make the choice to get up and get out of unbelieving, negative environments that tend to pull me down. I am laying aside every weight, and I am making a break from all unhealthy environments. With God's help, I make right choices and right friends. I do everything I can to stay in environments that help me keep my faith alive and well. I declare this by faith in Jesus' name!

You're Not a Spiritual Orphan

*I will not leave
you comfortless: I
will come to you.*

John 14:18

My Prayer for Today

Lord, I thank You that I am not a spiritual orphan in this world. You didn't abandon me or leave me to figure out everything on my own. You sent the Holy Spirit to be my Teacher and Guide. So right now I open my heart wide to the Holy Spirit, so He can be the Helper You sent Him to be in my life. I give You thanks for sending this divine Helper, and I ask You to teach me how to lean upon Him more and more in the course of my life. I pray this in Jesus' name!

My Confession for Today

I boldly declare that the Holy Spirit is my Helper, my Teacher, and my Guide. Everything Jesus did for the disciples, the Holy Spirit now does for me. He leads me, He teaches me, and He shows me everything the Father wants me to know. I am not a spiritual orphan! I am a child of God who is fully befriended, indwelt, empowered, and led by the Spirit of God. I declare this by faith in Jesus' name!

A Royal Ambassador for Christ

> *Now then we are ambassadors for Christ....*
>
> *2 Corinthians 5:20*

My Prayer for Today

Lord, I thank You for the tremendous privilege of representing You on this earth. Please forgive me for the times I have overlooked the honor of being a child of God. I am sorry for the moments when I've been negative about myself, talked badly about myself, and did not acknowledge who You have made me to be in Jesus Christ. Today I am asking the Holy Spirit to help me see and truly perceive that You have made me to be an ambassador in this world. I pray this in Jesus' name!

My Confession for Today

I confess that I am important to the plan of God. I am an ambassador! I represent Jesus Christ to my family, to my place of employment, and to my neighborhood. I have been invested with royal powers, including the name of Jesus and the authority of the blood, and I may call upon Heaven to assist me at any given moment! All angelic powers and all the vast resources stored in the treasury of Heaven are available for my use when I am representing Jesus to this world. I declare this by faith in Jesus' name!

Dealing With Sin From God's Perspective

And others save with fear, pulling them out of the fire; hating even the garment spotted by the flesh.

Jude 1:23

My Prayer for Today

Lord, help me see sin the way You see it so that I have no stomach for it in my life. I know that as long as I view sin only as a mistake or a weakness, I will be tempted to tolerate it. So I ask You to teach me to see sin exactly the way You do so my desire for change will grow. Holy Spirit, help me see the truth and know the proper steps I need to take in order to make those needed changes. I pray this in Jesus' name!

My Confession for Today

I confess that I understand the consequences of sin and that I hate even the smallest hint of sin in my life. I will deal with sin while it is still a small, superficial problem so that it never becomes a much deeper problem. The Holy Spirit opens my eyes to those areas of my life that need attention and correction. He lovingly shows me what needs to change, and I willingly obey Him as He shows me how to change. I declare this by faith in Jesus' name!

Free From the Captivity of Sin

My Prayer for Today

Lord, I thank You for coming into my life and for breaking the power of sin that used to hold me captive. I remember the futility I felt as I tried to change myself but couldn't do it. But when You came into my life, everything changed! I praise You for loving me so much that You left Heaven and descended into a world filled with sin and depravity. You did that for me, and I thank You so much! I pray this in Jesus' name!

But God be thanked, that ye were the servants of sin, but ye have obeyed from the heart that form of doctrine which was delivered you.

Romans 6:17

My Confession for Today

I confess that I am free because of the death and resurrection of Jesus Christ. The shedding of His blood paid the ransom for me. The hold Satan used to have on me is broken, and I am liberated and set free! Now God's divine power operates mightily in me, and I have authority over the enemy who used to control me. I declare this by faith in Jesus' name!

Let God's Word Feel at Home in Your Life

Let the word of Christ dwell in you richly....

Colossians 3:16

My Prayer for Today

Lord, how can I ever thank You enough for the power of Your Word? I am so honored that You would place such a gift in my life. Help me to appreciate it, value it, and give it the kind of reception it deserves. I want to make Your Word a top priority in my life; I want it to feel welcomed, wanted, and deeply loved. Starting today, I open my heart wider than ever before and ask that Your Word come to richly dwell inside me. I pray this in Jesus' name!

My Confession for Today

I confess that the Word of God dwells richly in me. It has such a grand reception in my life that it literally feels at home in me. Because I give it this place of prominence in my life, it produces phenomenal amounts of spiritual wealth in my life. I have so many spiritual riches inside me that they continually flow forth to enrich those around me. I declare this by faith in Jesus' name!

Bought With a Great Price

My Prayer for Today

Lord, I want to thank You for loving me so much that You gave Your precious blood on the Cross for me. I was so lost and so hopeless, but You came for me—and when You came into my life, everything in me changed. Hope, joy, and peace came into my heart, and today I am completely different from the person I used to be. All this happened because of Your shed blood, Jesus, so today I want to take this moment to thank You for doing what no one else could do for me. I pray this in Jesus' name!

Who gave himself for us, that he might redeem us from all iniquity, and purify unto himself a peculiar people, zealous of good works.

Titus 2:14

My Confession for Today

I declare that Jesus' blood purchased my deliverance and lasting freedom from the demonic powers that had previously held me captive. Jesus loves me so much that He was willing to do for me what no one else was willing to do. He went into the slave market, found me, and bought me for Himself. For the rest of my life, I will live to serve and glorify Him. I declare this by faith in Jesus' name!

Keep Envy and Strife Out of Your Life

For where envying and strife is, there is confusion and every evil work.

James 3:16

My Prayer for Today

Lord, I ask You to forgive me for the times I have allowed strife to get into my heart. Also, please forgive me for those occasions when I have been the origin of strife and fighting. Help me grow in discernment so I can quickly recognize when the devil is trying to create division. Show me how to be a peacekeeper and a source of harmony rather than a player in the midst of others' wrong attitudes. I pray this in Jesus' name!

My Confession for Today

I confess that I do not yield to envy and strife. When the opportunity for strife arises, I beat Satan at his own game by choosing to respectfully make room for the ideas, thoughts, and opinions of others. Even if I don't agree with what they say, I let them know that I value their right to have a differing opinion. I maintain an attitude of staying on the same side with my fellow believers; therefore, I put the devil on the run and keep him out of my relationships. I declare this by faith in Jesus' name!

Equipped With the Armor of God

My Prayer for Today

Lord, help me not to get so brain-heavy with facts, knowledge, and information that I forget I must have more than brain power. I am asking You to help me focus on my spiritual side and to stay equipped with the spiritual weapons You have provided for me, for I know that knowledge alone is not enough to keep the devil under my feet. Today I choose to pick up those weapons and to walk in the whole armor of God. I pray this in Jesus' name!

Finally, my brethren, be strong in the Lord, and in the power of his might.

Ephesians 6:10

My Confession for Today

I confess that I have spiritual weapons to defeat the enemy. I walk in those weapons and use them every time the devil tries to attack my life or the lives of those I love. Because I have the whole armor of God, I am fit and equipped to shove back every assault the devil may try to bring against me. God has more than adequately outfitted me with every weapon I need to maintain the victory Jesus obtained for me. I declare this by faith in Jesus' name!

The Revealing Work of the Spirit

*But as it is written,
Eye hath not seen,
nor ear heard,
neither have entered
into the heart of
man, the things
which God hath
prepared for them
that love him. But
God hath revealed
them unto us by his
Spirit: for the Spirit
searcheth all things,
yea, the deep
things of God.*

1 Corinthians 2:9,10

My Prayer for Today

Lord, now I understand that I've been trying to find answers I'll never discover by myself. The things I long to know can only be revealed by You, so today I ask You to pull back the veil that has concealed those things I long to understand. I know that when You get involved, my eyes will be opened and my ignorance will evaporate. I sincerely ask You in faith to speak to me and to show me those things I need to know. I pray this in Jesus' name!

My Confession for Today

I affirm that with the help of the Holy Spirit, I clearly see and understand everything the Holy Spirit wants me to know. The day of ignorance has been removed because the Holy Spirit has come to reveal the benefits Jesus has provided for me. Now I have access to the secrets that were previously hidden to my natural mind and perception. I am thankful for the Spirit's revealing work in my life, and I declare that I never have to claim ignorance again. I declare this by faith in Jesus' name!

The Gift of a Sound Mind

For God hath not given us the spirit of fear; but of power, and of love, and of a sound mind.

2 Timothy 1:7

My Prayer for Today

Lord, I thank You by faith that I am NOT going crazy and I am NOT losing my mind. The stress and pressure I've been facing is going to pass, and I know You will bring me through these challenging times. You promised me a sound mind, and that is exactly what You have given me. I can't ever thank You enough or fully express my gratitude for the power, love, and sound mind You have given to me that will carry me safely through these times. I pray this in Jesus' name!

My Confession for Today

I declare that my mind is guarded by the Word of God. God's Word works in my mind; safeguards my emotions; defends my mind from demonic assault; and shields me from the arrows the enemy tries to shoot in my direction in order to arouse a spirit of fear inside me. When the devil tries to convince me that I'm losing my mind or to confuse me with stressful situations, I get alone with the Lord and give my concerns to Him. As I focus on Jesus and release all those burdens, I find that my mind is working fine. I declare this by faith in Jesus' name!

Your Victory Has Already Been Won

And having spoiled principalities and powers, he made a shew of them openly, triumphing over them in it.

Colossians 2:15

My Prayer for Today

Lord, I thank You for the victory You obtained by Your resurrection from the dead. No one else could have done what You did for us. You invaded hell; broke the power of its demonic forces; seized their artillery; and bound the devil. And because You did all this, You set us free! You are our great Victor, our great Champion, and You are the Lord of all lords. Thank You for cleansing me with Your blood and granting me the honor to be called a son of God and a joint-heir with You. I pray this in Jesus' name!

My Confession for Today

I confess that Satan is not a force I am trying to defeat because he is already defeated. I use my God-given authority to resist him, and he flees from me. No matter what demonic strategy may come against me this day or how many demons may try to assemble together for my destruction, I NEVER have to go down in defeat. When I look into the mirror, I see someone who already has the victory. I possess the authority necessary to keep Satan under my feet where he belongs! I declare this by faith in Jesus' name!

You Have a Razor-Sharp Sword in Your Hands

My Prayer for Today

Lord, I know that Your Spirit has the very answer I need for any situation I may confront in life. When He speaks to my heart, it places a razor-sharp sword in my hands that I can use against my spiritual enemies. Help me keep a sensitive ear to the Holy Spirit so I can recognize those moments when He is trying to give me a "rhema" that will put the devil on the run! I pray this in Jesus' name!

And take the helmet of salvation, and the sword of the Spirit, which is the word of God.

Ephesians 6:17

My Confession for Today

I confess that I can hear the Holy Spirit's voice when He drops a word into my heart at the exact moment I need it. Those quickened words impart special power and authority to me. They are so powerful that it is as if a sword has been placed in my hands. When I receive that kind of word from the Lord, I insert it, twist it, and do as much damage as possible to the devil until he's sorry he ever messed with me! I declare this by faith in Jesus' name!

Chosen by God

And base things of the world, and things which are despised, hath God chosen....

1 Corinthians 1:28

My Prayer for Today

Lord, I am so thankful that You chose me! Even though the devil has tried to use people to tell me that I would never be worth anything, You wanted me and sought me out until I finally heard Your voice and surrendered to Your call. I am so grateful that the opinion of the world about me wasn't true. I'm so glad that You pursued me with such a mighty love and that You refused to give up on me. What else can I say to express my heart to You? I can only say, "Thank You, Jesus!" I pray this in Jesus' name!

My Confession for Today

I confess that because I am in Christ Jesus, I have no reason to be ashamed of who I am. I do not allow other people to affect my self-image and confidence. Because I know who I am in Jesus Christ, I hold my head high and refuse to be embarrassed or to let anyone make me think I am inferior or less than who Jesus made me to be. I am exactly the kind of person God wants to use. He has BIG plans to use me in a mighty way! I declare this by faith in Jesus' name!

God Will Reward Your Faithfulness

My Prayer for Today

Lord, I am thankful that You reward us when we are faithful to fulfill the assignments You've given us to do. I know that by serving You, I will never suffer real loss or lack because You always take good care of those who do Your will. I trust that You will see to it that I am fully reimbursed for everything I've spent to complete my assigned tasks. I believe that You will make a settlement for past expenses that will make me shout with joy! You've never overlooked what I've done for You in the past, and I trust that You will take care of me now as well. I pray this in Jesus' name!

And whatsoever ye do, do it heartily, as to the Lord, and not unto men; Knowing that of the Lord ye shall receive the reward of the inheritance: for ye serve the Lord Christ.

Colossians 3:23,24

My Confession for Today

I confess that God is mindful of the time, love, patience, and money I have invested as I've served Him. Hebrews 6:10 says God never overlooks or fails to remember what I have done for Him. This means I can rest assured that as I work long hours on His behalf; invest my personal energies; give 100 percent of my heart and soul to my assigned task; and give sacrificially of my finances, God will never forget any of it. He rewards those who diligently seek Him, so I'm a candidate for one of His rewards! Therefore, I will not get tired; I will not give in to discouragement; and I will keep pressing forward to do what God has called me to do, believing that He will take care of me all the way through to the end. I declare this by faith in Jesus' name!

Set the Spiritual Hostages Free

...For this purpose the Son of God was manifested, that he might destroy the works of the devil.

1 John 3:8

My Prayer for Today

Lord, please help me to be conscious of the people I meet who are bound by the devil in their minds. I know that You want to use me to touch them and to bring them the freedom that can be found only in You. I am so sorry for the times I get so busy that I fail to recognize opportunities to speak Your name and to share Your love with people who are lost and bound. Please help me to become consistently alert to the people for whom You died and to go out of my way to tell them the Good News that will deliver them and set them free. I pray this in Jesus' name!

My Confession for Today

I confess that I am alert to the people around me who are held as hostages in their minds. I see their struggles; I recognize their fears; and I use every available opportunity to speak words of freedom and release into their lives. I have received so much from the Lord; now it is my responsibility to share this same liberty with others who come into my life. I know this is what God is asking of me, and I choose to start obeying this mandate today. I declare this by faith in Jesus' name!

God's Peace in the Midst of the Storm

My Prayer for Today

Lord, thank You for teaching me that Satan often attacks right when I'm on the verge of a major breakthrough. This knowledge helps me so much because it causes me to recognize that Satan loves to make all hell break loose in my life just before a big victory. Now that I know this, please help me keep this in mind when a turbulent wind blows into my life. Help me to look at that storm and say, "I know that the devil must be upset; otherwise, he wouldn't be messing with me right now. I must be right on track with God!" With this understanding, I will keep pressing ahead, regardless of what I see, feel, or hear. I pray this in Jesus' name!

And there arose a great storm of wind, and the waves beat into the ship, so that it was now full.... And He [Jesus] arose, and rebuked the wind, and said unto the sea, Peace, be still. And the wind ceased, and there was a great calm.

Mark 4:37,39

My Confession for Today

I declare that every attack of the devil is my opportunity to see a demonstration of the power of God. What the devil meant for my harm, God will turn for my good. This is my opportunity to rise up, speak the name of Jesus, use my God-given authority, and declare to the spiritual realm that the Lord of lords whom I serve is by far the One with the most spiritual power! I declare this by faith in Jesus' name!

You Are the Treasury of God's Spirit

But we have this treasure in earthen vessels, that the excellency of the power may be of God, and not of us.

2 Corinthians 4:7

My Prayer for Today

Lord, how can I ever say thank You enough for putting Your Spirit inside me? It is so amazing to think that You would want to live inside someone like me. Yet this was Your choice, and for this I am eternally grateful. Help me live a life that is worthy of Your Presence inside me. Forgive me for times when I've treated You wrongly by defiling my mind or my body with things that are not worthy of You. Help me stay constantly aware that I am a carrier of the greatest gift the world has ever known. I pray this in Jesus' name!

My Confession for Today

I joyfully declare that I carry the Presence of God in my life. I am the temple of the Holy Spirit—a treasury where God has placed His power, His gifts, His grace, His fruit, and His character. Resident within me is enough power and answers to change both my environment and the environment of anyone to whom God uses me to speak the words of life. I declare this by faith in Jesus' name!

Learning To Lean on the Holy Spirit

My Prayer for Today

Lord, help me to be mindful that the Holy Spirit lives inside me and wants to possess more and more of me every day. Please help me learn how to surrender to the Spirit's power and to yield to His sanctifying Presence. I know that as I yield to Him, He will fill me full of every good thing I need to live a happy and successful life in this world. I want to begin today by opening myself to the Holy Spirit completely. Holy Spirit, I ask You to fill me anew right now. I pray this in Jesus' name!

Do ye think that the scripture saith in vain, The spirit that dwelleth in us lusteth to envy?

James 4:5

My Confession for Today

I confess that the Holy Spirit loves me! He thinks of me, dreams of me, and wants to fill me with His Presence and power. The Holy Spirit was sent into this world to be my Helper, my Guide, my Teacher, and my Leader. Therefore, I am learning to lean on Him and to let Him lead me through all my affairs in this life. I surrender to Him, yield to Him, and depend on Him for everything I need. I declare this by faith in Jesus' name!

Mighty in the Spirit

For though we walk in the flesh, we do not war after the flesh.

2 Corinthians 10:3

My Prayer for Today

Lord, help me remember that real spiritual battles are fought and won in the Spirit. I'm so often tempted to focus on my physical appearance and the condition of my body. I even frequently judge myself by how physically "in shape" I am. But the fight I need to win isn't going to be won by my physical appearance. Yes, I want to be in good physical shape, and I ask You to help me achieve that goal. But please keep me from getting distracted by the less-than-pleasurable aspects of my physical body. Help me stay focused on the spiritual realm where the real battle is being waged. I pray this in Jesus' name!

My Confession for Today

I proclaim that regardless of what I look like in the natural realm, I am a menace to the devil in the spiritual realm. In that sphere, I am anointed and powerful, with the ability to pull down strongholds from peoples' lives and minds. I am so mighty in the Spirit that the devil and his forces flee when I resist them. I declare this by faith in Jesus' name!

Stay on Fire

Quench not the Spirit.

1 Thessalonians 5:19

My Prayer for Today

Lord, help me to quickly obey when the Spirit of God prompts me to do something. The last thing I want to do is throw water on the flames of the Spirit in my heart. Forgive me for suffocating the life of the Holy Spirit in me by refusing to do what He tells me to do. From this point onward, I make the choice to quickly obey, but I need Your strength to do this. So today I am asking You to fill me anew with brand-new courage to step out in faith, to quickly obey, and to leave the results with You. I pray this in Jesus' name!

My Confession for Today

I confess that I am quick to obey the voice of the Holy Spirit. When He tugs at my heart, pointing me in a specific direction or leading me to minister to a certain person, I do not hold back, hesitate, or resist. Instead, I say, "Lord, I'll do whatever You want me to do!" I then step out in faith and watch as His power is demonstrated to me and through me. I declare this by faith in Jesus' name!

Following the Example of Faith

Wherefore seeing we also are compassed about with so great a cloud of witnesses....

Hebrews 12:1

My Prayer for Today

Lord, thank You for reminding me that I am not the first to walk by faith. Others have walked this walk before me, and they did it with power and with grace. If they were able to do it, I know I can do it too, but I must have Your assistance to make it all the way through. So today I look to You to give me everything I inwardly need to keep marching ahead in order to achieve the things You have ordained for me. I pray this in Jesus' name!

My Confession for Today

I confess that I can do whatever God asks me to do! He wouldn't ask me if He didn't think I could do it. Rather than doubt my abilities, I confess that His ability is working inside me. I lean on the Holy Spirit—His mind, His power, and His grace—and these divine forces enable me to successfully achieve the things He has designed for me to do today. I declare this by faith in Jesus' name!

God Wants To Use You

My Prayer for Today

Lord, help me see myself with the full potential I have in Jesus Christ. My temptation is to see myself according to my past, but starting today I ask You to help me see myself through the promises of Your Word. I know that with Your grace and power, I can rise above any weakness or infirmity that has hindered me in the past. I turn to Your grace, and I ask You to release Your power in me so I can step into the reality of the person You have made me to be. I pray this in Jesus' name!

...God hath chosen the weak things of the world to confound the things which are mighty.

1 Corinthians 1:27

My Confession for Today

I confess that I am NOT substandard, second-rate, low grade, or inferior. I am filled with the Spirit of God, and I have the call of God on my life. Even if my gifts and talents seem small in comparison to others, I have all that I need in order to do what God has asked me to do. God wants to use me to baffle the "know-it-alls" and to bewilder people who are more talented than I but who do not trust in the Lord. He wants to get glory because of what He does through me! I declare this by faith in Jesus' name!

Diligent To Pursue Success

*But without faith
it is impossible
to please him:
for he that cometh
to God must
believe that he is,
and that he is a
rewarder of them
that diligently
seek him.*

Hebrews 11:6

My Prayer for Today

Lord, I ask You to please help me become more serious as I adjust my level of commitment to a higher level. Help me give full attention to what You have called me to do. I realize that diligence cannot be a sideline issue in my life. In order for me to succeed at what You have asked me to do, I must give it my full consideration, my undivided attention, and my mental and spiritual concentration. But I can only keep pressing toward this higher level of commitment if I have the divine energy of the Holy Spirit propelling me forward. As I reach upward to become all that You want me to be, I ask You for divine assistance. I pray this in Jesus' name!

My Confession for Today

I agree that God is no respecter of persons. What He does for one, He will do for all. Every believer possesses the same promises, the same faith, the same power, the same Spirit, and the same Jesus who sits at the right hand of God to make intercession for us. These promises belong to me today! Because I choose to put my whole heart into my assigned task and to do more than average work, I know I will reap more than average results. I am deeply committed to the task and willing to do whatever is necessary to realize the goals and aspirations God has given to me. I declare this by faith in Jesus' name!

The Convicting Power of the Holy Spirit

And when he [the Holy Spirit] is come, he will reprove the world of sin....

John 16:8

My Prayer for Today

Lord, thank You for the convicting power of the Holy Spirit, for it was this act of the Spirit that first brought me to the place of my salvation. When I do wrong and the Holy Spirit convicts me of what I have done, help me be sensitive enough to recognize that He is pricking my heart to get my attention. Help me slow down to see what He is wanting to show me and to take the necessary time to properly repent and deal with the issues He is wanting me to change. I pray this in Jesus' name!

My Confession for Today

I confess that I am sensitive to the Holy Spirit and live a life that pleases Him. But when I fail to do what is right, I am sensitive to His voice and quickly repent for the wrong I have done. My heart's desire is to please Him, and I will do everything I can to live a life that honors His Presence inside me. I declare this by faith in Jesus' name!

Divine Strategies From the Holy Spirit

For the weapons of our warfare are not carnal, but mighty through God to the pulling down of strong holds.

2 Corinthians 10:4

My Prayer for Today

Lord, I know that today I'm going to need a supernatural strategy to do what I need to do. My own natural mind is working all the time to come up with solutions. I'm doing the best I can do, but now I need extra help. I need a divine strategy—a divine idea so powerful and effective that no force will be able to resist it! I know that these kinds of strategies are imparted by the Holy Spirit, so right now I open my heart wide to Him. Holy Spirit, I ask You to drop a supernatural idea into my spirit and soul. Please help me to properly discern it, understand it, and then follow through with obedience. I pray this in Jesus' name!

My Confession for Today

I declare by faith that the Holy Spirit gives me the strategies and ideas I need. I am willing and ready to do whatever He tells me to do. The Spirit of God was sent into this world to be my Helper and my Guide, and I know I can fully rely on Him. I must have His direction, or I won't know what to do. So today He will speak to my heart; I will perceive what He tells me to do; and then I will obediently carry out His good plan for me! I declare this by faith in Jesus' name!

Power To Defeat the Enemy

My Prayer for Today

Lord, I know that Your Word has the power to defeat every adversary in my life. As I take it into my heart and get it deep into my soul, I know it will empower me to speak Your Word with mighty strength and authority. Forgive me for the times I have just skimmed over Your Word rather than planting it deep in my heart. I realize that the answers I seek are in Your Word—and that Your Word, when spoken from my mouth, releases authority against the devices the devil tries to use against me. So today, Lord, I make the decision to plant Your Word deep in my spirit man and then to speak it and release its power in my life. I pray this in Jesus' name!

For the word of God is quick, and powerful, and sharper than any two-edged sword....

Hebrews 4:12

My Confession for Today

I confess that God's Word is a mighty and sharp two-edged sword that releases His power when I speak it out of my mouth. I read the Word; I take it deeply into my heart; and then I release its power from my mouth to thwart the enemy's strategies and bring victory into every situation I'm facing today. I declare this by faith in Jesus' name!

Your Divine Partner in Life

The grace of the Lord Jesus Christ, and the love of God, and the communion of the Holy Ghost, be with you all. Amen.

2 Corinthians 13:14

My Prayer for Today

Holy Spirit, I want to thank You for being my Partner in this world. I need Your partnership. I know that without You, I am so limited in what I am able to do. You see what I can't see; You know what I don't know; You have wisdom and insight that I don't have. I simply must have Your help if I am going to do what God has asked me to do. I ask You to please forgive me for all the times I have gotten in such a hurry that I didn't take time to fellowship with You. From this moment on, I promise I will do my best to consult You before I make a decision or take a single step. I pray this in Jesus' name!

My Confession for Today

I confess that I am led by the Spirit of God. I am careful not to make big decisions without consulting Him first. The Holy Spirit is my Leader, my Teacher, and my Guide; therefore, I look to Him to help me make the right decisions and take the right actions in every sphere of my life—my family, my business, and my ministry. Every day I experience more and more victory because I allow the Holy Spirit to direct all my steps. I declare this by faith in Jesus' name!

Lay Aside Unnecessary Weights

My Prayer for Today

Lord, I know that You're on my side and that You want to help me. So today I'm asking You to help me lay aside the attitudes, negative thought patterns, and bad habits that keep pulling me back down into miserable defeat. I'm exhausted from trying to live for You while dragging along these old weights behind me at the same time. I need to drop them and leave them behind! So today I am asking You to help me make the big break. Help me make this the day I permanently drop all the unnecessary weights that hinder me and walk away from them forever! I pray this in Jesus' name!

> *Wherefore seeing we are compassed about with such a great cloud of witnesses, let us lay aside every weight....*
>
> *Hebrews 12:1*

My Confession for Today

I confess that I live a life of obedience. Sin, bad habits, negative attitudes, and fear have no influence in my life. Because I am free of these things, I am able to run my race of faith without any hindrances caused by my own actions. Because I want to please God, I do not tolerate things in my life that make it difficult for me to walk by faith or to please God. Absolutely nothing is more important to me than knowing God's will and doing it in a way that brings pleasure to the Lord. I declare this by faith in Jesus' name!

Your Heart Is Home to the Holy Spirit

What? know ye not that your body is the temple of the Holy Ghost which is in you, which ye have of God, and ye are not your own? For ye are bought with a price: therefore glorify God in your body, and in your spirit, which are God's.

1 Corinthians 6:19,20

My Prayer for Today

Lord, I am so excited to think that You made my heart Your home. It is so overwhelming to think that You want to live inside me. Help me see myself as Your dwelling place and to honor Your Presence inside me by the kind of life I lead. I want to bless You and honor You, so please help me do the right things that bring You the greatest pleasure and joy. I pray this in Jesus' name!

My Confession for Today

I gratefully acknowledge that my body is the temple of the Holy Spirit. Yes, the Holy Spirit lives inside me. My heart is not a hotel where He occasionally visits; rather, my heart has become His home. He has invested His power, His gifts, His fruit, and the life of Jesus Christ in me. Inwardly I am highly adorned with the goodness of God. My spirit is so marvelously created in Christ Jesus that God Himself is comfortable to live inside me! I declare this by faith in Jesus' name!

Make Prayer a Pillar of Your Life

Praying always,
with all prayer....

Ephesians 6:18

My Prayer for Today

Lord, forgive me for the times I get so busy that I neglect my prayer life. I really want this inconsistency in my life to be broken; I want my prayer life to get stronger and more stable. I realize that when I don't spend time alone with You, I make it difficult for You to tell me what You want me to know. Inconsistency is a work of the flesh, so I am asking You to help me break this pattern and learn how to make prayer one of the most important pillars of my life. I pray this in Jesus' name!

My Confession for Today

I declare by faith that prayer is a central and significant part of my life. God has great spiritual adventures planned for me, and He wants to reveal them to me during my time of prayer. I am steadfast, immovable, and consistent in my time with God. Nothing is as important to me as those moments I enjoy with Him. As I spend time with Him each day, He refreshes my spirit and enlightens my mind with the knowledge that He wants me to know. My prayer time is a key to the success God is giving me in my life. I declare this by faith in Jesus' name!

You're Not Who You Used To Be

Wherein in time past ye walked according to the course of this world, according to the prince of the power of the air, the spirit that now worketh in the children of disobedience.

Ephesians 2:2

My Prayer for Today

Lord, as I read this today, it makes me so thankful that I am not the person I used to be! Thank You for sending someone to me to share the Good News of the Gospel. My life has been transformed, and now I'm on the path that You planned for my life. I ask You to forgive me for not telling others about the saving message of Jesus Christ. I have freely received, and now I have a responsibility to freely give. So today I thank You that I have all the power I need to be a witness to my lost family and friends. I pray this in Jesus' name!

My Confession for Today

I confess that I am a witness for Jesus Christ. When I was filled with the Holy Spirit, I received power to tell my friends and family about the Good News of the Gospel. I have no reason to be afraid of their reaction, and I refuse to allow a spirit of fear to keep me from giving them the truth that will set them free! I declare this by faith in Jesus' name!

Your Redemption Is a Done Deal

My Prayer for Today

Lord, I thank You that my redemption is a done deal! It's not something I'm trying to get; it's something You've already purchased and accomplished in my life. Help me renew every area of my mind so I can enjoy the liberty You purchased for me. Give me a desire to experience Your freedom in every sphere of my life and a determination to reject any form of bondage that tries to hang on to me. I pray this in Jesus' name!

Christ hath redeemed us from the curse of the law, being made a curse for us: for it is written, Cursed is every one that hangeth on a tree.

Galatians 3:13

My Confession for Today

I confess that I am free! Sin has no more hold on me! Bondages and habits from the past have no more legitimate right to exercise their control over me! I rejoice that God sent Jesus to buy me out of my slavery and place me in His family as His own child. I declare that I am forever removed from the curse of sin. I agree that it's a done deal! I declare this by faith in Jesus' name!

Set Your Affection on Jesus

*...A friend of
the world is the
enemy of God.*

James 4:4

My Prayer for Today

Lord, I pray that my passion for You will grow stronger and stronger and that I will remain untainted from the world. Please show me if there are any places in me that are drawn to things that displease You. It may be hard for me to hear, but if there is anything in me that seeks to slip back into the life from which You delivered me, please reveal it to me. If my affection for anything else in this world is greater than my affection for You, please show me! I pray this in Jesus' name!

My Confession for Today

I declare by faith that I am more deeply in love with Jesus Christ today than at any previous moment in my life. My affection for Him is so deep that I will never turn back to the life from which I've been delivered. I have no relational obligations greater than the sense of obligation that I feel for Jesus Christ. He saved me, redeemed me, delivered me, and changed me—and I vow to serve Him for the rest of my life! I declare this by faith in Jesus' name!

God's Power Is Yours for the Taking

My Prayer for Today

Lord, how can I ever thank You enough for making Your power so available to me? I need this power so much in my life, and I'm grateful You have made it so easy for me to receive it. Therefore, I open my heart right now by faith, and I ask You to give me a fresh infilling of Your Spirit. I pray this in Jesus' name!

Finally, my brethren, be strong in the Lord, and in the power of his might.

Ephesians 6:10

My Confession for Today

I confess that a fresh infilling of the Holy Spirit's supernatural power is never far away from me. A fresh surge of this power is as accessible to me as my very next breath of air! It's just as normal for me to receive a new infilling of the Spirit as it is for a fish to freely swim around in its tank. In fact, it's difficult for me NOT to receive this impartation of super-human, supernatural strength for the fight. Because my heart is open to receive it, I ask God to release it into my life, and by faith I now receive this divine power. It's mine for the taking! I declare this by faith in Jesus' name!

Stand Against Satan's Attacks

Lest Satan should get an advantage of us: for we are not ignorant of his devices.

2 Corinthians 2:11

My Prayer for Today

Lord, I thank You for opening my eyes and illuminating my understanding to recognize Satan's attacks against my life. Thank You also for giving me the understanding to know how to stand against these demonic attacks. I am so grateful that You have sent the Holy Spirit to be my Teacher and Guide and to equip me to stand against every assault that comes against my life, my family, my church, my business, and all my relationships. Armed with the power and insight of the Spirit, I never have to allow the enemy to take advantage of me again. So I open my heart today, and I ask the Holy Spirit to teach me everything I need to know to stand against the wiles the devil wants to employ against me. I pray this in Jesus' name!

My Confession for Today

I declare that I am not ignorant of Satan's devices. Because the Holy Spirit is my Teacher, I know how to recognize the onset of Satan's attack as he starts maneuvering to frustrate my plans. I am not in the dark about the devil; therefore, the enemy finds it very difficult to take advantage of me. Because my mind has been illuminated to see how the devil operates, his evil plots against my life are aborted by the power of God. I will not be taken down by any strategy the enemy tries to use against me. I declare this by faith in Jesus' name!

Access to the Riches of Heaven

My Prayer for Today

Lord, I'm so glad You saved and delivered me from the life I used to lead. Thank You for making me a joint heir with Jesus and for allowing me to have access to the riches of Heaven! I ask You to forgive me for the times I've lived so far below what You provided for me. I sincerely ask You to help me explore the spiritual riches I possess. Help me to release those riches so my own life can be enriched and so You can use me to enrich the lives of people around me. I pray this in Jesus' name!

...In every thing ye are enriched by him, in all utterance, and in all knowledge; even as the testimony of Christ was confirmed in you.

1 Corinthians 1:5,6

My Confession for Today

I boldly declare that the day I was born again and placed into Jesus Christ was the richest day of my life. On that day, I literally became a joint heir with Jesus Christ and obtained the legal right to claim all the promises of God. From that day until now, I have been constantly enriched by His Presence in my life. I no longer have to settle for spiritual poverty, because I have every right to expect an abundance of manifested promises, power, and spiritual gifts in my life. I possess more spiritual treasure than I'll ever be able to explore or fully exhaust! I declare this by faith in Jesus' name!

Regain Your Zeal

That ye be not slothful, but followers of them who through faith and patience inherit the promises.

Hebrews 6:12

My Prayer for Today

Lord, help me understand how totally unacceptable it is for me to lose my passion, momentum, and desire. I ask You to forgive me for allowing any hint of slothfulness to operate in my life. Today I repent and deliberately turn from slothfulness. Holy Spirit, I turn to You now and ask You to stir and reignite the fire in my heart. Please help me regain the zeal, the thrust, and the fire I once possessed. Help me to keep that fire burning this time, never to lose it again. I pray this in Jesus' name!

My Confession for Today

I declare by faith that I am NOT spiritually neutral for Jesus Christ. The Holy Spirit burns brightly in my life, and I am more excited about serving Jesus Christ than at any other time in my life! The fire of God is burning brightly inside me, evident for all to see. I am an example of what it means to be passionate, committed, and on fire about the things of God. I am stirred up and ready to take on any assignment God gives me—and I will do it with all my heart. I declare this by faith in Jesus' name!

Leavee Lukewarm Attitudes Behind

My Prayer for Today

Lord, I never want to be lukewarm so that You find me to be an unpleasant taste in Your mouth. Instead, I ask You to help me be a fountain from which healing waters flow to the sick and a source of refreshment to anyone who needs strength and encouragement. Help me to never allow a lukewarm attitude to take hold in my life! If there is any area of my life where I've already slipped into a lukewarm state, please reveal it to me so I can repent and get back to where I ought to be. I pray this in Jesus' name!

So then because thou art lukewarm, and neither cold nor hot, I will spue thee out of my mouth.

Revelation 3:16

My Confession for Today

I confess that I am a fountain of healing and a source of refreshment to everyone who comes into my life. When people come near me, they receive exactly what they need. Healing flows from me to everyone who needs a healing touch. Those who are spiritually tired become refreshed when they spend time with me. I allow no middle ground in my life—no neutrality, no lukewarm attitude—and I am therefore continually filled with everything needed to meet the needs of people who come across my path. I declare this by faith in Jesus' name!

Take Up Acting...Like God

*Be ye therefore
followers of God,
as dear children.*

Ephesians 5:1

My Prayer for Today

Lord, help me make the decision to put my unsanctified emotions, thoughts, feelings, and behavior aside and to start acting like You. I know that if I approached every problem "acting" like You, it would make a huge difference in my life. You see everything from a viewpoint of power and victory, so please help me to see like You, think like You, and act like You. Help me make the decision to change my way of thinking—to learn how to respond as You do to every situation I am confronted with in life. I pray this in Jesus' name!

My Confession for Today

I declare by faith that I am going to take up acting! In every situation I face, I am going to imitate the character of my Heavenly Father, successfully replicating Him in every sphere of my life. I know it will require a great deal of time and commitment for me to arrive at this high level of duplication, but I resolve to start where I am today and then do more each day from this moment forward. And I'll keep up my efforts to act like God until I finally begin to think like Him, talk like Him, sound like Him, and carry myself in His confidence. I declare this by faith in Jesus' name!

Set Your Desires and Affections on the Holy Spirit

My Prayer for Today

Lord, if I ever turn my devotion to the world, please move on the scene like a Divine Lover who has come to defend and rescue that relationship You hold so dear. Help me never to forget that You are preoccupied with me and want to possess me totally. I know that You want my desires and affection to be set on You, so if I begin to walk and talk like an unbeliever and give my life to the things of this world, please nudge me and bring conviction to my heart to change. And if I refuse to listen, I ask You to please move with divine malice toward those things that have usurped Your role in my life. I pray this in Jesus' name!

Do ye think that the scripture saith in vain, The spirit that dwelleth in us lusteth to envy?

James 4:5

My Confession for Today

I confess that I respect the Holy Spirit's Presence in my life; therefore, I am careful in the way I think, the way I speak, and the way I connect with the world around me. I do not grieve the Spirit of God by allowing worldliness to become a part of my life. He fiercely wants more of me, and I want more of Him. The Holy Spirit is the top priority in my life, and I never do anything that would make Him feel wounded, grieved, or envious. I live a life that pleases Him! I declare this by faith in Jesus' name!

Relax From the Stresses of Life

*And to you who
are troubled rest
with us....*

*2 Thessalonians
1:7*

My Prayer for Today

Lord, I admit that I've been carrying the worries, stresses, and pressures of life for too long. Before I do anything else, I want to cast these burdens over onto You today. I am tempted to worry that the problems I'm facing won't work out, but taking them into my own hands and worrying about them isn't going to make the situation any better. So I repent for letting myself become consumed with worry about things I cannot change, and I turn them all over to You today. Please help me stay free of anxiety as I learn to relax and enjoy life a little more than I've been enjoying it lately. I pray this in Jesus' name!

My Confession for Today

I confess that I need to set aside time for relaxation and recreation. Starting today, I'm going to take a break from my problems. I am casting my burdens on the Lord; as a result, I know I will be refreshed, recharged, and given a renewed vision. After a little rest, I will see my challenge with new eyes, and I'll face it with new strength. I know my survival depends on this, so today I choose to take a break from the constant stress I've been dealing with before I get worn down and become easy prey for the devil. God will give me the strength and energy I need to get up and get going so I can complete the work He has entrusted into my hands. I declare this by faith in Jesus' name!

Designed To Live in the Last Days

This know also, that in the last days perilous times shall come.

2 Timothy 3:1

My Prayer for Today

Lord, You designed me to live in these last days according to Your great plan. Because You are in charge of my life, I know it's no mistake that I am alive in this generation. Since these days are filled with greater risk than any other generation has ever known, I need faith to face these times victoriously. I need wisdom to minister to others who are wounded and hurt. So today I ask You to help me embrace this time as a part of my destiny and to become strong in faith so I can reach out to those who are near me and who need spiritual assistance. Help me to recognize their need and to know exactly how I should respond to help them. I pray this in Jesus' name!

My Confession for Today

I declare by faith that I am chosen and equipped to live in this last generation. The Word of God protects my mind, my family, and everything that is a part of my life. I will renew my mind with the Word of God and get God's perspective about what His role is for me in these last days. Therefore, I will be a blessing and a help to people who have been victimized by these difficult and trying times. Rather than hide in fear, I will move out with the power of God and stay ever-ready to minister to those who have suffered harm because of the times in which we live. I declare this by faith in Jesus' name!

Don't Budge an Inch

My brethren, count it all joy when ye fall into divers temptations; knowing this, that the trying of your faith worketh patience. But let patience have her perfect work, that ye may be perfect and entire, wanting nothing.

James 1:2-4

My Prayer for Today

Lord, help me stand my ground and defend what I have gained, no matter how difficult it might be to do this. I know that with Your supernatural help, I can outlive and outlast the resistance. With Your Spirit's power working inside me, I know I can indefinitely and defiantly stick it out until the enemy realizes he cannot beat me and decides to retreat. I pray this in Jesus' name!

My Confession for Today

I confess that I am steadfast, consistent, unwavering, and unflinching. I don't care how heavy the load gets or how much pressure I'm under, I am not budging one inch! This is my spot, and there isn't enough pressure in the whole world to make me move and give it up! I have supernatural endurance—staying power, hang-in-there power—and an attitude that holds out, holds on, outlasts, and perseveres until the victory is won and the goal is reached. I declare this by faith in Jesus' name!

You Are a Part of God's Team

My Prayer for Today

Lord, give me the grace to recognize both my abilities and limitations. Help me be unafraid to admit when I've overstepped my bounds and tried to tackle something bigger than my abilities. In those moments, please enable me to ask others to join the project and to help me do what I cannot accomplish by myself. I really need You to help me overcome my weaknesses and my fears that others may be better gifted than I am. I know You have placed people all around me to be blessings in my life, so today I am turning to You. Help me recognize these people and receive them as the blessings You intend for them to be. I pray this in Jesus' name!

For I say, through the grace given unto me, to every man that is among you, not to think of himself more highly than he ought to think; but to think soberly, according as God hath dealt to every man the measure of faith.

Romans 12:3

My Confession for Today

I confess that I am part of a team as God intended for me to be! I don't think too highly of myself, nor do I attempt to go it alone with every project I undertake. I have a team mentality. I recognize my limitations and seek out those who have the gifts and talents I need. Rather than try to figure out everything by myself, I let the people around me contribute their thoughts, views, and insights. I want them to use the talents and abilities God gave them, because we can do a whole lot more as a team than I can do by myself. I declare this by faith in Jesus' name!

Created To Be One of God's Pillars

Therefore, my beloved brethren, be ye steadfast, unmovable, always abounding in the work of the Lord....

1 Corinthians 15:58

My Prayer for Today

Lord, I want to be the person You and others can depend on. Forgive me for any instability in my life, and help me overcome every weakness in my character. Just as I have looked for others to be "rocks" in my life, I want to be a "rock" to other people. I have a lot of room for development in my life, but I am willing to be changed. I want to be taught, corrected, and taken to a higher level. Today I ask You to do whatever is necessary to make me the strong and reliable kind of person You want me to be. Please do Your special work inside me! I pray this in Jesus' name!

My Confession for Today

I confess that God's Word overcomes the weaknesses in my personality and character. God calls me to be "steadfast"—and I AM steadfast. God and people see me like a pillar that stands in its place and helps to hold things together. I am so dependable that people can lean on me, counting on the fact that I will always be there to help keep things together. When events occur that shake up the world around me, I am not easily excited, shaken, or affected. Praise God, I am becoming more and more dependable all the time! When people hear my name, they think of someone on whom they can rely. I declare this by faith in Jesus' name!

You Are Worthy To Receive From God

My Prayer for Today

Lord, I have been made worthy by the blood of Jesus Christ to receive every good thing You have planned and prepared for me. Forgive me for the times I have placed limitations on Your ability to bless me because I thought I wasn't good enough. It is clear that You want to bless me IN SPITE of me! You are so good to do all the wonderful things You do in my life. Today I thank You for choosing to bless me with the extra strength I so desperately need in my life right now. Thank You for making this power completely available for free! I pray this in Jesus' name!

...God would count you worthy of this calling, and fulfil all the good pleasure of his goodness, and the work of faith with power.

2 Thessalonians 1:11

My Confession for Today

I declare that thoughts of unworthiness have no place in me. What Jesus does for me, He does for free—just because He loves me. I do not have to worry that I'm not good enough to receive of His goodness, because my feelings don't have a thing to do with His good pleasure to bless my life. He wants to bless me regardless of anything I do, because it is God's nature to bless and to do good in my life. Today I receive the power God wants to give me by His grace. I receive it without hesitation, knowing that this is His good pleasure for me! I declare this by faith in Jesus' name!

Payday Is on the Way

Cast not away therefore your confidence, which hath great recompence of reward.

Hebrews 10:35

My Prayer for Today

Lord, I am so thankful that You are always mindful of the time, money, and talents—as well as the blood, sweat, and tears—that I've poured into my life assignment. Sometimes when it gets hard or when I get physically or emotionally exhausted, I am tempted to think no one sees or appreciates what I have done. But You have seen it all, and You are faithful to see that I am rewarded for what I have done. I thank You for being so steadfast and faithful and for promising that I will be recompensed for everything I've done with a right heart. I pray this in Jesus' name!

My Confession for Today

I boldly declare that God is going to reward me! God's Word promises that He sees what I have done and that He will see to it that I am fully recompensed for all I have done in His name. Because I am convinced that God will take care of me, I boldly, frankly, and confidently declare that my payday is on the way! He knows about everything I have done in faith, and He will reward and reimburse me for all the time, energy, commitment, and money I've given to His work over the years. I declare this by faith in Jesus' name!

God's Conquering Peace Empowers You

My Prayer for Today

Lord, I thank You for the peace You have placed in my life. This powerful spiritual weapon protects me from the assaults of life, enabling me to stand fixed, even in the face of the occasional storms that try to blow into my life, my family, my church, my friendships, and my business. How can I ever express how much I need this peace or how grateful I am to You for covering me with this protective shield that fortifies me and makes me strong? When adverse situations arise against me, help me remember to immediately release this divine force to safeguard my life. I pray this in Jesus' name!

Stand therefore, having your loins girt about with truth, and having on the breastplate of righteousness; and your feet shod with the preparation of the gospel of peace.

Ephesians 6:14,15

My Confession for Today

I confess that God's peace rules my mind and emotions, protecting me from the ups and downs of life. When storms are trying to rage against me and situations are hostile toward me, God's peace covers and safeguards me from all harm. Because divine peace is operating in me, I am not easily moved, quickly shaken, or terrified by any events that occur around about me. This mighty and powerful piece of spiritual weaponry is mine to use day and night. Therefore, although the devil may try to kick, punch, pull, and distract me, that conquering peace empowers me to keep marching ahead, oblivious to the devil's attempts to take me down! I declare this by faith in Jesus' name!

Whose Faith Are You Following?

That ye be not slothful, but followers of them who through faith and patience inherit the promises.

Hebrews 6:12

My Prayer for Today

Lord, I need an example that I can follow and imitate! Your Word commands me to imitate strong and successful spiritual leaders, so I am asking You to help me find that exact leader whom You want me to follow and imitate. Give me the grace to do what he does, say what he says, and act the way he acts, until finally I no longer have to act because I have become like the person I have been imitating. Holy Spirit, I want to be obedient to God's Word. Since God tells me to mimic those who through faith and patience inherit the promises of God, I'm asking You to please help me recognize the people whom I should look to as spiritual examples in my walk with God. I pray this in Jesus' name!

My Confession for Today

I confess that I do not have to find my way by myself! By locating godly examples, I can imitate these people's lives and produce the same fruit they produce in their lives. So right now I choose to follow the examples of those who have preceded me—acting like them and replicating both their acts and their godly fruit in my life. God's Word says this is what I am to do, so I will do it as I am commanded. The Holy Spirit will help me know exactly who should be the supreme examples in my life, and He will help me follow their example as I ought to do. I declare this by faith in Jesus' name!

Stick Your Neck Out—
Commit Yourself to Someone

My Prayer for Today

Lord, help me overcome the hurts and disappointment I've experienced because of people who proved to be unfaithful. When I am tempted to judge those who have wronged me, help me remember those whom I myself have wronged in the past. Just as I never intended to hurt anyone, help me realize that my offenders probably didn't intend to hurt me either. As I was forgiven then, I am asking You now to help me forgive—and not just to forgive, but to stick out my neck again and begin to rebuild my life with other people in the Body of Christ. I pray this in Jesus' name!

And the things that thou hast heard of me among many witnesses, the same commit thou to faithful men, who shall be able to teach others also.

2 Timothy 2:2

My Confession for Today

I confess that I don't hold grudges or bitterness against anyone who has wronged me in the past. Just as I've been forgiven, I freely forgive. As others gave me a second chance, I give people the benefit of the doubt and allow them to prove themselves even if they've done something to hurt me. The devil can't paralyze me with fears of being hurt again, because I refuse to allow that kind of fear to operate inside me. I have too much to do to let the devil immobilize me with something that happened to me in the past, so I confess right now that I am freed from every past hurt, and I am moving forward to possess all that God has for me. I declare this by faith in Jesus' name!

Strive To Get Along

From which some having swerved have turned aside unto vain jangling.

1 Timothy 1:6

My Prayer for Today

Lord, help me to never be viewed as an argumentative, belligerent, disagreeable person by those who know me—especially by those who are working with me toward a common goal. If I've done anything to be perceived this way, I am sincerely asking You to forgive me right now. But I know that I don't just need Your forgiveness; I also need to ask for forgiveness from those who felt uncomfortable with my wrong behavior so my relationship with them can be made right. I need Your help to keep a right attitude, Lord, so I am asking You to help me to stay open-minded and correctable. Help me to always maintain a humble spirit and to strive to get along with the key people You have placed in my life. I pray this in Jesus' name!

My Confession for Today

I confess that I have a teachable, correctable spirit. People love to work with me because I strive to be cooperative and to show appreciation for those who are working with me toward a common goal. When an idea is presented that is new or different to me, I think carefully before I open my mouth to respond. Even if I disagree, I don't show disrespect for anyone in the group. I realize that I am not always right and that others may be correct, so I make room for others to express themselves and to speak their hearts, and I honor their right to hold a position that is different from mine. I declare this by faith in Jesus' name!

The Necessary Attitude for Success

My Prayer for Today

Lord, as I step out in faith to do something new, I realize there will always be obstacles that try to get in my way. So today I am asking You to help me stay tougher than any problems that may arise. Help me maintain the attitude that says, "I'm not moving until I see my dream come to pass!" I understand that if I am going to do great things for You, I must be constant, stable, dependable, inflexible, unbending, and unyielding in the face of challenges. With Your help, I know this is exactly the kind of person I will be! I pray this in Jesus' name!

Therefore, my beloved brethren, be ye steadfast, unmovable, always abounding in the work of the Lord....

1 Corinthians 15:58

My Confession for Today

I declare that I am steadfast and immovable! I have a non-negotiable attitude of absolute determination to do what God has called me to do. I am fixed, solid, grounded, established, anchored, unvarying, permanent, and stable in my tenacity to grab hold of all that God has destined for me to accomplish with my life. I will not stop, give in, give up, or surrender to anything that tries to discourage me or to throw me off track. I am committed to stay in the race until I've made it all the way to the end. I declare this by faith in Jesus' name!

Refuse To Ever Let Go of Your Dream

Let us hold fast the profession of our faith without wavering;(for he is faithful that promised;).

Hebrews 10:23

My Prayer for Today

Lord, I am well aware that events will occur in life that will tempt me to release the dream You put in my heart. So right now I ask You to fill me with the courage I need to refuse to let go of my dream. Even though my mind and the circumstances around me may send signals that the dream will never come to pass, I know that You are faithful to what You have promised. Help me wrap my arms of faith around Your promises and never let go until I see them come into manifestation! I pray this in Jesus' name!

My Confession for Today

I boldly declare that my word from God will come to pass! It may take a little while for it to happen, but I will firmly hang on to the promise God has given me. And because I refuse to let the dream slip from my heart, I stand by faith and declare that it is only a matter of time until I see the manifestation of what I'm believing God for. I declare this by faith in Jesus' name!

Esteem the Whole Family of God

My Prayer for Today

Lord, I want to have an appreciation for the entire Body of Christ and not hold others in judgment because they worship differently than I do. Please forgive me for the times I've been so judgmental, narrow-minded, and closed to anyone who does things differently than what I am accustomed to doing. Help me see the wonderful flavors You have placed in Your Church and to learn to appreciate and enjoy the wonderful blend and varieties that exist in Your family. I pray this in Jesus' name!

As every man hath received the gift, even so minister the same one to another, as good stewards of the manifold grace of God.

1 Peter 4:10

My Confession for Today

I confess that I am tolerant and nonjudgmental toward those who worship God differently than my friends and I. As long as they worship Jesus and do it with all their hearts, I thank God for them. I choose to do everything within my power to show respect for and to honor the way others feel most comfortable in their worship of God. If God sees their heart and receives their worship, I am in no position to judge or condemn. For the rest of my life, I will no longer take a contentious position against those who represent parts of the Church that are different from mine. I declare this by faith in Jesus' name!

Pray for Those Whom God Places on Your Heart

I thank God, whom I serve from my forefathers with pure conscience, that without ceasing I have remembrance of thee in my prayers night and day.

2 Timothy 1:3

My Prayer for Today

Lord, I thank You so much for people who have prayed for me. I know their prayers were a vital force to keep Heaven in remembrance of the needs and situations I was facing in life at the time. Forgive me for not being more grateful for people who loved me enough to pray. Now I ask You to help me faithfully pray for those You place on my heart, just as others have prayed for me. Help me keep Heaven in remembrance of these people and their needs. I pray this in Jesus' name!

My Confession for Today

I declare that I am faithful to pray for the people I love! Just as others have prayed for me, I take time to pray for those whom God places on my heart, even mentioning them by name to the Lord. My prayers are powerful and effective for them, causing Heaven to be constantly confronted by the situations and needs they are facing right now. I make a difference in their lives by taking time to pray. I declare this by faith in Jesus' name!

Be Bold To Ask God

My Prayer for Today

Lord, I'm so glad that I can be bold and straight to the point when I come into Your Presence. I am so thankful that You want me to boldly present my needs to You and expect You to answer my requests. Jesus told me to boldly ask, so it is right for me to do just that! Today I come before You to tell You about some big needs I have in my life—and because I know You want to bless and help me, I am releasing my faith, fully expecting to receive what I request of You today. I pray this in Jesus' name!

If ye abide in me, and my words abide in you, ye shall ask what ye will, and it shall be done unto you.

John 15:7

My Confession for Today

I confess that I am bold when I come to God in prayer. Because Jesus beckons me to come to the Father with bold, frank, and confident requests, I make my needs known to God and fully expect Him to answer me. He is my Father, and I am His child. He WANTS me to be bold enough to ask Him to meet my needs, and He promises never to withhold any good thing from me! I declare this by faith in Jesus' name!

God's Word–Your Most Important Weapon

*Stand therefore,
having your loins
girt about with
truth....*

Ephesians 6:14

My Prayer for Today

Lord, I know that Your Word is the most important weapon You have given to me. Forgive me for the times I have not made it a priority in my life. Today I make the decision to never ignore Your Word again. Holy Spirit, help me stay true to this decision. Please remind me every day to open my Bible and take the time needed to wrap that Word around my life. I pray this in Jesus' name!

My Confession for Today

Because God's Word has a central place in my life, I have a sense of righteousness that covers me like a mighty breastplate. God's Word is operating in my life, giving me a powerful sword to wield against the enemy—that rhema word quickened by the Spirit of God to my heart in my time of need. And because God's Word also dominates my thinking, I have peace that protects me from the attacks of the adversary and shields my mind like a powerful helmet. I declare this by faith in Jesus' name!

Keep the Devil Where He Belongs—Under Your Feet

And the God of peace shall bruise Satan under your feet shortly....

Romans 16:20

My Prayer for Today

Lord, the next time the devil tries to get in my way or to block my path, help me to raise my feet high, pound down as hard as I can, and stomp all over him as I march forward unhindered to do Your will. I thank You that because of Your victory, Satan has no right to exercise this kind of control over my life anymore! With You working as my Partner, I can stare that old enemy in the face and command him to move. And if he tries to put up a fight, I can push him out of the way and walk on through! I pray this in Jesus' name!

My Confession for Today

I boldly declare that Jesus destroyed Satan's power over me! Through Jesus' death and resurrection, the devil was utterly smashed, crushed, and bruised. Now my God-given mission is to reinforce that glorious victory and to demonstrate just how miserably defeated Satan already is. The enemy may try to lord himself over me, but he has no authority to exercise any control in my life. I declare this by faith in Jesus' name!

The Lord Will Reckon With You When He Comes

After a long time the lord of those servants cometh, and reckoneth with them.

Matthew 25:19

My Prayer for Today

Lord, help me live with the awareness that a day of reckoning is in my future. Your Word makes it clear that on the day I stand before You, I will answer for what I did in this life. I will give account for the gifts, talents, abilities, ideas, and assignments You entrusted to me. On that day, I want to look into Your face with confidence, so help me NOW to faithfully use the abilities You've given me to execute every task You have asked me to do. I pray this in Jesus' name!

My Confession for Today

I boldly acknowledge that a day of reckoning is coming in my future. On that day, I will give account for what I did or didn't do in this life. Therefore, I will use the gifts, talents, and abilities Jesus has given to me. I will faithfully execute every assignment He has asked me to do. I will do everything within my power to please Jesus in the way that I serve Him. I will make sure that my conscience is clear with God and with myself. I declare this by faith in Jesus' name!

You Are in the Race of Your Life–So Run

My Prayer for Today

Lord, I want to set my eyes on the finish line and never lose my focus until I know that I've accomplished the task You have given me to do. I know it's going to take all my spiritual, mental, and physical energies to get this job done. So I am turning to You now, Holy Spirit, and I'm asking You to empower me and to help me make it all the way to the completion of the dream You have given to me. I pray this in Jesus' name!

Know ye not that they which run in a race run all, but one receiveth the prize? So run, that ye may obtain.

1 Corinthians 9:24

My Confession for Today

I declare that I have a divine purpose in life! I am not half-hearted, mealy-mouthed, touchy, or easily discouraged. I am like a runner who is seriously running a race. Because I'm serious about achieving God's plan for my life, I am shifting into high gear and putting all my spiritual, mental, and physical energies into getting the job done. I declare this by faith in Jesus' name!

From 'Amateur' to 'Professional'

And if a man also strive for masteries, yet is he not crowned, except he strive lawfully.

2 Timothy 2:5

My Prayer for Today

Lord, I want You to see me as a professional! Therefore, I choose to put away amateurish Christian attitudes and behaviors. For me to be all You want me to be, I understand that it's going to require more of me. Right now I am making up my mind to move to a higher level of commitment with God, to give Him all that I have, and to never stop until the job is done and the assignment is complete. Help me move into the "professional league" as a believer and to leave the life of the amateur behind forever! I pray this in Jesus' name!

My Confession for Today

I confess that I am a serious contender for doing the will of God. In spite of what the devil and life may try to throw at me, I will walk away as the winner. I will survive hard times and thus prove the sincerity of my faith. Mine isn't a flawed faith that tucks its tail and runs. I am the kind of Christian who sticks it out to the end! I declare this by faith in Jesus' name!

The Supernatural Intercessory Ministry of the Holy Spirit

My Prayer for Today

Lord, I thank You that the Holy Spirit joins me in the challenges I am facing in my life today. You sent Him to be my Helper, my Guide, my Teacher, and my Intercessor—the One who meets my problems head-on and helps me to overcome them. Rather than try to work out those problems by myself, I open my heart today for the Holy Spirit to join me as my Divine Partner so I can be more than a conqueror in every situation! I pray this in Jesus' name!

Likewise the Spirit also helpeth our infirmities: for we know not what we should pray for as we ought: but the Spirit itself maketh intercession for us with groanings which cannot be uttered.

Romans 8:26

My Confession for Today

I confess that the Holy Spirit is my leading Partner in this life. When I need help, He is right by my side, ready to help me and to pull me through each challenge that I face. I know His voice; I partner with Him; and as a result, I enjoy continuous victory in my life. I declare this by faith in Jesus' name!

Letting God Transform You

But as we were allowed of God to be put in trust with the gospel, even so we speak; not as pleasing men, but God, which trieth our hearts.

1 Thessalonians 2:4

My Prayer for Today

Lord, thank You for considering my character so carefully. I know that You want to change me and conform me into the image of Jesus more than anything else. I often feel rushed to get things moving, but I know that You are looking to see if I have the character I need so I can successfully do what You've called me to do. I yield my heart to You and ask You to do Your work inside me. Change me so You can use me as You wish! I pray this in Jesus' name!

My Confession for Today

I declare by faith that I am being changed so God can use me to the degree He desires. Yes, I have areas in my life that need to be transformed, but because I renew my mind with the Word of God and spend time in prayer, God is free to work on me and get me ready for the big job He has designed for my life. I know that as I stay open and willing to change, my character will be transformed into the image of Jesus so I can complete my task successfully and to the glory of God. I declare this by faith in Jesus' name!

Learn To Work With the Holy Spirit

My Prayer for Today

Lord, help me learn how to work with the Holy Spirit. I don't want to waste time grieving over what I missed by not living two thousands years ago, so I ask You to teach me how to let the Spirit lead and guide me. Your Word teaches that because the Holy Spirit is with me, the ministry of Jesus can continue uninterrupted in my life today. Holy Spirit, I ask You to bring me into a greater knowledge of how to work with You so that the ministry of Jesus can continue through me. I pray this in Jesus' name!

And I will pray the Father, and he shall give you another comforter....

John 14:16

My Confession for Today

I declare by faith that the Holy Spirit works mightily in my life. I know His voice, I discern His leading, and I boldly do what He tells me to do. Because I am obedient to His voice, the life of Jesus Christ is manifested in me. Having the Holy Spirit work with me is just like having Jesus right by my side all the time. Just as Jesus worked miracles in the book of Acts, the Holy Spirit works miracles through me today—healing the sick, casting out demons, and bringing salvation to the lost through Jesus Christ. I declare this by faith in Jesus' name!

Forgiveness for Wrongdoing

And supper being ended, the devil having now put into the heart of Judas Iscariot, Simon's son, to betray him.

John 13:2

My Prayer for Today

Lord, please forgive me for the times I've allowed the devil to put a wedge between me and the people You have placed in my life. Help me go to them and ask forgiveness for the things I did wrong. Help me also to extend patience, forgiveness, and love to others who have done wrong to me or who will wrong me in the future. I never want the devil to be in charge of my emotions or my thought life, so I am asking You to help me think clearly and to know how to recognize those times when the devil tries to upset me and ruin my relationships. I pray this in Jesus' name!

My Confession for Today

I confess that my mind is free of offense, unforgiveness, and strife. Because I walk in mercy and forgiveness, the devil has no entrance or open door to find his way into my mind and emotions. The Spirit of God dominates my thinking and helps me see things very clearly. I declare this by faith in Jesus' name!

Jesus Understands Your Feelings

My Prayer for Today

Lord, I need a little relief from the stress and pressure I've been under lately. I'm so thankful You understand what I'm feeling and going through in my life right now. Sometimes I feel so lonely in my situation. Even when my friends want to help, I don't know how to express myself. But I know that You understand me, even when I can't get the right words out of my mouth. So, Lord, today I am asking You to come alongside me in a special way. Undergird me with Your strength, power, and wisdom. Thank You for understanding me and for helping me today! I pray this in Jesus' name!

And there appeared an angel unto him from Heaven, strengthening him. And being in an agony he prayed more earnestly: and his sweat was as it were great drops of blood falling down to the ground.

Luke 22:43,44

My Confession for Today

I boldly confess that Jesus Christ understands and emphasizes with me and the situations I am facing right now. Because He understands, I go to Him and talk to Him, knowing that He hears me when I pray. And not only does He listen to me, but He also answers the prayers and the cries of my heart. I do not have to face my challenges today alone because Jesus is with me, empowering me to stand tall, to stand firm, and to hold my head high! With Him as my Helper, I will not only survive but will thrive and prosper in spite of what the devil has tried to do to me. I declare this by faith in Jesus' name!

Supernatural Assistance for Every Burden

And there appeared an angel unto him from Heaven, strengthening him.

Luke 22:43

My Prayer for Today

Lord, I thank You for Your Word that speaks so directly into my life today. It's true that I feel very alone and trapped in the situation I'm facing right now. I don't know what to do, what step to take, what to say, or where to turn. I've tried to give the problem to You, but in some way I've continued to carry part of the load by myself, and it is starting to break me. Right now—at this very moment—I am throwing the full weight of my burden and cares on Your huge shoulders! I thank You for taking this burden from me and for filling me with the strength I need to press through this time in my life. I pray this in Jesus' name!

My Confession for Today

I confess that God is committed to seeing me through the situation I am facing right now. He is providing all the supernatural assistance I need to get recharged and to keep me moving full steam ahead. Even though I am tempted to feel isolated and alone, I am not alone. God is filling me with power; He is surrounding me with angels; and He is ready to provide me with anything else I need to keep moving forward to fulfill His will for my life. I declare this by faith in Jesus' name!

Walking in the Power of Your High Priest

My Prayer for Today

Lord, I am so thankful You possess the greatest power in the whole universe! I'm not serving a dead god; I'm serving a living Lord who is interceding for me at the right hand of the Father at this very moment. Jesus, I come to You as my great High Priest, and I ask You today to fill me with Your power 24 hours a day, 365 days a year. I don't want to just intellectually know about You; I want to truly know You. I want to experience Your power and walk in Your ways. I pray this in Jesus' name!

For we have not an high priest which cannot be touched with the feeling of our infirmities; but was in all points tempted like as we are, yet without sin. Let us therefore come boldly unto the throne of grace, that we may obtain mercy, and find grace to help in time of need.

Hebrews 4:15,16

My Confession for Today

I declare by faith that the Greater One lives inside me. I am a world overcomer! The same power that raised Jesus from the dead now lives inside me and is at my disposal 24 hours a day. When I'm faced with a situation that requires power, I open my heart and release the immense power of Jesus Christ that is stored up deep inside me. This power is continuously resident in my heart and is more than enough to face and overcome any obstacle the devil ever tries to throw in my way. I declare this by faith in Jesus' name!

Show Mercy in Your Relationships

Be ye therefore merciful, as your Father also is merciful.

Luke 6:36

My Prayer for Today

Lord, help me learn how to avoid misjudging and misperceiving other people. I know that when I misjudge someone, it affects my opinion of that person in a way that can open a door to the devil in our relationship with each other. I don't want to give the devil an inch in any of my relationships, so I need You to help me think cautiously, to take time to get to know people, and to give them the benefit of the doubt when I don't understand something they say or do. Help me give people the same mercy I would expect them to give me. And help me get started on this path today! I pray this in Jesus' name!

My Confession for Today

I confess that it doesn't ruffle my feathers or upset me when I hear that someone has a wrong perception about me. I know I've made this same mistake about others in the past, so I am filled with mercy for those who misjudge or have misconceptions about who I am. I choose to be thankful for this situation and to see it as my opportunity to show people who I really am. I also take this opportunity to see what needs to be changed in my life and then to make the necessary adjustments so people never misperceive me in this way again. I declare this by faith in Jesus' name!

The Judas Kiss

My Prayer for Today

Lord, forgive me for the times I've been a Judas! I am so sorry for the times I've been unfaithful or hurtful to people who thought they could trust me. I truly repent for repeating things that were told to me in confidence, for I know it would have hurt me deeply if someone had done the same thing to me. Help me go back to those whom I have hurt and ask for their forgiveness. Please restore my fellowship with those people, and help me never to repeat this wrong behavior again. I pray this in Jesus' name!

And he that betrayed him had given them a token, saying, Whomsoever I kiss, that same is he: take him, and lead him away safely. And as soon as he was come, he goeth straightway to him, and saith, Master, master; and kissed him.

Mark 14:44,45

My Confession for Today

I confess that I use wisdom in the way I choose my closest friends. Because the Holy Spirit is constantly illuminating my mind with insight, I discern who is a real friend and who isn't. Even more, I confess that I am a real friend and not a betrayer of the people who are dear to me. When the devil tempts me to open my mouth and repeat things that were told to me in confidence, I do not do it! I am a friend who can be trusted. I will never be known as a betrayer to the friends God has brought into my life! I declare this by faith in Jesus' name!

Submission to Spiritual Authority

Obey them that have the rule over you, and submit yourselves: for they watch for your souls, as they that must give account, that they may do it with joy, and not with grief: for that is unprofitable for you.

Hebrews 13:17

My Prayer for Today

Lord, thank You for the spiritual authorities You have placed in my life. Help me learn how to honor them, respect them, and truly submit to their spiritual authority. If there is any defect in my character that would cause me to rebel or to act in an ungodly fashion, please expose it in me now so I can deal with it and change. I want to make sure that my commitments are real and not artificially contrived, so please work in me and bring to light every area that needs work and attention. I pray this in Jesus' name!

My Confession for Today

I confess that God is helping me submit to the spiritual authorities He has placed in my life. I am having a change of heart and a true turn-around, and I'm learning to be faithful in my relationships with those who are over me. God has tapped me on the shoulder and instructed me to stop rebelling against my authorities and to start acting in a godly fashion toward them. I choose to be thankful that God has entrusted to my spiritual authorities the responsibility of watching over my soul, for that is profitable for me. God is working in every area of my life that needs change, and I am able to honor, respect, and submit to those He places in authority over me. I declare this by faith in Jesus' name!

Knocked Flat by the Power of God

My Prayer for Today

Lord, I am so glad that You are the great "I AM" and that You have power over every force in the universe. When You speak, demons tremble, sickness flees, poverty is vanquished, and Your Kingdom rules and reigns! Because You live inside me, Your power is resident in me and ready to set me free from any force that tries to come against me. I stand on Your Word, Lord. I speak it out loud by faith and therefore expect to see mountains move out of the way for me! I pray this in Jesus' name!

Jesus therefore, knowing all things that should come upon him, went forth, and said unto them, Whom seek ye? They answered him, Jesus of Nazareth. Jesus saith unto them, I am he.... As soon then as he had said unto them, I am he, they went backward, and fell to the ground.

John 18:4-6

My Confession for Today

I declare that there is no force strong enough to resist God's power in my life. No sickness, financial turmoil, relational problems, political force—absolutely NOTHING has enough power to resist the supernatural power of Jesus Christ that is resident in me! When I open my mouth and speak the Word of God, every power that attempts to defy His Word is pushed backward and shaken till it staggers, stumbles, and falls to the ground. When my mouth gets into agreement with God's Word, I see His power unleashed against the forces that try to come against me! I declare this by faith in Jesus' name!

Releasing Grudges

When they which were about him saw what would follow, they said unto him, Lord, shall we smite them with the sword? And one of them smote the servant of the high priest, and cut off his right ear. And Jesus answered and said, Suffer ye thus far. And he touched his ear, and healed him.

Luke 22:49-51

My Prayer for Today

Lord, I ask You to help me be more like Jesus! Help me release the grudges and deeply-held resentments that I am tempted to carry toward people. Instead of rejoicing when they get in trouble or when something bad happens to them, help me to reach out to them, to see what I can do to help, and to become the hand of God in their lives. Forgive me that I haven't already acted as Jesus would act, and help me learn how to put any negative emotions aside so I can reach out to them in the name of Jesus. I pray this in Jesus' name!

My Confession for Today

I confess that I do not hold grudges, nor do I allow deep-seated resentments to reside in my heart, mind, and emotions. I have the mind of Christ, and I think just like Jesus thinks. What Jesus does is what I do. What Jesus says is what I say. How Jesus behaves is how I behave. Because the Holy Spirit is working to produce the life of Jesus Christ in me, I can be the extended hand of Jesus to everyone around me, including those who have been opposed to me. I declare this by faith in Jesus' name!

Jesus Cleans Up Your Mess

My Prayer for Today

Lord, I am so thankful for the many times You have stepped into my life to clean up the messes I've created by myself. Had I been more patient and waited on You, I could have avoided the problems that stole my time, my thoughts, my energies, and my money. Forgive me for being impetuous, and help me learn to wait on You. When I see others make the same mistakes I've made, help me remember the times You have helped me so I can respond with a heart filled with compassion and not with judgment, reaching out to help them recover from the mistakes they have made. I pray this in Jesus' name!

And Jesus answered, Suffer ye thus far. And he touched his ear, and healed him.

Luke 22:51

My Confession for Today

I confess that I am merciful and compassionate to people who have messed up their lives. Their problems are my opportunities to allow God to use me in their lives by helping them recover from their mistakes. God loves these people so much that He wants to send me alongside them to assist, teach, and do whatever I can to help them get back on their feet again. I have been so touched by God's mercy myself that judgment and condemnation cannot operate inside me. Rather than lecture people about their mistakes so they feel even worse about what they have done, I am God's mercy extended to support them in their time of trouble. I declare this by faith in Jesus' name!

Let Jesus Solve Your Problems

Then Simon Peter having a sword drew it, and smote the high priest's servant, and cut off his right ear. The servant's name was Malchus. Then said Jesus unto Peter, Put up thy sword into the sheath: the cup which my Father hath given me, shall I not drink it?

John 18:10,11

My Prayer for Today

Lord, I am so glad You have the power to put an end to my problems! So many times I've acted just like Peter, swinging furiously in the strength of my own flesh as I've tried to solve my problems without Your help. Forgive me for wasting so much time and energy! Today I ask You to speak to my heart and tell me what I am supposed to do; then help me follow Your instructions to the letter. Give me the patience to wait while You supernaturally work behind the scenes to resolve my questions. I pray this in Jesus' name!

My Confession for Today

I boldly and joyfully affirm that Jesus Christ has all the power needed to fix my problems! I am not smart enough by myself to figure out how to get out of my messes, so I turn to Him to give me wisdom, insight, power, and the answers I need to get from where I am to where I need to be. His power works mightily through me, and that divine power is being released right now to tackle the challenges I face in life and bring me to a peaceful place of resolution in every situation. I declare this by faith in Jesus' name!

Thankful for the Cross

My Prayer for Today

Lord, You are so amazing! How can I ever thank You enough for coming into this world to give Your life for me? I'm sorry for the times I get so busy that I fail to remember the incredible love You willfully demonstrated to me by going to the Cross. You didn't have to do it, but You did it for me. I thank You from the depths of my heart for loving me so completely! I pray this in Jesus' name!

For God so loved the world, that he gave his only begotten Son, that whosoever believeth in him should not perish, but have everlasting life.

John 3:16

My Confession for Today

I boldly declare that God values me! He loves me so much that He sent Jesus into the world to take my place on the Cross. He took my sin, He carried my sickness, and He bore my shame. Because of Jesus' work of redemption on the Cross, today I am saved, I am healed, and I am not ashamed! I declare this by faith in Jesus' name!

Kept by God's Peace

Thou wilt keep him in perfect peace, whose mind is stayed on thee: because he trusteth in thee.

Isaiah 26:3

My Prayer for Today

Lord, in times when I find myself stuck in a situation I don't like or enjoy, help me lift my eyes and look to You for strength. I know that You love me and are looking out for my life, so in those moments when I am tempted to be nervous or afraid, I ask You to help me rest in the knowledge that You will take care of me. I pray this in Jesus' name!

My Confession for Today

I declare by faith that I am kept by the peace of God. Even when I find myself in situations that seem unjust, undeserving, and unfair, God is secretly working to turn things around for my good. He loves me, He cares for me, and He wants to see the very best for my life. Therefore, I entrust my job, my income, my marriage, my children, my health, and everything else in my life into the hands of my Heavenly Father! I declare this by faith in Jesus' name!

Unshaken Love

My Prayer for Today

Lord, thank You for being such a good example of love that is unshaken and unaffected by other people's actions. You have loved me with a consistent love, even in times when I've acted badly and didn't deserve it. Thank You so much for loving me in spite of the things I've done and the things I've permitted to go on in my life. Today I want to ask You to help me love others just as consistently as You have loved me. Forgive me for being on-again, off-again in my love. Help me become rock-solid and unwavering in my love for others, including those who haven't treated me too nicely. I know that with Your help, I can love them steadfastly no matter what they do! I pray this in Jesus' name!

Then said Jesus, Father, forgive them; for they know not what they do. And they parted his raiment, and cast lots.

Luke 23:34

My Confession for Today

I confess that what other people have done to me doesn't affect my desire or my commitment to love them. My love for people is consistent, unwavering, unshaken, and unaffected. The same Holy Spirit who lived in Jesus now lives in me—and just as the Spirit of God empowered Jesus to love everyone consistently, now the Holy Spirit empowers me to do the same! I declare this by faith in Jesus' name!

Don't Play Games in Your Walk With God

And the men that held Jesus mocked him, and smote him. And when they had blindfolded him, they struck him on the face, and asked him, saying, Prophesy, who is it that smote thee?

Luke 22:63,64

My Prayer for Today

Lord, I never want to play games with You. I am asking You right now to forgive me for any time that I have lied to You and to myself, deceiving myself into believing that things were all right in my life when, in fact, they were not inwardly good at all. Please shine Your light deep into my soul to show me any areas of my life that need immediate attention. And, Lord, I also ask that You give me a strong desire to read through all four of the Gospels so I might better know the life of Jesus and how I can be more like Him. I pray this in Jesus' name!

My Confession for Today

I declare by faith that God gives me the wisdom to know how to respond when I am in a difficult predicament. I know when I should speak, when I should be quiet, and exactly what steps I must take. When I find myself in a tight place, I don't give way to my emotions. Instead, I guard my mouth and let the Spirit dictate my emotions so I can demonstrate the love of God even to those whom the devil is trying to use against me! I declare this by faith in Jesus' name!

Knowing God's Plan for Your Life

My Prayer for Today

Lord, I want to be so confident of Your plan for my life that I refuse to let anything move me! Just as Jesus refused to be swayed away from Your plan for Him, I want to be fixed and committed to do exactly what I've been born to do. Help me know Your plan for my life—and once I really understand it, please give me the strength and power until I see that plan come to pass in my life! I pray this in Jesus' name!

And when they had bound him, they led him away, and delivered him to Pontius Pilate the governor.

Matthew 27:2

My Confession for Today

I boldly declare that God has a wonderful plan for my life! God's Spirit is revealing that plan to me right now. I am willing to do what He's called me to do; I'm willing to go where He tells me to go; and I'm willing to pay any price I have to pay to accomplish the life-assignment God has pre-ordained for me. My greatest priority and obsession is to do the will of the Father! I declare this by faith in Jesus' name!

Have the Mind of Christ

For who hath known the mind of the Lord, that he may instruct him? but we have the mind of Christ.

1 Corinthians 2:16

My Prayer for Today

Lord, I am so glad You understand when I feel confused about the person I am supposed to report to and to whom I am supposed to be accountable at work and at church. Sometimes I feel like my leaders send me back and forth, not knowing what to do with me or to whom I am supposed to report, which makes it hard for me to do my job. I know that those who are over me have their own challenges, so I want to be helpful to them, not judgmental of them. Please give me the wisdom to know how to behave in a godly manner in this environment. I pray this in Jesus' name!

My Confession for Today

I confess that I have the mind of Christ for my situation. I am not in confusion; rather, I walk in peace in every situation. Because Jesus has been in my same place, I go to Him to tell Him about my situation, and He gives me all the mercy and grace I need to be successful in this place where He has called me. I declare this by faith in Jesus' name!

Quiet and Self-Controlled

My Prayer for Today

Lord, help me control myself when a project into which I've put my whole heart and soul goes unappreciated and rejected by my boss, my parent, my pastor, my fellow workers, or my friends. Help me take advantage of moments like these to learn how to be quiet and controlled. Please use these times in my life to help me mature and to learn how to keep my mouth shut. I know You understand the emotions that accompany this kind of disappointment, so who else can I turn to but You to help me in these kinds of ordeals? I pray this in Jesus' name!

And beside this, giving all diligence, add to your faith... temperance [self-control]; and to temperance [self-control] patience; and to patience godliness.

2 Peter 1:5,6

My Confession for Today

I confess that I am self-controlled when people get angry or upset with me. Even when others vent their anger by yelling and screaming, I don't yell and scream back at them. In these moments, the Spirit of God rules my heart, mind, and emotions, and I am able to remain quiet and controlled. When I find myself in this situation, I hide myself away in prayer for a few minutes and call out to the Lord. He helps me understand the right way and the right time to respond. I declare this by faith in Jesus' name!

The Wonder of Redemption

Neither by the blood of goats and calves, but by his own blood he entered in once into the holy place, having obtained eternal redemption for us.

Hebrews 9:12

My Prayer for Today

Lord, I want to take this moment to say thank You for everything You went through for me. It is amazing that You loved me so much that You were willing to endure all of this for me. I know that my salvation was purchased with Your blood and that I could never pay for my salvation. But I want to tell You that I will serve You faithfully for the rest of my days as a way to show You my gratitude. Jesus, thank You for loving me so much! I pray this in Jesus' name!

My Confession for Today

I confess that I am redeemed by the blood of Jesus Christ! God loved me so much that He sent His only begotten Son to take away my sin, my sickness, my pain, my lack of peace, and my suffering on the Cross. Because of Jesus, today I am forgiven; I am healed; I am free of pain; I am filled with peace; and I am a joint heir with Him! I declare this by faith in Jesus' name!

Never Back Down

My Prayer for Today

Lord, forgive me for the times I've denied You and the principles of Your Word because I was afraid I'd jeopardize my popularity if I remained faithful to You. I am truly sorry for this, and today I repent for my wrong behavior. The next time I'm put on the spot and required to make this kind of choice, please help me put aside any worry about saving my own popularity or reputation and make the decision that honors You. I pray this in Jesus' name!

And about the space of one hour after another confidently affirmed, saying, Of a truth this fellow also was with him: for he is a Galilaean. And Peter said, Man, I know not what thou sayest. And immediately, while he yet spake, the cock crew. And the Lord turned, and looked upon Peter. And Peter remembered the word of the Lord, how he had said unto him, Before the cock crow, thou shalt deny me thrice.

Luke 22:59-61

My Confession for Today

I confess that living for Jesus Christ is the most important thing in my life. I will stand for Him, live for Him, speak up for Him, and never back down. Regardless of the pressure that comes to push me away from this rock-solid position, I will not move from my wholehearted commitment to Jesus. His power strengthens me and helps me remain strong even in the face of opposition and conflict. I declare this by faith in Jesus' name!

By His Stripes You Are Healed

...And when he had scourged Jesus, he delivered him to be crucified.

Matthew 27:26

My Prayer for Today

Lord, I had no idea how much pain You endured to pay the price for my physical healing. Forgive me for the times I've tolerated sickness and didn't even pray to be healed. Now I understand that Your desire to see me healed is so great that You paid a price far beyond anything I will ever be able to comprehend. Since my physical well-being is that important to You, starting today I determine to walk in divine health and healing. I am taking a stand of faith to walk in healing and to fully possess the health You bought for me that day when You were so severely beaten. I pray this in Jesus' name!

My Confession for Today

I boldly confess that I am healed by the stripes of Jesus Christ. The agony He endured was for me and my health. I don't have to be sick; I don't have to be weak; and I don't have to live at the mercy of affliction anymore. The stripes on Jesus' body were for me, so today I release my faith and commit that I will not be satisfied with anything less than God's best—divine healing and health every day of my life! I declare this by faith in Jesus' name!

Empowered With God's Spirit

My Prayer for Today

Lord, open my eyes to those around me who are unsaved and in need of salvation. You died for them because You want them to be saved. I know that You are trusting me to tell them the Good News that they can be saved. Please empower me strongly with Your Spirit, giving me the boldness I need, to step out from behind intimidation and to tell them the truth that will save them from an eternity in hell. Help me to start telling them the Good News immediately, before it is too late. I pray this in Jesus' name!

And when they had prayed, the place was shaken where they were assembled together; and they were all filled with the Holy Ghost, and they spake the word of God with boldness.

Acts 4:31

My Confession for Today

I declare by faith that I am a strong witness for Jesus Christ. My eyes are opened and my spirit is attentive to recognize opportunities to speak the Gospel to people who are unsaved. When I speak to them, they listen with an open heart and want to hear what I have to say. Because of my bold witness, my family, friends, acquaintances, and fellow workers are getting saved. I declare this by faith in Jesus' name!

Freedom Through Christ

And when they were come unto a place called Golgotha, that is to say, a place of a skull, They gave him vinegar to drink mingled with gall: and when he had tasted thereof, he would not drink. And they crucified him, and parted his garments, casting lots: that it might be fulfilled which was spoken by the prophet, They parted my garments among them, and upon my vesture did they cast lots.

Matthew 27:33-35

My Prayer for Today

Lord, how can I ever adequately say thank You for all that You did for me at the Cross? I was so undeserving, but You came and gave Your life for me, taking away my sin and removing the punishment that should have passed to me. I thank You from the depths of my heart for doing what no one else could do for me. Had it not been for You, I would be eternally lost, so I just want to say thank You for laying down Your life that I might be free. I pray this in Jesus' name!

My Confession for Today

I confess that I am washed in the blood of Jesus Christ. His blood covered my sin, washed me whiter than snow, and gave me right standing with God. I have no need to be ashamed of my past sins, because I am a new creature in Christ Jesus—marvelously made brand new in Him. Old things have passed away, and all things have become new because I am in Jesus Christ. That's who I am! I declare this by faith in Jesus' name!

No One Else

My Prayer for Today

Lord, help me never to forget the price You paid on the Cross for my salvation. Please forgive me for the times my life starts moving so fast that I fail to remember what You did for me. No one else could have taken my place. No one else could have paid the price for my sin. So You went to the Cross, bearing my sin, my sickness, my pain, and my lack of peace. That Cross was the place where the price was paid for my deliverance. Today I want to thank You from the very depths of my heart for doing this for me! I pray this in Jesus' name!

And when they had crucified him, they parted his garments, casting lots upon them, what every man should take. And it was the third hour, and they crucified him.

Mark 15:24,25

My Confession for Today

I boldly and thankfully confess that the blood of Jesus Christ was shed for me! That precious blood covered my sin and washed me clean, and today it gives me a right standing before God. Because of the Cross, I am redeemed from sin, sickness, pain, and torment. Satan no longer has a right to lay any claim on me! From a grateful heart, I will faithfully serve Jesus the rest of my days. I declare this by faith in Jesus' name!

APRIL 25

No More Separation

Jesus, when he had cried again with a loud voice, yielded up the ghost. And, behold, the veil of the temple was rent in twain from the top to the bottom; and the earth did quake, and the rocks rent.

Matthew 27:50,51

My Prayer for Today

Lord, I thank You for destroying the veil that separated me from Your Presence. By taking away the veil, You made it possible for me to come boldly before Your throne of grace to obtain mercy and receive help in my time of need. Because of what You did for me, today I am coming boldly to tell You what I need in my life. I present my case to You, and I thank You in advance for helping me just as You promised in Your Word. I pray this in Jesus' name!

My Confession for Today

I confess that I have a God-given right to come directly into the Presence of God. Jesus removed the wall of separation—and because of what He did, I have no reason to feel unworthy or beggarly when I come before the Lord. Indeed, I am washed by the blood of Jesus, and God beckons me to come to Him with confident expectation. Therefore, I boldly come and make my requests known to God, and He answers me when I pray. I declare this by faith in Jesus' name!

Heavenly Treasure

My Prayer for Today

Lord, I want to become a better and bigger giver! I love You with all my heart, and I want to demonstrate my love with my finances. Your Word says where my treasure is, that is where my heart is also. What I do with my treasure reveals what is precious to me and the true condition of my heart. Therefore, I want to give more to You; I want to live better for You; and I want to serve You more fully than ever before. I am making the decision today to make You and Your Kingdom the highest priority when it comes to how I spend my personal finances. I pray this in Jesus' name!

Lay not up for yourselves treasures upon earth, where moth and rust doth corrupt, and where thieves break through and steal: But lay up for yourselves treasures in heaven, where neither moth nor rust doth corrupt, and where thieves do not break through nor steal: For where your treasure is, there will your heart be also.

Matthew 6:19-21

My Confession for Today

I boldly declare that Jesus Christ and His Kingdom are the highest priorities in my life. I faithfully tithe and give special offerings to help advance the message of Jesus Christ around the world. There is no higher priority in my life than getting the Gospel to the ends of the earth, so I use my finances wisely and carefully, making certain that I am able to give my maximum gift to Jesus. Because I give so faithfully, I am blessed! I declare this by faith in Jesus' name!

The Risen Lord–Your High Priest

Then cometh Simon Peter following him, and went into the sepulchre, and seeth the linen clothes lie, And the napkin, that was about his head, not lying with the linen clothes, but wrapped together in a place by itself. Then went in also that other disciple, which came first to the sepulchre, and he saw, and believed. For as yet they knew not the scripture, that he must rise again from the dead.

John 20:6-9

My Prayer for Today

Lord, I refuse to struggle in my own strength any longer, acting like I can handle every problem and challenge in my life by myself. You were raised from the dead to become my High Priest. I am so sorry for the times You have waited in vain for me to come to You because I lingered, thinking I didn't need Your help. Starting right now, I am changing this in my life—and when I have a need, I'm going to come straight to You because You are there waiting to help me! I pray this in Jesus' name!

My Confession for Today

I boldly declare that Jesus is my High Priest and that He hears me when I pray. I go to Him and tell Him about my needs and challenges, and He answers me! He gives me strength, power, wisdom, and all the guidance I need to make right decisions and choices. As a result of Jesus helping me, I am strong; I am wise; and I make right decisions and choices in my life today. I declare this by faith in Jesus' name!

The Power To Witness

My Prayer for Today

Lord, I am concerned for my family, friends, acquaintances, and fellow workers who still don't know You as their personal Savior. I've been concerned that if I tried to talk to them, I wouldn't make sense, so I've shied away from witnessing to them. But I know You can make sense out of anything I say. Today I am leaning on You to help me witness to people in my life. I need You to speak to their hearts at the same time I'm speaking to their ears. Please help me tell them about Your saving grace! I pray this in Jesus' name!

But ye shall receive power, after that the Holy Ghost is come upon you: and ye shall be witnesses unto me both in Jerusalem, and in all Judaea, and in Samaria, and unto the uttermost part of the earth.

Acts 1:8

My Confession for Today

I confess that I am a witness for Jesus Christ! I open my mouth and speak the truth in love, and people want to hear what I have to tell them. This is the best news in the whole world—and when I tell it, people get excited and want to give their lives to Jesus. I am not afraid to speak up, to speak out, and to speak on behalf of my precious Savior. What He has done for me, He will do for others, for He is not a respecter of persons. Therefore, I will boldly tell of the grace of God and what He has done for me! I declare this by faith in Jesus' name!

He Will Rescue You

The Lord is my rock, and my fortress, and my deliverer; my God, my strength, in whom I will trust; my buckler, and the horn of my salvation, and my high tower. I will call upon the Lord, who is worthy to be praised: so shall I be saved from mine enemies.

Psalm 18:2,3

My Prayer for Today

Lord, it is true that You have worked so many miracles in my life. If I were to try to recount all the times You have saved me, delivered me, rescued me, gotten me out of trouble, put me on a right path, and blessed me when I didn't deserve it, I wouldn't have enough time to recite them all! So how could I ever question that You would be with me right now in my present challenge? Of course You are with me and will help me. Forgive me for being so hard-hearted as to forget what You have already done for me. And I thank You right now that You are going to help me this time too! I pray this in Jesus' name!

My Confession for Today

I confess that I am not forgetful of the many ways God has worked in my life. I am mindful of His mercy and grace, and I praise Him for it every day. I am a living testimony of His power. He is my Redeemer, my Healer, my Deliverer, and my Provider. He is the One who rescues me from harm and who meets my every need. I am fully supplied in every area of my life because of the promises God has made to me in His Word. I declare this by faith in Jesus' name!

Knowing the Voice of Jesus

My Prayer for Today

Lord, thank You for being my Good Shepherd! I am so thankful You speak to me and lead me through life. I'm sorry I haven't listened to You so many times when You have tried to warn me, help me, and guide me. I have lost so much because I didn't listen when You spoke. But rather than focus on my past losses, I determine to do everything within my ability to hear You now and to obediently follow what You tell me to do. I pray this in Jesus' name!

Jesus saith unto her, Woman, why weepest thou? whom seekest thou? She, supposing him to be the gardener, saith unto him, Sir, if thou have borne him hence, tell me where thou hast laid him, and I will take him away. Jesus saith unto her, Mary. She turned herself, and saith unto him, Rabboni; which is to say, Master.

John 20:15,16

My Confession for Today

I boldly confess that I know the voice of Jesus! He is my Shepherd, and I am His sheep. He promises that I will know His voice and that the voice of a stranger I will not follow. Therefore, I declare by faith that I recognize the voice of Jesus when He speaks to me. I am not hesitant to follow, but I am bold and quick to obey what He speaks to my heart. I declare this by faith in Jesus' name!

Let Jesus Be Real in Your Life

*Then saith he to Thomas,
Reach hither thy finger,
and behold my hands; and
reach hither thy hand, and
thrust it into my side: and
be not faithless, but
believing. And Thomas
answered and said unto
him, My LORD and my
God. Jesus saith unto him,
Thomas, because thou
hast seen me, thou hast
believed: blessed are they
that have not seen, and
yet have believed.*

John 20:27-29

My Prayer for Today

Lord, I want You to be so real in my life. I know that You are willing to make Yourself known and felt in any part of my life that I will surrender to You. So I choose right now to surrender more of me so I can experience more of You in every sphere of my existence. Jesus, please have Your way in my life. Do whatever You deem necessary to make me the kind of person I need to be to know and experience You better. I pray this in Jesus' name!

My Confession for Today

I confess that the Presence of Jesus Christ is felt in almost every area of my life. I am surrendering more and more of me to Him every day, and as a result, I am expecting a stronger Presence of God in my life. As I give more of me to Him, He gives more of Himself to me! I declare this by faith in Jesus' name!

God's Word—Top Priority in Your Life

My Prayer for Today

Lord, I've been asking You for power and strength, not realizing that I have the source of Your power and strength sitting right in my house. Forgive me for not spending enough time in my Bible to tap into the power that is held within it. Starting today, I want to make Your Word a priority in my life. When I am tempted to be lazy and to put off reading my Bible, please help me say no to my flesh. Help me choose to pick up my Bible and read it whether I feel like it or not, taking it deep into my heart and letting the power inside the Word begin to work in me and in my situation. I pray this in Jesus' name!

All scripture is given by inspiration of God, and is profitable for doctrine, for reproof, for correction, for instruction in righteousness.

2 Timothy 3:16

My Confession for Today

I confess that I have determined to read and meditate on the Word of God on a regular basis. The power of the Word works mightily inside me because I take it deeply into my heart. It transforms my thinking, renews my vision, forces darkness out of my mind, and blows like a mighty force into every part of my life. There is nothing stronger at my disposal than God's Word, so I make it a priority in my life. I declare this by faith in Jesus' name!

Run the Race Set Before You

*I have fought
a good fight,
I have finished
my course, I have
kept the faith.*

2 Timothy 4:7

My Prayer for Today

Lord, help me to keep my focus and to not allow the challenges I face to distract me from fulfilling Your will for my life. I know that the enemy keeps surrounding me with distractions because You have called me to do something important. Rather than let these nuisances break me and steal my joy, help me keep my eyes focused on that day when I will stand before You. I ask that Your Spirit supernaturally energize me to push beyond the obstacles and keep pressing forward to the high calling You have designed for my life. I pray this in Jesus' name!

My Confession for Today

I boldly declare that I am a winner and not a loser. I don't throw in the towel and quit when it gets hard; instead, I dig in my heels and refuse to surrender the territory that God has called me to conquer and possess. I live my life seriously and with balance and commitment. Because of God's Spirit inside me, I am tougher than any challenge and stronger than any foe. I fight a good fight and run a good race—and I successfully guard and hold tight to the assignment God has given to my life. I declare this by faith in Jesus' name!

Powerful Gifts Are Yours

My Prayer for Today

Lord, I thank You for the ministry of the Holy Spirit and for His powerful gifts that make Jesus so real to me. Help me understand my need for the Spirit's gifts. Arouse a spiritual hunger inside me that makes me earnestly yearn to experience more of these gifts in my life and in my church. I know You gave the gifts of the Spirit because we need them, so today I am choosing to open my heart so I can experience more of Your power as these supernatural gifts begin to flow through me. I pray this in Jesus' name!

That in every thing ye are enriched by him, in all utterance, and in all knowledge; Even as the testimony of Christ was confirmed in you: So that ye come behind in no gift; waiting for the coming of our Lord Jesus Christ: Who shall also confirm you unto the end, that ye may be blameless in the day of our Lord Jesus Christ.

1 Corinthians 1:5-8

My Confession for Today

I confess that I am a vessel for the gifts of the Holy Spirit. These gifts operate through me and bring the living reality of Jesus Christ to me and to those who are around me. I am not afraid to obey what the Holy Spirit prompts me to say. I am not hesitant to act when the Spirit prompts me to step out in faith. Because I obey the leading of the Spirit, God's power mightily flows through me to others who are in need. I declare this by faith in Jesus' name!

Rejuvenated and Recharged

But if the Spirit of him that raised up Jesus from the dead dwell in you, he that raised up Christ from the dead shall also quicken your mortal bodies by his Spirit that dwelleth in you.

Romans 8:11

My Prayer for Today

Lord, I admit that I need a fresh surge of supernatural power in my life right now. I ask You to release the resurrection power of Jesus Christ that resides in my spirit. Let it flow up into my body and mind so I can be rejuvenated and recharged with enough power to fulfill all the responsibilities and duties that lie before me. I know that in my own strength, I can't do everything that is required of me in the days ahead. But I also know that with Your supernatural power working in me, I will be able to do everything You have asked me to do! I pray this in Jesus' name!

My Confession for Today

I confess that God's Spirit is quickening my mortal flesh and rejuvenating me with enough strength to fulfill all the duties and responsibilities that lie ahead of me. I am not weak. I am not tired. I am refreshed. I am strengthened. I am filled with power. Because the Holy Spirit dwells in me, there is not a single moment when I don't have everything that I need! I declare this by faith in Jesus' name!

Sensitive to Others' Needs

My Prayer for Today

Lord, forgive me for being so self-centered that I forget to think about other people's needs. I get so fixated on my own problems that I forget I am not the only person in the world who is struggling with a situation. Help me to take my eyes off myself and to look around me to see who needs a special word of encouragement. Holy Spirit, open my eyes and help me be sensitive in my spirit to recognize people who need a tender touch. So many times I've freely received help from others. Now I want to freely give what I have received. I pray this in Jesus' name!

And let us consider one another to provoke unto love and to good works.

Hebrews 10:24

My Confession for Today

I declare by faith that I am sensitive to the needs of others. God uses me to encourage people who are around me. As I become more Christ-like, I am less aware of me and more aware of those who are around me. Because God's Spirit lives inside me, all the wonderful fruit of the Spirit—love, joy, peace, patience, gentleness, goodness, faith, meekness, and temperance—reside in me and flow through me to others. I am aware of others. I think of them; I ask about them; I pray for them; and I treat them with the greatest love, care, and attention. I declare this by faith in Jesus' name!

True Profession Is From the Heart

Let us hold fast the profession of our faith without wavering; (for he is faithful that promised;).

Hebrews 10:23

My Prayer for Today

Lord, I want to get Your Word so deep into my heart that it becomes my word! I want to see things the way You see them, hear things the way You hear them, and feel things the way You feel them. I want to get so aligned with You that our hearts beat in syncopation together. I thank You that once Your Word gets that deeply rooted in my heart, my spoken words will release rivers of power and authority against the works of the devil that he has designed for my destruction. I thank You that just as Your words created the universe, my spoken words of faith create a change in my atmosphere. I pray this in Jesus' name!

My Confession for Today

I boldly confess that God's Word is deeply rooted inside my heart and soul. My mind is being renewed to the truth, and I am being changed. What I used to think, I no longer think; what I used to believe, I no longer believe. Now I base my life on the eternal truths contained in God's Word. I take the Word deep into my heart and soul where it inwardly transforms me. When I open my mouth to speak, I don't speak empty, mindless words; instead, my words come from a deeply held conviction and therefore release power to set the answers I need in motion. I declare this by faith in Jesus' name!

Calm, Kind, and Gentle

My Prayer for Today

Lord, please help me to be calm, kind, and gentle when I find it necessary to correct people who are under my care. Forgive me for any time that I've allowed myself to become angry and exasperated and for those times when I have said things I shouldn't have allowed myself to speak. Help me act like a real leader, taking a parent-teacher role. I know I am called to help take people to a higher level in their work, their attitudes, and their lives. So help me to be more like You in the way I deal with people who are under my authority and care. As I learn to bring correction to others the way You bring correction into MY life, I will become a good example and the kind of leader You have called me to be. I pray this in Jesus' name!

And the servant of the Lord must not strive; but be gentle unto all men, apt to teach, patient.

2 Timothy 2:24

My Confession for Today

I confess that I have the mind of Christ for every situation I face in life. When it is necessary for me to speak correction to a member of my team, I speak with compassion and love from my heart. I desire the best for every person whom God has placed under my authority and care. Therefore, when I deal with these individuals, I approach them from a standpoint of how I can best help them grow, help them develop, and help them become all God has called them to be. I don't get angry, frustrated, or exasperated if they get upset; instead, I remain calm, kind, and gentle as I deal with the people whom God has entrusted to my care. I declare this by faith in Jesus' name!

Dressed in the Whole Armor of God

*Put on the whole
armor of God, that
ye may be able to
stand against the
wiles of the devil.*

Ephesians 6:11

My Prayer for Today

Lord, how can I ever thank You enough for providing me with everything I need to successfully stand against each and every attack the devil tries to bring against my life? I thank You for loving me enough to equip me with these kinds of spiritual weapons. Because of what You have provided for me, I can stand fast, confident that I can withstand every assault, drive out the enemy, and win every battle. Without You, this would be impossible; but with Your power and the weapons You have provided for me, I am amply supplied with everything I need to push the enemy out of my way and out of my life. I pray this in Jesus' name!

My Confession for Today

I joyfully declare that I am dressed in the whole armor of God. There isn't a part of me that hasn't been supernaturally clothed and protected by the defensive and offensive weapons God has provided for me. I proceed with my loinbelt of truth; I walk in my shoes of peace; I boldly wear my breastplate of righteousness; I hold up my shield of faith; I am clad in my helmet of salvation; I make use of my sword of the Spirit; and I have a lance of intercession that deals a blow to the enemy from a distance every time I aggressively pray. I declare this by faith in Jesus' name!

Peace That Passes Understanding

And the peace of God, which passeth all understanding, shall keep your hearts and minds through Christ Jesus.

Philippians 4:7

My Prayer for Today

Lord, I thank You for placing Your wonderful, powerful, protective peace in my life. I am grateful that You have positioned it to stand at the entrance of my heart and mind and that it dominates my mind and controls my life. Because what is inside me is what rules me, I choose to let this peace rise up and conquer me. With this peace standing at the gate of my heart and mind, I know it will disable the devil's ability to attack my emotions and will not permit his lies and accusations to slip into my mind. Thank You for loving me enough to put this powerful peace in my life! I pray this in Jesus' name!

My Confession for Today

I confess that I am guarded and protected by the powerful peace of God that works in my life. It rises up to dominate my mind; it controls my thinking; and it determines the condition of my life and the environment where I live and work. I am unaffected by the circumstances that surround me, for this supernatural peace stands at the gate of my mind and emotions to monitor everything that tries to access me. Because no fretting, anxiety, panic, or worry is allowed to enter me, I remain free, calm, and peaceful—even in difficult situations that in the past would have upset me! I declare this by faith in Jesus' name!

Cast All Your Care on the Lord

*Casting all your
care upon him; for
he careth for you.*

1 Peter 5:7

My Prayer for Today

Lord, I regret having carried burdens and worries so long by myself when, in fact, You were always ready to take them from me and to carry them on my behalf. But it's never too late to do what is right, so right now I make the decision to yield to You every one of these matters that are bothering me. Thank You for coming alongside me to take these weights from my shoulders. Because You are so loving and attentive to me, I can now go free! I pray this in Jesus' name!

My Confession for Today

I confess that Jesus is standing right at my side, yearning to help me and inviting me to shift the weight from my shoulders to His shoulders so I can go free! By faith I have already cast my cares onto Jesus. As a result, I am liberated from stress, anxiety, worries, pressures, and all the other things that have been bothering me. I declare this by faith in Jesus' name!

Be a Source of Blessing, Not of Offense

My Prayer for Today

Lord, I want to repent for ever being a source of offense to anyone. I am asking You to forgive me for fighting to prove my point in the past when I should have just gone to that other person and apologized, asking for his forgiveness. If I ever find out I've offended someone again, please help me deal with it more maturely than I have in the past. Jesus, I also need You to help me remember that when others do things that make me sad or that disappoint me, they probably didn't mean to do it. Help me give them the same mercy and grace that I hope others will give me. I pray this in Jesus' name!

Then said he unto the disciples, It is impossible but that offences will come but woe unto him, through whom they come!

Luke 17:1

My Confession for Today

I confess that I am a source of blessing and not a cause of offense! I do everything in my power to communicate correct messages, and I immediately move to bring healing and restoration whenever misunderstanding and offense has occurred between myself and someone else. I do everything I can to bury that offense and to destroy what the devil is trying to do. I make it my aim to walk in the Spirit, to speak the love of God into every situation, and to refuse to let the devil use me to cause others to trip and fall. I declare this by faith in Jesus' name!

Vibrant Life

Go ye therefore, and teach all nations, baptizing them in the name of the Father, and of the Son, and of the Holy Ghost.

Matthew 28:19

My Prayer for Today

Lord, I am so grateful that You accepted me when I was dead in sin and washed me with Your precious blood. When I was placed inside You, everything old passed away and everything in me became brand new. For this great gift of life and salvation, I want to serve You the rest of my days. I am so thankful to You for giving me a new view of life and a whole new reason to live. When You came to dwell in me through the Person of the Holy Spirit, the drab, dark days of sin passed away, and a new world of light and color filled my life. For this, I am forever thankful! I pray this in Jesus' name!

My Confession for Today

I boldly declare that I am a new creature in Jesus Christ. Old things have passed away, and all things have become new! I am not who I used to be anymore. I don't think like that old man; I don't see like that old man; I don't talk like that old man; and I don't behave like that old man anymore. Now I am in Jesus Christ, and I think like Him, see like Him, talk like Him, and behave like Him. I have come alive with vibrant life because of His resurrection power that works inside me! I declare this by faith in Jesus' name!

Raising Godly Children

One that ruleth well his own house, having his children in subjection with all gravity.

1 Timothy 3:4

My Prayer for Today

Lord, I thank You for speaking to me about teaching my children the responsibilities of life. I want my children to be godly and successful, so I want to lead them and teach them from the Word of God. I know that my personal example is the strongest message I have to preach to my children, so help me be real and authentic, not hypocritical, in my Christian life. Parenting is such a huge responsibility that I must have Your help to do it properly. I look to You and Your Word to guide me as I rear the children You have placed in my care. I pray this in Jesus' name!

My Confession for Today

I declare by faith that I am a godly parent and I lead my children in the way of righteousness! I am not afraid to step up to the plate and take my leadership role. I do it boldly, proudly, and reverently, realizing that this is one of the greatest honors and responsibilities of my life. I recognize that my children are gifts from God, and I treat them with the greatest respect as I teach them how to become successful young adults. With the help of God's Spirit and the guidance of His Word, I am doing exactly what I must for my children to be anointed, godly, and blessed. I declare this by faith in Jesus' name!

Petition of Surrender

*Praying always
with all prayer
and supplication
in the Spirit,
and watching
thereunto with
all perseverance
and supplication
for all saints.*

Ephesians 6:18

My Prayer for Today

Lord, I come before You right now with the specific petition that is on my heart. I know that You want to answer my prayers and fulfill my requests, but You also want me to surrender more of myself to You. Before I ask You to meet my needs today, I first want to consecrate myself more fully to You. Forgive me for hanging on to parts of my life that I've needed to surrender to You. Right now I yield these areas of my life to You, and I ask You in exchange to please fill me with more of You. I thank You in advance for answering that prayer. I also thank You for hearing my specific prayer request and for fulfilling the needs I am confronted with today. I pray this in Jesus' name!

My Confession for Today

I confess that I am surrendered and yielded to the Lord. Every part of my life is becoming more yielded to Him every day. As the Holy Spirit shows me areas that I need to release to Him, I do it quickly and without delay. Because I have given my life to Him, He is filling me with more and more of Himself. He hears me when I pray, He accepts my thanksgiving, and He fulfills the needs that I present to Him today. I declare this by faith in Jesus' name!

Put Your Foot Down!

My Prayer for Today

Lord, I've tolerated the devil's lies long enough. Today I am making the decision to put my foot down. I'm going to tell the enemy to shut his mouth and flee from me! I have made my choice that I will stand by Your promise and will never retreat from what You have told me to believe and confess. You are not a man that You should lie, and I believe Your Word to be true for my life. Holy Spirit, give me the strength I need to stay fixed, immovable, and steadfast until I finally see the manifestation of those things that I believe. I pray this in Jesus' name!

Let us hold fast the profession of our faith without wavering; (for he is faithful that promised;).

Hebrews 10:23

My Confession for Today

I confess that I don't waver or bend and that I am fixed and unmoving as I stand on the promises of God. What God promises, He will perform. It may take awhile for that promise to come into manifestation, but I know it is on the way right now. I dig in my heels, I drive down my stake, and I tell the devil that I am NOT going to move from my position of faith! I declare this by faith in Jesus' name!

Encouraged by Remembrance

But call to remembrance the former days, in which, after ye were illuminated, ye endured a great fight of afflictions.

Hebrews 10:32

My Prayer for Today

Lord, help me to never forget those early experiences I had with You after I first got saved. I'm so sorry I've allowed the complexities of life to steal my joy, and today I ask You to help me return to the simplicity of faith I once enjoyed. I admit I've been discouraged, but today I am deciding to get encouraged! Thank You for helping me to refocus and to remember that Your Word is unchanging and Your promises are true. I pray this in Jesus' name!

My Confession for Today

I boldly confess that discouragement has no place in me! God's Word is true, the devil is a liar, and my circumstances are not permanent. And with God's power, I will rise above the situations I face today! I decide it, I declare it, and I pronounce it to be true! I declare this by faith in Jesus' name!

Intellectual Power Is Not Sufficient

My Prayer for Today

Lord, I want to tell You that I am sorry for the many times I've tried to present the Gospel to others in the power of my intellect and flesh, failing to let the Holy Spirit confirm the Word with signs following. I have been timid and shy about moving in the power of God, but I know it's time for me to push that timidity aside. To the best of my ability and with sincerity of heart, I am telling You today that I want Your Gospel-proving power to flow through me. I pray this in Jesus' name!

And I, brethren, when I came to you, came not with excellency of speech or of wisdom, declaring unto you the testimony of God. For I determined not to know any thing among you, save Jesus Christ, and him crucified.

1 Corinthians 2:1,2

My Confession for Today

I declare by faith that I am not timid or afraid! God wants to pour His power through me, and I am receptive and open to His using me in this wonderful way. People need the power of God, and God wants to use me to bring His miraculous touch into their lives. I am bold and confident—and I am growing bolder and more confident every day! I declare this by faith in Jesus' name!

Your Part in God's Plan

There is a lad here, which hath five barley loaves, and two small fishes: but what are they among so many?

John 6:9

My Prayer for Today

Lord, I want to thank You for allowing me to be a part of Your great plans. You could use someone else, but You have chosen to use me. For this, I am so thankful to You. If there is any faith deficiency in me, please expose it NOW so I can get it fixed and be prepared for any assignment You give to me in the future. I pray this in Jesus' name!

My Confession for Today

I confess that I am ready for God to use me! My faith is growing. It's getting stronger, and the deficiency in my faith is being reduced day by day. There was a time when I was weak, but now God's Word is making me stronger. There was a time when I would have doubted and feared, but now I am filled with faith. In fact, I'm excited about taking on ANY assignment Jesus Christ wants to give me! I declare this by faith in Jesus' name!

Tap Into God's Power

My Prayer for Today

Lord, I thank You for making such power avail-able to me. Now I see that I have no excuse to ever complain that I am weak, for You have placed at my disposal the very power of the res-urrection itself. Teach me how to tap into that power so it can be released in my life. I know that this power is the answer for many people's needs and that You want it to flow through me. Holy Spirit, as my Great Teacher, please teach me how to open my heart wide so the river of Your divine goodness can flow through me. I pray this in Jesus' name!

Finally, my brethren, be strong in the Lord, and in the power of his might.

Ephesians 6:10

My Confession for Today

I confess that God's indomitable, overpowering, conquering, and irre-sistible power flows through me! The very power that raised Jesus from the dead resides and operates in my life. It is an eruptive power; it is a demonstrated power; and it is an outwardly visible power—the strongest kind of power known to God or man. With this empowering Presence of the Holy Spirit working in me, I expect the power that raised Jesus from the dead to operate in my life. I deliberately turn up my level of expecta-tion and anticipate this mighty power of God to begin to flow through me. I declare this by faith in Jesus' name!

God's 'Muscle Power'

*Greater is he
that is in you,
than he that is
in the world.*

1 John 4:4

My Prayer for Today

Lord, I am so thankful that Your muscles are the backup for the power that operates in my life! Just as Your mighty arm created the universe, divided the Red Sea, destroyed the Egyptians, ripped Jesus from the throes of hell, and raised Him from the dead, I know that now this mighty power also works in me. Help me learn how to flow with this power and allow it to be released through my life so I can be a bigger blessing to people who are around me. I pray this in Jesus' name!

My Confession for Today

I boldly confess that all that God is, all the power He possesses, and all the energy of His muscular, mighty ability now energizes me! With this power at my disposal, I confront every spirit that comes to wage war against me. I lay hands on the sick and see them recover; I pray with power and authority; I speak the word of faith to every situation I face. Therefore, mountains move on my behalf! Greater is He who is in me than he that is in the world. I have no need to be afraid, and I don't shrink back in timidity, because there's enough power at work in me to resist any force that comes against me and to supernaturally remedy anything that is out of God's order in my life. I declare this by faith in Jesus' name!

Become a Better Listener

My Prayer for Today

Lord, it is true that I need to learn how to be a better listener. Forgive me for the times I've inconvenienced others and messed up their plans because I didn't carefully listen to the instructions that everyone else obviously understood. I recognize that this is a flaw in my life. Starting today, I want to discipline myself to become a top-notch listener. For me to do this, I know I'll have to break the habit of thinking about other things when people are trying to talk to me. So I'm turning to You to help me silence my mind, listen to others, digest what they are saying, and become a better team player. I pray this in Jesus' name!

Wherefore, my beloved brethren, let every man be swift to hear, slow to speak, slow to wrath.

James 1:19

My Confession for Today

I confess that I am quick to hear what others are trying to tell me, and I don't interrupt them when they are speaking. I am a first-place runner when it comes to listening to others. Because God's Spirit is helping me, I am getting better and better in this area of my life. As a result, I am an effective team player, and others enjoy working with me. I declare this by faith in Jesus' name!

Meeting Others' Needs

Bear ye one another's burdens, and so fulfil the law of Christ.

Galatians 6:2

My Prayer for Today

Lord, I am asking You to help me be sensitive to the needs of other people. Help me to stop being so self-consumed with my own concerns that I am negligent in recognizing the needs of people around me who need help and prayer. Holy Spirit, help me see through the masks people tend to wear to cover up what is really happening in their lives. Give me the wisdom to know how to approach people who need strength and encouragement. I pray this in Jesus' name!

My Confession for Today

I confess that I am sensitive to the needs of people who are around me. I see when they hurt; I recognize the times when they're struggling; and I am a blessing to them in their time of need. God's Spirit is helping me to become a better minister and servant to help meet the needs in other people's lives. I am attentive, caring, and Christ-like in the way I deal with others. What Jesus does for me is what I am becoming to other people. I declare this by faith in Jesus' name!

Helping Others To Become Responsible

My Prayer for Today

For every man shall bear his own burden.

Galatians 6:5

Lord, I know some people who need to grow up and start taking on more of the responsibilities of life. I must admit that I've gone to their rescue too many times and that I've probably enabled them to continue their wrong behavior and inappropriate lifestyle. Saying no is so hard for me to do, but I am asking You to help me stop empowering them to keep living irresponsibly as they have been doing. Holy Spirit, please give me Your mind and Your power, and help me to do what is right on this issue. I pray this in Jesus' name!

My Confession for Today

I confess that I have the mind of Christ to help me know when I am to help and when I am to say no. The Holy Spirit speaks to my heart and shows me what to do in every situation. God's Spirit advises me about what I should do. I am obedient to Him and am NOT led by my emotions. I declare this by faith in Jesus' name!

Stir Up Your Desire To Move Up Higher

This is a true saying, If a man desire the office of a bishop, he desireth a good work.

1 Timothy 3:1

My Prayer for Today

Lord, thank You for speaking to me so strongly today about my personal level of desire. For me to be what You have called me to be, I know that I have to develop a stronger inner desire than I am demonstrating in my life at this moment. Holy Spirit, please stir my heart so fiercely that I won't be satisfied with my current level of life. Please give me a godly discontentment with the level I've already achieved so I'll be motivated to keep reaching for higher levels in my personal life. I pray this in Jesus' name!

My Confession for Today

I confess that I am filled with desire! I am fixed on the goal God has given me to achieve, and my actions demonstrate that I am committed to achieving God's plan for my life. I read, study, work, and develop myself regularly so I can become better and achieve higher results. Because I will never become someone great or achieve anything special by doing what everyone else does, I do more than what others do. Because I have desire, I will make it! I declare this by faith in Jesus' name!

Being a Good Example

My Prayer for Today

Lord, I thank You for placing me under people who helped me grow when I was a young Christian. Their influence was important in my spiritual development, so I thank You for them right now—for their patience, their love, their kindness, and their willingness to let me get close enough to really learn how to walk with You. Now it's time for me to do this for someone else, so please lead me to a young disciple whom I can begin to show how to walk in the power and authority of Your Word. I pray this in Jesus' name!

So being affectionately desirous of you, we were willing to have imparted unto you, not the gospel of God only, but also our own souls, because ye were dear unto us.

1 Thessalonians 2:8

My Confession for Today

I confess that I am a good example to other believers. Because I walk in the truth of what I preach, my life makes the message even stronger. People need a good example they can follow, and that means they need me! The Holy Spirit empowers me to preach, to teach, and to boldly model my life before others with confidence and grace. I declare this by faith in Jesus' name!

Receive a Fresh Anointing

*...I shall be
anointed with
fresh oil.*

Psalm 92:10

My Prayer for Today

Lord, I am asking You to lay Your hand upon me in a brand-new way today. Rub the oil of Your Spirit deep into my life—and let the powerful fragrance of the anointing be felt, sensed, and seen by others who are near me. I want to carry Your power and demonstrate the aroma of Your Presence, so please lay Your hand on me today and let the anointing deeply penetrate me. I pray this in Jesus' name!

My Confession for Today

I confess that God's hand is on my life. Because of this, the Spirit of the Lord rests mightily upon me. Just as He anointed Jesus, I am also anointed to preach the Gospel to the poor; to heal the brokenhearted; to preach deliverance to the captives; to give recovery of sight to the blind; and to preach the acceptable year of the Lord. I carry the power of Jesus Christ, and I give off the aroma of God's Presence! I declare this by faith in Jesus' name!

The Shield of Faith

My Prayer for Today

Lord, I want to thank You for giving me spiritual weapons! Today I am especially grateful that You have equipped me with a shield of faith that covers me from head to toe. Because You have been so gracious to provide everything I need, there is never a reason that Satan's fiery darts should get through to me. So I ask You to help me hold my faith up high, keep it out in front, and march forward without any fear of what Satan might try to do to me. I pray this in Jesus' name!

Above all, taking the shield of faith, wherewith ye shall be able to quench all the fiery darts of the wicked.

Ephesians 6:16

My Confession for Today

I confess that I am dressed in the whole armor of God! There isn't a part of me that hasn't been covered by the spiritual weaponry God has placed at my disposal. My shield of faith is working fine! It is anointed; it is strong; it is ready for any confrontation; and it will cause any dart that the enemy tries to throw at me to ricochet off without doing harm. I declare this by faith in Jesus' name!

Becoming a Better Parent

One that ruleth well his own house, having his children in subjection with all gravity.

1 Timothy 3:4

My Prayer for Today

Lord, I ask You to help me truthfully evaluate the situation in my life and honestly analyze how I am doing at rearing my children. It is difficult for me to be honest with myself about my performance as a parent, so I need You to give me the grace to see the truth as You see it. After You show me where I have erred, please quickly teach me how to bring correction into the situation. I am willing to be corrected, and I am waiting for You to help me clearly see the situation. I determine this day to do whatever is required to put my home in good working order. I pray this in Jesus' name!

My Confession for Today

I confess that I am growing and developing as a parent. My parental skills are getting better and better all the time. My home is filled with love; my children speak with kindness and respect; and I am rearing them to be godly leaders for the next generation. With God's Word as my guide and the Holy Spirit as my Teacher, I am leading my family in a way that pleases God and that is an example to others. I declare this by faith in Jesus' name!

Free From All Strongholds

My Prayer for Today

Lord, help me to see any area of my life that is dominated by rational or irrational strongholds. Forgive me for allowing the devil to sink his lies into my mind, and help me now to uproot and cast down every one of his lies. I know that Your Word will renew my mind to think in accordance with You, so I am asking You today to help me make Your Word a priority in my life. I pray this in Jesus' name!

For though we walk in the flesh, we do not war after the flesh: (For the weapons of our warfare are not carnal, but mighty through God to the pulling down of strong holds;)

2 Corinthians 10:3,4

My Confession for Today

I boldly declare that my mind is free from the devil's lies! I think God's thoughts; I meditate on God's Word; and my brain is spot-free from the rational and irrational strongholds that Satan would like to plant inside me. Because of God's Word working in me, I am completely free! I declare this by faith in Jesus' name!

Darkness Cannot Overcome the Light

And the light shineth in darkness; and the darkness comprehended it not.

John 1:5

My Prayer for Today

Lord, I thank You that darkness doesn't have the power to overcome me. It may try, but Your Word guarantees that darkness doesn't have the ability to overcome the light. I am so thankful that I am Your child and that I live on the winning side. When the devil tries to discourage me, help me remember that in the end, we win! I pray this in Jesus' name!

My Confession for Today

I boldly confess that even if I occasionally get knocked down, I never get knocked out! I possess the supernatural ability to keep getting up again because I am born of God and I overcome the world. Regardless of what weapon Satan uses or how he attempts to combat me, my faith overrides and supersedes any event, any circumstance, and any difficult dilemma Satan would try to employ against me. I declare this by faith in Jesus' name!

Praying With Faith

My Prayer for Today

Lord, I can remember times in my past when I've prayed the right thing the wrong way, and it resulted in unanswered prayer. I ask You to help me ask correctly when I pray, and to ask in a spirit of faith and not in a spirit of fear, dread, or anxiety. I never realized before now how important it is to ask in the right way. Holy Spirit, I ask You to help me ask correctly and pray appropriately from this moment forward. Whenever I start praying wrongly or out of a wrong spirit, please stop me. I ask You to correct me and teach me how to pray in line with Your Word from a heart of faith. I pray this in Jesus' name!

But let him ask in faith, nothing wavering. For he that wavereth is like a wave of the sea driven with the wind and tossed.

James 1:6

My Confession for Today

I confess that God's Word is my guide to help me ask correctly when I pray. I declare that I am motivated by faith and not by fear, dread, or anxiety when I pray. Because I ask according to God's will, He hears me when I pray. Because He hears me, I know that I have the petitions I ask of Him. God acts promptly to answer my prayers because I ask with a heart filled with faith in accordance with His will. Because I make sure that what I pray is correct and how I pray is appropriate, I am receiving more and more results from my prayers all the time! I declare this by faith in Jesus' name!

Prepare for Your Fruit-Producing Season

Rooted and built up in him, and established in the faith, as ye have been taught, abounding therein with thanksgiving.

Colossians 2:7

My Prayer for Today

Lord, I thank You for not sending success to me too quickly. I know that if I had achieved success earlier, I wouldn't have been ready for it. In fact, I might have destroyed it due to my own lack of experience and my immaturity. Help me embrace this time in my life as a time of preparation. Help me to truthfully analyze every part of my life in order to see what areas need to be more deeply rooted in You. I want my roots to go down so deeply that no storms of life and no attacks from the devil will be able to move me from the place where You have called me. Help me to stay so fixed, firm, strong, and stable that once I enter the fruit-producing season, I will never leave it! I pray this in Jesus' name!

My Confession for Today

I confess that I am firmly and deeply rooted in God's Word. As a result, I am fixed, steady, stable, and strong like a tree whose roots go down deep. I am tapped into the life of Jesus Christ, and He has become my Source of nourishment. I am held so securely in place that I am unaffected by the storms of life and the pestilence that the devil tries to use to attack me. I will outlast every season, every foul climate, and every storm. I am about to enter into the finest fruit-producing season of my life, my ministry, my family, and my business. My fruit-producing season is getting ready to begin! I declare this by faith in Jesus' name!

You Are Sealed With God's Spirit

My Prayer for Today

Lord, I am so thankful today that You have sealed and guaranteed me! Forgive me for those times when I speak badly of myself, judge and condemn myself, or put myself down in front of others. I should be proud of and thankful for who I am, because the blood of Jesus has cleansed and redeemed me. You were so convinced that I was free of defects that You sealed me with Your Spirit, giving me Your ultimate seal of approval. Help me appreciate the great work You have done inside me! Thank You for guaranteeing, overseeing, and assuring me that no force on earth and no demonic powers can stop me from arriving at my ultimate heavenly destination. I pray this in Jesus' name!

In whom ye also trusted, after that ye heard the word of truth, the gospel of your salvation: in whom also after that ye believed, ye were sealed with that holy Spirit of promise.

Ephesians 1:13

My Confession for Today

I confess that I am "sealed" with the Holy Spirit. My contents are intact and in order. I am approved, endorsed, recognized, affirmed, sanctified, and notarized by the Spirit of God. Because God has "sealed" me, it is guaranteed that I am going to make it to my final destination. When demons see the seal of God on me, they know they are not to mess around with me! I am a special package, to be treated with special care. Angels watch over me and guard my safe passage from one place to the next. Evil forces may attempt to mess with me, but the seal of God guarantees that I'll arrive safely and complete! I declare this by faith in Jesus' name!

Taking Hold of God's Call

For ye see your calling, brethren, how that not many wise men after the flesh, not many mighty, not many noble, are called: But God hath chosen the foolish things of the world to confound the wise....

1 Corinthians 1:26,27

My Prayer for Today

Lord, help me stop making excuses for why I think God shouldn't use me! It's time for me to stop ignoring the call of God and to accept the fact that He has laid His hand upon me and wants to use me in this world. Forgive me for putting this off for so long, but today I accept Your call. I reject all excuses for any further delay, and I gladly embrace what You are telling me to do. I pray this in Jesus' name!

My Confession for Today

I boldly confess that I am exactly the kind of person Jesus Christ wants to use! I may not have the blue blood of nobility flowing through my veins, but I have been touched, cleansed, and redeemed by the blood of Jesus Christ. That blood qualifies me! With the Word as my guide and the Holy Spirit as my Teacher, I have everything I need to do anything Jesus ever requires of me. I am quick to obey, I do not hesitate, and I am faithful to carry out every assignment that He gives me. I boldly declare this in Jesus' name!

You Are Not an Accident

My Prayer for Today

Lord, I am so glad that You knew me and called me even before I was conceived in my mother's womb. According to Your Word, I am no mistake; therefore, I ask You to help me start looking at my life with respect, esteem, and honor. You called me, and You have an awesome plan for my life. I ask You to help me uncover that plan so I can get started on the road of obedience toward the fulfillment of what You brought me into this world to do. I pray this in Jesus' name!

According as he hath chosen us in him before the foundation of the world, that we should be holy and without blame before him in love.

Ephesians 1:4

My Confession for Today

I boldly declare that I am no accident and no mistake! God knew me before the earth was created; He called me before I was formed in my mother's womb; and He has long awaited my arrival on planet earth. God has a plan for me! I am purposeful; I am respectful of myself; and I walk in a way that honors the One who called and anointed me to be enlisted in His service. I declare this by faith in Jesus' name!

Striving Toward Excellence

And whatsoever ye do, do it heartily, as to the Lord, and not unto men.

Colossians 3:23

My Prayer for Today

Lord, I am sorry for any laziness that I've allowed in my life. Yes, I know I can do so much more than I've done. I haven't applied myself with all my heart and strength; instead, I've permitted myself to slip by at a mediocre level. I have done enough to keep my job, but I haven't done enough to deserve a promotion or a salary increase. Forgive me for complaining that I don't make enough money when the truth is that I haven't done my best work. I sincerely ask You to help me change my attitude and to increase my level of work performance. I pray this in Jesus' name!

My Confession for Today

I confess that I am a good worker and that I have a great attitude! I am exactly the kind of person God can use and bless—and I am exactly the kind of employee my employer is thrilled to have in his department, organization, or business. I work so hard and do such good work that I bring many blessings and benefits to those who are over me in authority. Because I am around, I make them look better! God rewards me for being faithful. My striving toward excellence today will lead to my promotion and financial increase tomorrow. I declare this by faith in Jesus' name!

Becoming a Profitable Servant

And cast ye the unprofitable servant into outer darkness: there shall be weeping and gnashing of teeth.

Matthew 25:30

My Prayer for Today

Lord, help me understand how to act on the ideas You have placed in my heart. I don't want to be like the unprofitable servant who was thrown into outer darkness and experienced weeping and gnashing of teeth. I want to stand in the reality of the dream You have put in my heart. Please give me wisdom and courage to step out and begin to fulfill the dream You birthed so deeply inside my soul. I need You, Holy Spirit. I ask You to stir up Your courage inside me and help me to get moving! I pray this in Jesus' name!

My Confession for Today

I confess that I'm not lazy or afraid to step out in faith. I am filled with God's wonderful ideas, and I will do what He has put in my heart. I am not hesitant or fearful but rather bold, courageous, and ready to go! God is my Helper; therefore, I will not be afraid. I will not fear what man can do to me, for the Lord is with me! He directs my mind, He guides my steps, and His Word lights my path before me! I declare this by faith in Jesus' name!

Make a Difference in Someone's Life

And of some have compassion, making a difference.

Jude 22

My Prayer for Today

Lord, please forgive me for being hardhearted, condemning, and judgmental toward people who have needed my prayers and intercession. Instead of wasting all my time judging them, I could have been praying for them. Now I see my mistake, and I truly repent for it. Starting today, I pledge to change my attitude—to open my heart and let the compassion of Jesus Christ flow through me to help set their deliverance in motion. Let Your compassion begin flowing through me today! I pray this in Jesus' name!

My Confession for Today

I boldly confess that compassion flows through me like a river! Condemnation and judgment have no place in my life, in my thinking, or in the way I relate to other people. I am filled with the love of God, and I allow that love to touch others who are near me. The bowels of my heart release the compassion of Jesus Christ, touching the lives of people caught in the deception of sin and darkness and setting them free! I declare this by faith in Jesus' name!

Controlling Your Mind

Casting down imaginations, and every high thing that exalteth itself against the knowledge of God, and bringing into captivity every thought to the obedience of Christ;

2 Corinthians 10:5

My Prayer for Today

Lord, I don't want to ever give the devil access to my mind. I ask for forgiveness for the times I've permitted wrong thinking to go on inside me when I knew it was wrong. Now I understand that these are the areas through which the devil seeks to find entrance into my life. Starting today, I am asking You to help me locate each "open door" in my mind; then help me seal those doors shut by the power of Your Spirit and Your Word. I pray this in Jesus' name!

My Confession for Today

I confess that my mind is dominated by the Word of God and that I am under the control of the Holy Spirit! I gird up the loins of my mind by reading my Bible and filling my mind with God's thoughts. God's Word strengthens me and keeps my mind free from unbelief and lying strongholds. I take God's Word deep into my mind, and it stops the devil from finding access into my life. I declare this by faith in Jesus' name!

Prevail Against the Enemy

For we wrestle not against flesh and blood, but against principalities, against powers, against the rulers of the darkness of this world, against spiritual wickedness in high places.

Ephesians 6:12

My Prayer for Today

Lord, help me start seeing myself as a mighty soldier in the army of God. You have provided every weapon I need to prevail against the enemies that come against my life, my family, my business, my friends, and my church. I want to stand tall and firm against the wicked plots the devil tries to exert against people's lives whom I love and need. Holy Spirit, give me the power and strength I need to successfully resist every attack and to drive all dark forces from my life and from the lives of those close to me. I pray this in Jesus' name!

My Confession for Today

I confess that I live a holy and consecrated life. There is no room for slackness in my life. I am serious about serving God as a real Christian soldier. I do everything that is required for me to walk with God and to hear the voice of His Spirit when He speaks to me. I am very serious about winning every conflict with evil forces. Because of my strong commitment to this fight of faith, I am more than a match for anything the devil tries to throw at me. I declare this by faith in Jesus' name!

Refuse To Be Moved

My Prayer for Today

Lord, help me keep my eyes and ears fixed on You and not on what I see and hear coming from people and circumstances around me. I believe that Your Word is true; therefore, I am standing firm on Your promise to me. Regardless of what people say or do, I choose to follow You! Please help me to stay put and to ignore other people's verbal accusations as I hold tightly to Your Word. I pray this in Jesus' name!

For ye have need of patience, that, after ye have done the will of God, ye might receive the promise.

Hebrews 10:36

My Confession for Today

I boldly declare that I will not move from the promise Jesus made to me. His Word is true, and His timing is right. Therefore, I am staying put until I see the manifestation of what I have believed. Although the devil tries to use people and circumstances to move me, I refuse to be moved from what Jesus has promised me. I declare this by faith in Jesus' name!

Producing Good Fruit

Wherefore by their fruits ye shall know them.

Matthew 7:20

My Prayer for Today

Lord, help me take a truthful look at the fruit produced in my life. After seeing the truth and coming to recognize areas of my life that produce bad fruit, please help me purge those bad places from my character so I can start producing good fruit in every part of my life. Without You, I can never be everything I need to be—but with Your help, I can become just like Jesus! So today I am asking You to help me get started purging and cleansing every part of my life that produces less-than-pleasing fruit. I pray this in Jesus' name!

My Confession for Today

I confess that I am a producer of good fruit! People see the character of Jesus Christ in me, and I demonstrate His love to everyone around me. Every day I am drawing closer to the Lord and becoming more like Jesus. The fruit produced by my life is so sweet that it causes others to draw near that they might experience the goodness of God as demonstrated through me. I declare this by faith in Jesus' name!

Win Your Race

Know ye not that they which run in a race run all, but only one receiveth the prize? So run, that ye may obtain.

1 Corinthians 9:24

My Prayer for Today

Lord, I ask You to help me become more fixed and focused on the goal You have given for my life. I don't want to allow distractions to pull me away from Your plan any longer. I want to shut my eyes and ears to the voices that beckon me to slow down and then set my face toward the goals You have given for my life. I can only do this with the help of Your Spirit, so today I turn to You to empower me to do this and to carry it all the way through to completion. I pray this in Jesus' name!

My Confession for Today

I confess that I am fixed and focused on God's plan for my life. I have set my face like flint; I am unflinching and unstoppable in my pursuit toward the goals God has set for me. I have strength of will, determination, a strong backbone, high morale, courage, devotedness, persistence, tenacity, and an unrelenting mindset. I have put my foot down and taken my stand. I am in the race, I have fixed my eyes on the goal, and I run with all my might so I can take the prize! I declare this by faith in Jesus' name!

Stay Watchful

Wherefore, let him that thinketh he standeth take heed lest he fall.

1 Corinthians 10:12

My Prayer for Today

Lord, help me stay watchful regarding the condition of my spiritual life. I recognize that sometimes I get too busy and fail to pray, wrongly presuming that I am strong enough to be able to survive in a state of prayerlessness. I realize that this kind of smugness and pride has always gotten me into trouble. Therefore, I turn from apathy and the wrong kind of confidence, and I turn to the Cross! Please examine my heart and help me identify those areas of my life that need to be fixed or corrected. Once You reveal to me what needs to be changed, please give me the power to apply the needed correction. I pray this in Jesus' name!

My Confession for Today

I declare by faith that I am sensitive to the Spirit of God. The Holy Spirit shows me every area of my life that is weak and that needs attention. When the Holy Spirit speaks to me, I am quick to listen and quick to obey. I urgently act to bring correction to every weakness in my character and my spiritual life where the enemy might try to penetrate. Therefore, the devil has no access to me! I declare this by faith in Jesus' name!

Discernment for Sharing

My Prayer for Today

Lord, I am asking You to help me discern when the holy things I share are being appreciated and valued, and when I am being ignored by those I am trying to help. Forgive me for investing too much of myself into people who aren't committed to applying what I have to teach them. I just wanted the best for them, and that's why it's been so hard for me to let them go. But today I am making a decision to start viewing myself, my experience, and my wisdom as treasures to be valued and held in esteem. From this moment onward, I ask You to help me invest these treasures into people who will listen, take what I have to share deeply into their hearts, and then apply those truths to their lives. I pray this in Jesus' name!

And whosoever shall not receive you, nor hear your words, when ye depart out of that house or city, shake off the dust of your feet.

Matthew 10:14

My Confession for Today

I confess that God has done wonderful things in my life that are a great blessing to others. I have something to share because Jesus has taught me so much. I am careful about what I say, and I allow the Holy Spirit to lead me to those I can open my heart to and pour out these treasures. God is helping me to be wiser about what I share and with whom I share it. I declare this by faith in Jesus' name!

Sharing the Pearls in Your Life

Give not that which is holy unto the dogs, neither cast ye your pearls before swine, lest they trample them under their feet, and turn again and rend you.

Matthew 7:6

My Prayer for Today

Lord, I want to thank You for forgiving me for all the times in my past when others did so much for me that I didn't appreciate. I was too young and too foolish to really appreciate what was being done for me, but now I understand. So today I want to thank You for everything that has been done for me. I thank You for every person You have sent to love me, to be patient with me, and to be used so mightily in my life. Now I ask You to help me be a blessing and a help to someone else who is just as I once was. I pray this in Jesus' name!

My Confession for Today

I confess that the pearls in my life are precious and have the power to help other people. I open my heart to share them with people who are serious about listening and growing. Because I'm putting so much time and energy into these people, they are going to grow in the Lord and become something truly great! They possess lots of potential, and their God-given gifts, talents, and abilities will be developed and released because God used me in their lives. I declare this by faith in Jesus' name!

Free of Strife

My Prayer for Today

Lord, I never want to be a source of strife. Please help me keep my heart free of strife and my mind clear of accusations so I can have relationships that are pleasing to You. I want to be a blessing to people—never a vehicle the devil uses to bring confusion or hurt to anyone. I am so thankful Your love has touched me and now flows through me to others. I truly desire for Your love to flow freely through me and to bring peace where strife and chaos once reigned supreme. I pray this in Jesus' name!

But if ye have bitter envying and strife in your hearts, glory not, and lie not against the truth.

James 3:14

My Confession for Today

I confess that the devil doesn't have the right to work in my mind and imagination. I refuse to permit him to divide me from the people I know, love, and need. My heart is free of strife and offense, and the door is closed to the devil so he cannot disrupt my relationships. When the devil does try to distract me with the temptation of strife, the Holy Spirit removes the blur of the disagreement and reminds me of how much I love and need that other person. I declare this by faith in Jesus' name!

From Dreams to Reality

Let a man so account of us, as of the ministers of Christ, and stewards of the mysteries of God.

1 Corinthians 4:1

My Prayer for Today

Lord, I am determining in my heart today to jump into the bottom of the boat, grab an oar, and start rowing with all my might. Doing the minimum is never going to get me where I need to go, so right now I am making the choice to put all my energies forward to achieve what You have planned for me. Help me to be faithful, steadfast, unmoving, and unflinching in the face of opposition. Help me to tell my flesh to be silent when it tries to scream out that I'm doing too much! I choose to crucify the flesh and press forward with all the strength You give me. As I do this, I believe that You will make my dreams come to pass. I pray this in Jesus' name!

My Confession for Today

I confess that I will see the fulfillment of the dream God has put in my heart. I am a hard worker, willing to do whatever it takes, and I have made a long-term commitment to achieve all that God wants to do through me. It will almost certainly take unbelievable strength and energy to move that vision from the realm of dreams to the realm of reality, but I can do all things through Christ who strengthens me. With God's Spirit working in me, I will see the fulfillment of my dreams! I declare this by faith in Jesus' name!

God's Delivering Power Is Yours

My Prayer for Today

Lord, You have never abandoned me, and You never will! When the devil tries to crush me with stress, I throw the weight of my cares upon You. I can't thank You enough for taking all those pressures off my shoulders and freeing me to walk in peace. My heart is simply overflowing with gratefulness for the strength and power You have released inside me. I know that with Your continued help, I shall be victorious, and these problems will flee! I pray this in Jesus' name!

For we would not, brethren, have you ignorant of our trouble which came to us in Asia, that we were pressed out of measure, above strength, insomuch that we despaired even of life: But we had the sentence of death in ourselves, that we should not trust in ourselves, but in God which raiseth the dead.

2 Corinthians 1:8,9

My Confession for Today

I confess that God's delivering power is mine! He has rescued me before, He will rescue me now, and He will rescue me when I need His power again in the future. I am "staying put" right where God called me. I refuse to move; I reject every temptation to give up; and I will never give in to the pressures to stop doing what God has told me to do. I will be faithful, and God will empower me to make it all the way through to my place of victory. I declare this by faith in Jesus' name!

Alive Unto God

Likewise reckon ye yourselves to be dead indeed unto sin, but alive unto God through Jesus Christ our Lord.

Romans 6:11

My Prayer for Today

Lord, I reckon myself dead to sin! It is no longer I who live, but Christ who lives in me. Since this is who You have made me to be, I ask You to help me say no to my flesh and to temptation and then to count myself alive unto You. Holy Spirit, energize me with Your strength and power to walk in the resurrection power of Jesus Christ. I pray this in Jesus' name!

My Confession for Today

I boldly declare that I reckon, deem, consider, regard, and count as a done fact that I am dead to sin! I take authority over the flesh and command it to shut its mouth, and I refuse to give it the right to rule and reign in my life. I am alive unto God through Jesus Christ. Sin is no longer my master; now I am the servant of Jesus Christ! I declare this by faith in Jesus' name!

You Are the Righteousness of God

My Prayer for Today

Lord, I need the Holy Spirit to open my eyes and convince me that I've become righteous through the blood of Jesus Christ. I've read and heard this truth, and I know it intellectually, but I need a revelation of it in my heart. So Holy Spirit, go to work in my heart. Open the eyes and ears of my spirit to see and to hear that I am the righteousness of God in Jesus Christ. Free me from religious thinking that holds me in bondage to feelings of unworthiness. Please do it today! I pray this in Jesus' name!

For if by one man's offence death reigned by one; much more they which receive abundance of grace and of the gift of righteousness shall reign in life by one, Jesus Christ.)

Romans 5:17

My Confession for Today

I confess that I am the righteousness of God in Jesus Christ. Jesus became sin for me so I could become the righteousness of God in Him. The Holy Spirit is the Great Convincer, and He is busy convincing me that I am free from defects and from sin, no longer the person I used to be. Because Jesus' blood touched, washed, and cleansed me, I am now free! I declare this by faith in Jesus' name!

Don't Throw Away Your Confidence

Cast not away therefore your confidence, which hath great recompence of reward.

Hebrews 10:35

My Prayer for Today

Lord, help me hold on tightly to the promises You have given me in Your Word. When I get physically tired or spiritually weary, please refill me with Your Spirit and recharge me with Your power so I can keep believing until I finally see the manifestation of my prayers. I know that You are faithful and that Your Word never fails, so help me remain true until I see all Your promises come true in my own life. With the assistance of Your Spirit and Your power, I can and I WILL stand firm to the end. I pray this in Jesus' name!

My Confession for Today

I confess that I have a faith that is unwavering! I stand firmly and solidly on the truths God has given me. The storms of life may come against me and the devil may try to move me, but I am not moving off the promises in God's Word. Those promises belong to me, and I claim them right now by faith. I am strong, and I am filled with the Spirit's power. Hell moves out of the way for me, because I take my stand on God's Word and refuse to move. I declare this by faith in Jesus' name!

You Are Not of This World

My Prayer for Today

Lord, I am running to You! I want to be as close to You as I can possibly be! I don't want even the smallest hint of worldliness in my life. I want to be like You, to think like You, and to please You in every part of my life—my family, my job, my relationships, and my finances. Holy Spirit, if there is any part of me that has been influenced wrongly by the world, I ask You to please show it to me and help me get it corrected. I pray this in Jesus' name!

Ye adulterers and adulteresses, know ye not that the friendship of the world is enmity with God? whosoever therefore will be a friend of the world is the enemy of God.

James 4:4

My Confession for Today

I confess that I am on fire for Jesus Christ! I am alive to God and dead to the world around me. Nothing means more to me than pleasing Jesus. Every day of my life, I live to serve Him and to do His will. Although I live in the world, I am not of the world. I am a citizen of Heaven, living with eternity at the forefront of my mind. I declare this by faith in Jesus' name!

Words of Life for Others

And the servant of the Lord must not strive; but be gentle unto all men, apt to teach, patient.

2 Timothy 2:24

My Prayer for Today

Lord, I ask You to help me be kind and patient when it is essential for me to bring correction. Help me to not be offended if the person I'm trying to help doesn't respond at first the way I wished he would have. Help me to put myself in that person's shoes and to sympathize with how he might feel. I ask You to give me the wisdom to know what to say, when to say it, and how to say it. I also ask that You give the other person the grace to hear what I am telling him so he might see that I have his best interest at heart and that I am only trying to help him. I pray this in Jesus' name!

My Confession for Today

I confess that I have the mind of Jesus Christ! When it is needful for me to speak correction to someone else, I do it with love, kindness, and patience. I refrain from allowing anger to rise up inside me. I am careful about the words that come out of my mouth, and I refuse to participate in vain arguing. I remain in control of myself as the Holy Spirit works mightily inside me. My words bring life to all who hear and receive them. I declare this by faith in Jesus' name!

Turn Every Attack Into an Opportunity

And he shook off the beast into the fire, and felt no harm.

Acts 28:5

My Prayer for Today

Lord, give me the attitude that turns every attack the devil sends into an opportunity for revival! Help me walk in such strong and consistent faith that I do not flinch at ANYTHING the devil tries to do to me. Rather than give in to my flesh and let worry conquer me, help me to remember the assignment You've given to me and to remain committed to finish my course on time. I pray this in Jesus' name!

My Confession for Today

I confess that revival happens everywhere I go! Every disaster the devil sends is my opportunity to advance the Gospel. I refuse to give in to my flesh and throw a pity party. Because I keep going and never give in or give up, God's power is always available to help me in every situation. There's too much at stake for me to let some little thing pull me down into defeat. With God's Spirit at work in me, I overcome each and every obstacle that tries to block my way. I declare this by faith in Jesus' name!

Considering Others' Needs

And let us consider one another to provoke unto love and to good works.

Hebrews 10:24

My Prayer for Today

Lord, forgive me for being so self-consumed that I have neglected to see the needs in people around me. I am sorry I've been so selfish that I haven't even recognized the times I could have been a blessing and an encouragement. I repent and I make the decision to reach out to those who are around me. Just as others have strengthened me, I want to be a source of strength to those around me. I pray this in Jesus' name!

My Confession for Today

I confess that I take the time to carefully consider other people's needs. I observe their ups and downs and their highs and lows. I study to find out what helps them feel encouraged. I am constantly observing and contemplating others to know how to encourage and provoke them to love and to good works. God uses me to come alongside those around me to help impel them to stay on track with God and with their God-given assignments. Because I am careful to notice other people's needs and I reach out to assist them with words of strength, they are becoming better, stronger, and bolder in the Lord. I declare this by faith in Jesus' name!

Renewing Your Mind and Emotions

My Prayer for Today

Lord, I ask You to help me tie up the loose ends that I've allowed to remain in my mind and emotions. Today I am making the deliberate choice to start submitting every area of my mind and emotions to the Word of God and to the sanctifying power of the Holy Spirit. Please let the power of Your Word and Spirit flow into every area of my mind and emotions, energizing them with Your Presence so that the devil can no longer access me through these areas of my life. I pray this in Jesus' name!

Wherefore gird up the loins of your mind, be sober, and hope to the end for the grace that is to be brought unto you at the revelation of Jesus Christ.

1 Peter 1:13

My Confession for Today

I confess that my mind and emotions are submitted to and renewed by God's Word. The devil has no access to my mind because my thought life is dominated by God's Word and by the power of the Spirit. I think God's thoughts, and I have the mind of Jesus Christ. Therefore, no entrance is available through which the devil can access me through my mind or emotions. I believe the truth, I think the truth, and I confess the truth about who Jesus Christ has made me to be! I declare this by faith in Jesus' name!

Speak God's Word

*Let the words of
my mouth, and
the meditation
of my heart, be
acceptable in thy
sight, O Lord, my
strength, and
my redeemer.*

Psalm 19:14

My Prayer for Today

Lord, I want my heart and mouth to say the right things! I know I need to spend more time filling my heart and mind with Your Word. I also know I need to be speaking positive confessions about myself, my family, my business, my future, my health, and everything else in connection with my life. Your Word has the promises I need for every sphere of my life, so I ask You to help me fill my heart with the truth and line up my mouth with what Your Word promises for my life. I pray this in Jesus' name!

My Confession for Today

I confess that I spend time meditating in the Word of God, and it renews my mind to God's way of thinking. God's Word brings a supernatural cleansing that washes my mind and emotions from the contamination of the world, the memories of past experiences, and the lies that the enemy has tried to sow into my brain. I make it a priority to fill my mind with truth from God's Word; therefore, I make it very difficult for the devil to penetrate my mind with his lies. I declare this by faith in Jesus' name!

Pray for Your Spiritual Leaders

My Prayer for Today

Lord, I am making the decision to stand with my pastor in prayer. I want to join him as a sincere prayer partner and support him spiritually by praying for him. I ask You to deliver him from people who have wrong motives. I also pray that his ministry will be well received; that he will have joy in his ministry; that he will make right decisions and stay in the will of God; and that he will always feel strong and refreshed in his spirit, soul, and body. Please richly bless my pastor, his wife, and his family. I pray this in Jesus' name!

Now I beseech you, brethren, for the Lord Jesus Christ's sake, and for the love of the Spirit, that ye strive together with me in your prayers to God for me; That I may be delivered from them that do not believe in Judaea; and that my service which I have for Jerusalem may be accepted of the saints; That I may come unto you with joy by the will of God, and may with you be refreshed.

Romans 15:30-32

My Confession for Today

I confess that I am a strong support to my pastor and his family. I regularly pray for him and for the other ministries and missionaries God has called me to support. They need my prayer power—and I stand with them in the Spirit for God's blessings to come upon their lives. I declare this by faith in Jesus' name!

Refrain From Gossip

Let no corrupt communication proceed out of your mouth, but that which is good to the use of edifying, that it may minister grace unto the hearers.

Ephesians 4:29

My Prayer for Today

Lord, I admit that I'm guilty of occasionally talking behind people's backs, and I'm wrong for doing it. I ask You to please forgive me for allowing the devil to use me in this way. I am asking You to help me keep a tight rein on my tongue and to refrain from gossiping about other people. When I find myself in a situation where the conversation turns to gossip, help me know how to graciously dismiss myself from the conversation so I can avoid participating in this sin and falling back into this trap. I repent for my activity in gossip, and I turn from it in Jesus' name. I pray this in Jesus' name!

My Confession for Today

I confess that I will no longer participate in the sin of gossip. If it can't be said publicly, I refuse to say it. If I have to whisper it, I will not repeat it. I refrain from gossip, and I stay away from those who practice it. Gossip is a sin, and I refuse to be a part of it. My mouth speaks only what is good for the use of edifying those who hear me. I declare this by faith in Jesus' name!

Glorifying God in Every Conversation

My Prayer for Today

Lord, I thank You for speaking to my heart today about gossip. Give me the power to tell others that I do not want to participate in talking about things that are not my business to decide or to discuss. Please forgive me for the times I've allowed myself to be caught up in conversations that didn't glorify You and that wouldn't be considered faithful by those who were being discussed. I repent for this, and today I am making the decision to walk away from such conversations from this moment forward. I pray this in Jesus' name!

But the tongue can no man tame; it is an unruly evil, full of deadly poison.

James 3:8

My Confession for Today

I confess that I refrain from gossiping and refuse to listen to it. I am a faithful friend, and I conceal a matter when it has been made known to me. I don't allow myself to fall into the trap of discussing and debating things that don't concern me. Because the Holy Spirit helps me, I know how to walk away from any conversation that doesn't glorify God. I do not listen to or participate in conversations that cause hurts and wounds in other people's lives. I declare this by faith in Jesus' name!

Let God's Spirit Control Your Tongue

But the tongue can no man tame; it is an unruly evil, full of deadly poison.

James 3:8

My Prayer for Today

Lord, I am submitting my tongue and my mouth to the Lordship of Jesus Christ today. I am unable to control my tongue by myself, so right now I deliberately make the decision to ask You to invade this area of my life with Your power and Your control. I confess that I need Your help, Lord; I can't do it on my own. Please help me learn how to overcome in this area of my life. I pray this in Jesus' name!

My Confession for Today

I boldly declare that my tongue is subdued, tamed, and brought under the control of the Holy Spirit. My lips speak words of kindness; my mouth releases praise; and I am known as one who says encouraging and helpful things to other people. My words are seasoned with grace, and my lips are constantly giving thanks to God. This is what my tongue speaks because it is submitted to the Lordship of Jesus Christ! I declare this by faith in Jesus' name!

Led by the 'Heart Tugs' of the Holy Spirit

As many as are led by the Spirit of God, they are the sons of God.

Romans 8:14

My Prayer for Today

Lord, I want to be led by the Holy Spirit in all that I say and do. When the Spirit "tugs" at my heart, trying to lead me in a new direction, please stir in me the courage I need to go wherever He leads me without being fearful, nervous, or concerned. I know the Holy Spirit is the Spirit of Truth and would therefore never mislead me. Help me become fearless to obey whatever He tells me and to go wherever He leads me. I know He has my victory in mind, so I follow Him where He leads. Thank You for helping me to be bold to follow. I pray this in Jesus' name!

My Confession for Today

I confess that I am led by the Spirit of God! The Holy Spirit "tugs" and "pulls" on my heart, and I cooperate by following Him as He gently leads me where He wants me to go. He prompts me, tugs at my heart, and pulls on my spirit to get my attention. Because I am sensitive to Him, the Holy Spirit leads me one step at a time to exactly where He wants me to go with my life. He sees and knows what I cannot see. He is leading me exactly where I need to be in order to reach my maximum potential in life. I declare this by faith in Jesus' name!

Our Mutual Ministry of Encouragement

But exhort one another daily, while it is called To day; lest any of you be hardened through the deceitfulness of sin.

Hebrews 3:13

My Prayer for Today

Lord, I want to be a major source of blessing to people in my life. Help me to quit being so fixated on myself and to see how I can become a strength and encouragement to others who are around me. Your Word commands me to be involved in giving daily encouragement. And since I am seriously committed to obeying Your Word, I intend to find a way to encourage someone who needs strength today. I pray this in Jesus' name!

My Confession for Today

I confess that I need to be encouraged! God's Word commands me to be encouraged daily, so I choose to believe that encouragement is what I need. I recognize my need for others, and I acknowledge that others need my encouragement as well. The daily exhortation and encourage-ment of other believers will stir up my faith and help me hold fast to my confession of faith. I declare this by faith in Jesus' name!

Missionary to Your World

My Prayer for Today

Lord, I ask You to use me to reach my city and the people who are in my sphere of influence. I've made the mistake of thinking that mission work only happens on the other side of the world and have therefore missed the vast mission field that surrounds my life every day. Now that I know You are calling me to invade every culture and ethnic group, give me the power and courage to start reaching them with the Good News. And now that I know I am to invade every sphere where I have influence, help me see myself as Your missionary, sent to these people whom I know so well. I surrender to the call—and today I acknowledge that I am Your missionary to my world. I pray this in Jesus' name!

Go ye therefore, and teach all nations....

Mathew 28:19

...Go ye into all the world, and preach the gospel to every creature.

Mark 16:15

My Confession for Today

I confess that I am God's missionary to my city and to the people I interact with in every area of life. Jesus expects me to take the Gospel to the different ethnic groups, cultures, and civilizations that are in my city and neighborhood. He expects me to invade every sphere where I have influence and to use that influence to share the Gospel with the people who live, work, and function in those places. My mission field is right down my street, and my assignment is to reach every person in every group where I have influence. So I choose this day to invest my time and energy into fulfilling that divine assignment to the glory of God. I declare this by faith in Jesus' name!

Be a Worthy Representative

...Go ye into all the world, and preach the gospel to every creature.

Mark 16:15

My Prayer for Today

Lord, I ask You to please help me become an honorable representation of who You are. I am sorry for allowing myself to live a low standard that gave a wrong impression about You. Now I understand that I am Your face and Your voice to the people around me. To the best of my ability, I want to speak courteously, act Christ-like, dress appropriately, and act professionally so I can accurately portray Your Word and Your heart. I know this is going to require some changes in my life, so today I am asking You to help me as I take steps toward becoming a worthy representative who brings only honor to the King of kings. I pray this in Jesus' name!

My Confession for Today

I confess that I am the spokesman of the Lord. As His representative, I live respectfully, honorably, and in a way that brings glory to His name. I behave professionally; I speak courteously and kindly to others; I dress appropriately as His representative; and I preach the Gospel with excellence by the way I live both my public and private life. As a believer, I accept my assignment to be one of God's messengers to my generation. I declare this by faith in Jesus' name!

Expect Signs and Wonders

And these signs shall follow them that believe....

Mark 16:17

My Prayer for Today

Lord, I prayerfully admit that I haven't been expecting signs and wonders to follow me as I ought to be expecting them. From this moment onward, I release my faith for the miraculous to follow me when I preach or share the Gospel with unbelievers. Holy Spirit, let the power of God flow and confirm the message! Let God's signature be all over the Gospel that I preach. Because I am constantly releasing my faith for the miraculous to follow me wherever I go, I expect to see people healed, blind eyes opened, and captives set free by the power of God! I pray this in Jesus' name!

My Confession for Today

I confess that signs and wonders follow me! I am intensely hungry to see the miraculous, and I am constantly believing for it to be in manifestation. Since everything in the Kingdom of God is activated by faith, I release my faith right now for supernatural signs to be manifested in my life. I am among those who are constantly believing for the miraculous to happen. When I preach the Gospel, I expect signs and wonders to follow that authenticate the message and supernaturally meet the needs of those who are listening to me. I declare this by faith in Jesus' name!

You Have Authority

And these signs shall follow them that believe; In my name shall they cast out devils....

Mark 16:17

My Prayer for Today

Lord, give me the courage to speak up and take authority over demons! Your Word declares that You have given me power over all unclean spirits. I am ready to use that power to bring freedom into people's lives who are bound. Help me know how to best minister to people who fall into this category so that their freedom can be full and complete. I pray this in Jesus' name!

My Confession for Today

I boldly confess that I have authority over all evil spirits. I have no reason to be afraid of them! Jesus gave me power and authority over all the works of the devil. When I am confronted with a demonic manifestation, I speak to it, take authority over it, and cast it out in Jesus' name! I declare this by faith in Jesus' name!

Speaking With a New Tongue

My Prayer for Today

Lord, I thank You for filling me with the Spirit and for giving me the ability to pray and to praise You in a supernatural language. My spirit longs to pray, to express itself, and to worship You. My own mind and intellect are so limited that I don't always know what to say or how to express myself. But when I pray and praise in the Spirit, I am very aware that I am praying perfectly and praising You on the highest level. Thank You for this wonderful ability. I want to pray in the Spirit and to worship You with all of my inner man! I pray this in Jesus' name!

And these signs shall follow them that believe; In my name shall they cast out devils; they shall speak with new tongues.

Mark 16:17

My Confession for Today

I confess that I am filled with the Spirit of God and that I regularly pray in the Spirit. God liberated my inner man to speak to Him on the day I was baptized in the Holy Spirit. From that time until now, I have had the ability to speak in a supernatural spiritual language. I refuse to neglect or ignore this ability God has given me; therefore, I regularly pray in tongues. As a result, I am growing stronger and more sensitive to the Holy Spirit, and I have a continual operation of divine, supernatural activity in my life. I declare this by faith in Jesus' name!

Divine Protection

He [God] is my refuge and my fortress: my God; in him will I trust. Surely he shall deliver thee from the snare of the fowler, and from the noisome pestilence. He shall cover thee with his feathers, and under his wings shalt thou trust: his truth shall be thy shield and buckler.

Psalm 91:2-4

My Prayer for Today

Lord, I believe Your Word to be true! By faith, I claim that there is nothing the enemy can do to injure or hurt me when I am traveling to take Your name to a new part of the world or to people who do not know You. Thank You for this promise of divine protection for my life! I am so grateful that You have shielded me with Your power and that the enemy cannot destroy me. I pray this in Jesus' name!

My Confession for Today

I confess that God's power shields and protects me from every attack of the enemy! If I am required to fly on rickety airplanes, drive on dangerous roads, pass through highly volatile areas, or work in regions that are considered dangerous, I will be safe. Regardless of the conditions I am forced to face in order to take the name of Jesus to people who have never heard, God will be with me. He will protect me every step of the way. I believe and claim God's protection; therefore, the enemy cannot do anything to hurt me! I declare this by faith in Jesus' name!

The Courage To Go Where God Sends You

My Prayer for Today

Lord, I thank You for giving me the courage to go wherever You want me to go. I rebuke fear; I reject intimidation; and I decide by faith that I can do anything and go anywhere Jesus wants to send me. Holy Spirit, fill me with Your power and help me think with a sound mind. There's so much that Jesus has for me to do, and I don't want to waste a single minute. Thank You for helping and strengthening me. I pray this in Jesus' name!

For God hath not given us the spirit of fear; but of power, and of llove, and of a sound mind.

2 Timothy 1:7

My Confession for Today

I boldly declare that I am protected from bad foods or fatal substances. When I sit down to eat, I take a few minutes to bless my food. I call it sanctified; I speak nutrition and health into it; and then I eat it, believing that it will only bless and strengthen my body. Jesus has provided supernatural protection from disasters, calamities, snakes, scorpions, and all the works of the enemy. He promised me traveling mercies and protection from acts of injustice. God isn't going to send me somewhere so I can die! I rebuke the spirit of fear—and I press forward into the divine life of Jesus Christ. I boldly declare this in Jesus' name!

Lay Your Hands on the Sick

...they shall lay hands on the sick, and they shall recover.

Mark 16:18

My Prayer for Today

Lord, I ask You for confidence to lay my hands on the sick. I want Your healing power to flow through me and to be deposited into sick bodies, attacking the enemy's work until finally those sick people are restored to health again. In Your Word, it is stated that when believers lay hands on the sick, the sick would be made well again. Today I am making the decision to pull my hands out of my pockets and to place them on the sick so Your healing power can be delivered to others through me. I pray this in Jesus' name!

My Confession for Today

I confess that God's power is released into the bodies of the afflicted when I lay my hands on them. Just as medicine slowly works to reverse a medical condition, the power of God that is deposited when I lay my hands on sick people begins to attack their affliction, causing them to be progressively restored to health and well-being. Healing the sick is part of my responsibility, so I boldly confess that I am going to lay my hands on sick people just as Jesus did when He was ministering on the earth— and I expect to see them get well! I declare this by faith in Jesus' name!

Moving to a Higher Realm

*This I say then,
Walk in the Spirit,
and ye shall not
fulfil the lust
of the flesh.*

Galatians 5:16

My Prayer for Today

Lord, help me walk in the Spirit and not in the flesh. I realize that I must make a choice to move up into this higher realm, so today I am telling You that I want to leave the low life I've been living and come up higher. You are beckoning me to come there, and I accept Your invitation. As I start taking steps to this higher sphere of life, help me resist the yearnings of the flesh that keep trying to pull me back down. I want to become so sensitive to You that the desires of the flesh altogether cease to have any effect on my life. I pray this in Jesus' name!

My Confession for Today

I confess that I am moving up into a higher realm! I fixate on the goal of walking in the Spirit. I am developing my own human spirit, and I am becoming more sensitive to the Spirit of God. Every day the voice of my flesh is getting weaker and weaker. I have accepted the call of God to leave the low life behind, and I am following the Spirit of God to a higher realm, where I will live in continual peace, joy, and victory! I declare this by faith in Jesus' name!

Alive Unto God

*For the flesh
lusteth against the
Spirit, and the
Spirit against the
flesh: and these are
contrary the one to
the other: so that
ye cannot do the
things that ye
would. But if
ye be led of the
Spirit, ye are not
under the law.*

Galatians 5:17,18

My Prayer for Today

Lord, help me to mortify the deeds of the flesh and to reckon myself alive unto God. I have walked in the flesh long enough; now I want to walk in the Spirit. I no longer want the flesh to have its way in my life. Instead, I want to let the Holy Spirit produce the life of Jesus Christ in me. I know that I ultimately make the decision of what is produced in my life, so please help me to consistently say no to the flesh and to say yes to the Spirit of God. I pray this in Jesus' name!

My Confession for Today

I confess that it is no longer I who live, but Jesus Christ lives in me! The life I now live in the flesh, I live for the Son of God, who loved me and gave Himself for me. I am His temple. I am His instrument. I refuse to allow the old flesh nature to dominate me. I willfully surrender my mind, my thoughts, my emotions, and my flesh to the sanctifying power of the Holy Spirit. As I yield to Him, He purifies me and makes me a worthy vessel for the work of God's Kingdom. I declare this by faith in Jesus' name!

Say No to Ungodliness

My Prayer for Today

Lord, I thank You for opening my eyes to the truth about how You see these works of the flesh. Forgive me for being too tolerant of these areas in my life. Help me to see these fleshly works the way You see them and to detest them as much as You detest them. Teach me to hate sin! Show me how to say no to ungodliness and to yield my mind and my body as instruments of righteousness. After what You have shown me, I never want to be the same! I pray this in Jesus' name!

Now the works of the flesh are manifest, which are these; Adultery, fornication, uncleanness, lasciviousness.

Galatians 5:19

My Confession for Today

I confess that I think clean thoughts and that I don't allow the devil to mess with my mind. My mind belongs to Jesus. It is filled with the Word of God. That Word renews my mind to think God's thoughts; therefore, Satan has no entrance into my mind or emotions to deceive me with thoughts of sin. I crucify my flesh, and I bring my body under the Lordship of Jesus Christ. I am no longer the servant of sin—I am the servant of righteousness! I declare this by faith in Jesus' name!

Walk in the Spirit

There is therefore now no condemnation to them which are in Christ Jesus, who walk not after the flesh, but after the Spirit.

Romans 8:1

My Prayer for Today

Lord, I want to walk in the Spirit and to mortify the deeds of the flesh. I don't want the flesh to have the superior role in my life that it has had in the past. I know that if Your Spirit empowers me, I can say no to the flesh and to its demands to control my life. I am tired of struggling with the same old sins again and again. So right now I am asking You to help me see the truth about what needs to change in my life. Once I see the problem, give me the courage to tell that work of the flesh that it is going to die. Then help me to fully embrace the new life You are wanting to release inside me. I pray this in Jesus' name!

My Confession for Today

I boldly declare that I am no longer dominated by the flesh; instead, I walk in the power of the Holy Spirit. There is therefore no condemnation for me! I am careful to read my Bible and to hear the truths that the Holy Spirit wants to show me. When I become aware of areas that need to be changed, I quickly ask Jesus to release His power to transform me. Instead of running from the truth, I run to the Cross to find permanent solutions for the problems I confront along the way. I declare this by faith in Jesus' name!

Crucifying the Works of Your Flesh

My Prayer for Today

Lord, I am surrendering my attitudes to You today. Hatred, variance, emulations, and wrath are so hurtful to my heart and destructive to my relationships. I don't want them to be a part of me any longer. I turn from these attitudes, Lord. I repent for allowing them to have any place in my life. I confess that they are wrong and are grievous both in Your sight and to my spirit. I ask You to give me the strength I need to crucify these works of the flesh and to let the life of Jesus flow through me! I pray this in Jesus' name!

And they that are Christ's have crucified the flesh with the affections and lusts. If we live in the Spirit, let us also walk in the Spirit.

Galatians 5:24,25

My Confession for Today

I confess that hatred, variance, emulations, and wrath have no place inside me. God's Spirit dwells in me and helps me keep these fleshly attitudes out of my heart so I can stay free. I am filled with love; I am thrilled when other people get blessed; and I never give way to rage or wrath. It simply has no place in me. Every day I am becoming more filled and controlled by the Spirit of God! I declare this by faith in Jesus' name!

Christ Lives in You

I am crucified with Christ: nevertheless I live; yet not I, but Christ liveth in me: and the life which I now live in the flesh I live by the faith of the Son of God, who loved me, and gave himself for me.

Galatians 2:20

My Prayer for Today

Lord, I don't want these works of the flesh to be active in my life! I stand against them in Jesus' name, and I yearn for the Holy Spirit to produce His divine fruit in me. Please help me to be sensitive to Your Spirit and to the needs of others, and to stay alert for those times when my flesh is trying to take me in one of these wrong directions. I pray this in Jesus' name!

My Confession for Today

I confess that I have the mind of Jesus Christ and I think the thoughts of God. I crucify the flesh, I mortify its deeds, and I release the resurrection life of Jesus Christ in me. Although I live in the flesh, it is no longer I who live, but Jesus Christ lives in me! I declare this by faith in Jesus' name!

Take Up Your Cross

My Prayer for Today

Lord, help me the next time I am tempted to get envious over someone else's blessing or position. Help me to keep my head on straight and not to allow things in my life that will recharge my flesh and stir me up to do things that are sinful or wrong. Forgive me for thinking that I constantly have to be entertained. I'm so sorry that I've wasted so much of my time and thrown away so much money on things that don't matter. I don't want to be dominated by my flesh anymore. Today I am calling on You to help me break away from my past patterns so I can start on a new and higher path. I pray this in Jesus' name!

Then said Jesus unto his disciples, If any man will come after me, let him deny himself, and take up his cross, and follow me.

Matthew 16:24

My Confession for Today

I confess that I am not dominated by the flesh but by the Spirit of God. I am completely committed to the Lordship of Jesus Christ and to doing what pleases Him most with my life. I refuse to let my flesh lead me astray, and I have decided to take up my cross and follow wherever Jesus leads me. I am serious about life; I am serious about doing what God wants me to do; and I am a good steward of my time, resources, and talents. I declare this by faith in Jesus' name!

Living To Please Your Heavenly Father

So then they that are in the flesh cannot please God. But ye are not in the flesh, but in the Spirit, if so be that the Spirit of God dwell in you...if the Spirit of him that raised up Jesus from the dead dwell in you, he that raised up Christ from the dead shall also quicken your mortal bodies by his Spirit that dwelleth in you.

Romans 8:8,9,11

My Prayer for Today

Lord, I thank You for saving me by the power of God. Help me put aside the works of the flesh once and for all. Please teach me to walk in the Spirit. I know that You have designed a powerful life for me, and I want to enter into that life in all its fullness. My heart's desire is to know You better and to walk with You, so today I am asking that Your Spirit propel me forward into this newer and higher way of living! I pray this in Jesus' name!

My Confession for Today

I confess that I do NOT routinely perform the works of the flesh. As a genuine child of God, I live to please my Heavenly Father, and I am repulsed by sin when it tries to operate in my life. My spirit is sensitive to God, and my heart is tender to the voice of the Holy Spirit. I hate sin and its consequences, and I do everything I can to live and to stay in the Presence of God. I declare this by faith in Jesus' name!

God's Divine Nature in You

My Prayer for Today

Lord, I thank You for placing Your divine life inside me! You have changed my whole view of life and given me new desires. I am so grateful to You for bringing about such change in me. I am truly a new creature with new desires, new longings, and new aspirations. I am so thankful that when I look at my life, I can see Your life and Your nature working in me! I pray this in Jesus' name!

Therefore if any man be in Christ, he is a new creature: old things are passed away; behold, all things are become new.

2 Corinthians 5:17

My Confession for Today

I confess that I have a new nature with new desires! I am not the person I used to be. By looking at me, it is evident that God's new nature is alive and working inside me. His divine seed is reproducing God's life in me so that every day I am thinking more like God, acting more like God, and possessing less tolerance for any sin that might still be active in my life. I don't have to wonder if I'm really saved, for my life gives proof that I have received a brand-new nature! I declare this by faith in Jesus' name!

Producing Divine Fruit

But the fruit of the Spirit is love, joy, peace, longsuffering, gentleness, goodness, faith, meekness, temperance: against such there is no law.

Galatians 5:22,23

My Prayer for Today

Lord, thank You for sowing Your Spirit and Word into my life. Forgive me for allowing the flesh to dominate so much of my life. Help me yield to the divine seed You have planted inside me. I know that Your life resides in me, longing to be released, so today I make the choice to let Your Spirit start working mightily inside me. Thank You for the life of God that is flowing up from my spirit right now, producing the life and the nature of Jesus Christ in me. I pray this in Jesus' name!

My Confession for Today

I confess that the Holy Spirit lives in me and is producing His fruit in my life. The flesh no longer rules or dominates me, for I yield to the peaceful fruit of the Holy Spirit in every sphere of my life. I demonstrate love, joy, peace, longsuffering, gentleness, goodness, faith, meekness, and temperance in my life. God has sown His Spirit and His Word into my heart; therefore, I expect this divine fruit to be produced inside me. I declare this by faith in Jesus' name!

The First Fruit Is Love

*But the fruit of the
Spirit is love....*

Galatians 5:22

My Prayer for Today

Lord, help me turn my attention to Your kind of high-level love and make it a part of my daily life. Forgive me for those times when I've fallen into low-level, "you scratch-my-back-and-I'll-scratch-yours" love that gets easily offended. Help me climb up to the higher realms of love that You desire to be manifested in my life. Holy Spirit, it is impossible to continually walk in this kind of love in the power of my flesh, so I turn to You to awaken this divine love inside me and to help me manifest it in my life. I pray this in Jesus' name!

My Confession for Today

I confess that I am hotly pursuing agape love in my life. I want to attain this high level of love and regularly walk in it, so I treat this fruit of the Spirit like it is one of the most important aims of my life. Because the seed of God's Spirit and Word is sown in my own human spirit, I have the potential for this divine love within me all the time. So right now I determine to shove the flesh aside and release the power of God from down deep inside. Because agape is the driving motivation of my life and the force behind all my relationships, I am the best, most devoted, faithful, and reliable friend anyone has ever known! I declare this by faith in Jesus' name!

Joy and Peace

*But the fruit of
the Spirit is love,
joy, peace....*

Galatians 5:22

My Prayer for Today

Lord, I am so thankful today that You haven't abandoned me to my flesh and my emotions. Because Your Spirit lives in me, I can be empowered to walk in joy and peace in any situation. Forgive me for pandering to the whims of my flesh and for allowing it to rant and rave when Your Spirit inside me is longing to cause His supernatural joy and peace to rule my life. I turn from my past habits of worry and fear, and I deliberately choose to let the Holy Spirit flood me with Your unquenchable joy and incomprehensible peace. I pray this in Jesus' name!

My Confession for Today

I confess that I am dominated by the fruits of joy and peace. Fear and anxiety have no place in my life; neither am I ruled by the temporary, fleeting emotions of happiness. Joy strengthens me and stabilizes me in every situation. Peace rules my emotions, helping me to maintain stability and eradicate emotional chaos from my life and surroundings. I am inhabited by the Spirit of God Himself—and as I yield to Him, He is controlling me more and more! I declare this by faith in Jesus' name!

Longsuffering and Gentleness

My Prayer for Today

Lord, I thank You that I don't have to walk in the works of the flesh. Because of Your grace, I can surrender to the power and Presence of the Holy Spirit inside me. As I surrender to the Spirit, I ask that His divine life release His supernatural fruits in me. I want to be more patient, longsuffering, and kind. I know that I need these attributes in my life and that I am lacking them right now. So rather than continue down the path I've been on, I am stopping everything right now to ask You to change me. Please produce the life of Jesus Christ and His wonderful character in me! I pray this in Jesus' name!

But the fruit of the Spirit is love, joy, peace, longsuffering, gentleness....

Galatians 5:22

My Confession for Today

I confess that I am loving, patient, and kind. I don't lose my temper. I am not quickly angered. I am forbearing of others, tolerant of their mistakes, and burning passionately to see them gain new levels of growth in their lives. Just as others have been patient and forbearing with me, I am very patient and understanding of others who are also trying to change. I am gentle, kind, and adaptable to those who are around me. As the Spirit of God works in me, I become all things to all men in order that I might gain some for the Kingdom of God. I declare this by faith in Jesus' name!

Goodness and Faith

But the fruit of the Spirit is love, joy, peace, longsuffering, gentleness, goodness, faith.

Galatians 5:22

My Prayer for Today

Lord, I want You to work so mightily in me that "goodness" and "faithfulness" become an integral part of my life. Please forgive me for the times I've been flesh-bound and insensitive to the human needs that are all around me. I have walked right past people with serious needs; yet I haven't even noticed. I am convicted by this, Lord, and I'm asking You to help me shift my focus from myself to those who are around me. I also ask You to help me become so faithful that people will know they can depend on me. I pray this in Jesus' name!

My Confession for Today

I confess that I am sensitive to the human needs of those who are around me. In addition to believing for my own needs to be met, I also believe for the financial resources to help meet the needs of others. Just as Jesus was a blessing in His generation, I am a blessing in my generation. I am stable, unwavering, and consistent in every area of my life, reflecting the life and character of Jesus Christ in all that I do. I declare this by faith in Jesus' name!

Meekness and Temperance

But the fruit of the Spirit is love, joy, peace, longsuffering, gentleness, goodness, faith, meekness, temperance....

Galatians 5:22,23

My Prayer for Today

Lord, I am so thankful that You are patient with me as I learn to walk in the Spirit and to produce the fruit of the Spirit in my life. Every day I am becoming more aware of my need to be changed. It is very evident that I cannot change myself without Your help. I know that I need meekness and temperance in my life. When I look at myself in the mirror, my physical image even tells me that temperance is greatly lacking in me. So today I am sincerely calling out and asking You to help me move up to a higher level of life. Produce these powerful, life-changing fruits in me. Change me, I pray! I pray this in Jesus' name!

My Confession for Today

I confess that I am becoming more and more controlled in my emotions and my physical life. Restraint, moderation, temperance, discipline, self-control—all of these are becoming a part of who I am and how I behave. The nature and character of Jesus Christ are being developed in me. The spiritual fruits of meekness and temperance are changing me—bringing peace to every situation I encounter and producing health in me as I learn to be moderate in everything that I do. I declare this by faith in Jesus' name!

Becoming 'Yoked' With Jesus

Come unto me, all ye that labour and are heavy laden, and I will give you rest. Take my yoke upon you, and learn of me; for I am meek and lowly in heart: and ye shall find rest unto your souls. For my yoke is easy, and my burden is light.

Matthew 11:28-30

My Prayer for Today

Lord, I admit that I've been trying to pull the whole load by myself, and I simply can't do it any longer. I have given every ounce of my strength; now I need You to come alongside me and help me finish the task that is before me. I'm willing to do it, but I must have Your help if I'm going to do it with all my heart and finish it all the way to the end. So today I am asking You to become "yoked" with me in my job, my business, my ministry, my family, and in all my personal affairs. I pray this in Jesus' name!

My Confession for Today

I confess that Jesus Christ is my Partner in life. He works with me, He walks with me, and He is my biggest Helper! Because of Jesus' strategic role in my life, my attitude, my environment, my work, and everything connected to me has become better, higher, finer, and more pleasurable. My life assignment is not a burden—it is truly a delight! I declare this by faith in Jesus' name!

God's Abounding Grace

My Prayer for Today

Lord, I thank You for pouring out Your grace in difficult, chaotic times. When sin abounds and darkness tries to reign, that is always when You reach out to seek and to save. Forgive me for giving way to fear and for thinking of retreating at this key moment when You are wanting to make a strategic advance. I choose to push away all my fears and to believe that You are going to do something miraculous to save the day! Let Your grace flow, Lord—-pour it on! Please shine Your light in this hour of darkness. I pray this in Jesus' name!

...But where sin abounded, grace did much more abound.

Romans 5:20

My Confession for Today

I confess that God's grace is poured out mightily to drive back the forces of darkness during times of difficulty and chaos. God uses these dark moments as opportunities to pour out His grace and to show others who He is. The world may reel in fear and uncertainty, but God is always near. I declare by faith that God will reveal His power and intervene with His grace to bring the solution for this difficult hour. I declare this by faith in Jesus' name!

God's Abundant Life

The thief cometh not, but for to steal, and to kill, and to destroy: I am come that they might have life, and that they might have it more abundantly.

John 10:10

My Prayer for Today

Lord, I am so thankful that You came to give me real life! You didn't save me so I could live the rest of my life in defeat and poverty. You didn't redeem me so I could be sick, depressed, and sad. You came to give me life, and I am determined to enter into the reality of that life You promised me. Forgive me for ever allowing the devil to talk me out of the blessings You have designed for my life and my family. I'm taking my eyes off the low road, and I'm headed for the high road of blessing You have planned for me! I pray this in Jesus' name!

My Confession for Today

I confess that Jesus Christ gives me a life that is filled with extraordinary abundance! He came that I might have, keep, and constantly retain a vitality, gusto, vigor, and zest for living that springs up from deep down inside me. He gives me a life that is not rattled or easily shaken by any outward event. I therefore embrace this unrivaled, unequaled, matchless, incomparable, richly loaded and overflowing life that Jesus came to give me. I declare this by faith in Jesus' name!

Wisdom in Leadership

My Prayer for Today

Lord, I ask You to please help me gauge how quickly others should be promoted in our church, organization, or business. I don't want to make the mistake of throwing people into situations where the devil will test them because I promoted them too quickly. Also, Lord, I ask You to please help me have a new appreciation for those who are over me and who are taking some time before promoting me. I want to be a blessing, and I never want the devil to have an opportunity to blur my vision because I think too highly of myself. Thank You for loving me enough to promote me in just the right time and in just the right way. I pray this in Jesus' name!

Not a novice, lest being lifted up with pride he fall into the condemnation of the devil.

1 Timothy 3:6

My Confession for Today

I confess that I use wisdom in the way I choose and promote leaders in my area of responsibility. I am careful, cautious, and hesitant about promoting people to high positions too quickly. Just as God watches and tests me before giving me greater responsibility, I watch, test, and wait to see if others are really ready before I assign them new and important tasks. Because I rely on the Holy Spirit's help in this matter, I am making fewer and fewer mistakes in choosing the right people to promote. I declare this by faith in Jesus' name!

Standing Firm

Wherefore take unto you the whole armour of God, that ye may be able to withstand in the evil day, and having done all, to stand.

Ephesians 6:13

My Prayer for Today

Lord, I receive Your Word today as strength for my life! You have called me to do something great for You, and I'm not going to let the devil or my circumstances chase me away from where I know I need to be. It's been very difficult, but this season will pass—and when it does, I'll be stronger, wiser, and more equipped for the future. I thank You for helping me to dig in, take a firm stand, and maintain the post You have assigned to me. I pray this in Jesus' name!

My Confession for Today

I confess that I am not moving from the place where Jesus called me. The devil and various circumstances have tried hard to move me, but I have made up my mind and have resolved in my heart that I am not flinching or moving from the place where Jesus called me to give my heart. This is my post, this is my ground, and I'm going to be around until I can say I've finished my part! I declare this by faith in Jesus' name!

Reaping What You Sow

> Be not deceived;
> God is not
> mocked: for
> whatsoever a man
> soweth, that shall
> he also reap.
>
> *Galatians 6:7*

My Prayer for Today

Lord, I want to be a faithful, consistent giver! I don't want to be on-again, off-again in the sowing of my financial seed. I know that this is a spiritual law that always works and will never change, so please help me renew my thinking to the truth of this law and come into a place of conformity with it. I want to habitually sow, and I want to habitually reap. Help me plant the right seeds into the right soil. Then I ask You to provide the right temperature, climate, and atmosphere to make my harvest grow. I pray this in Jesus' name!

My Confession for Today

I confess that I am NOT a one-time sower. I continually, habitually sow my seed into the Kingdom of God. God's Word promises that "whatsoever a man sows, sows, sows, and sows, and keeps on habitually sowing and sowing and sowing, that shall he also reap, reap, reap, and reap, and keep on habitually reaping and reaping and reaping." Because I am a habitual sower, I will be a habitual reaper! The level at which I sow determines the level at which I will reap. If I sow a little, I will reap a little. If I sow a lot, I will reap a lot. If I sow inconsistently, I will reap inconsistently. If I sow regularly, I will reap regularly. Knowing this to be true, I choose to make my giving one of the most important and consistent things I do in my life. I declare this by faith in Jesus' name!

Filled With Supernatural Endurance

Truly the signs of an apostle were wrought among you in all patience, in signs, and wonders, and mighty deeds.

2 Corinthians 12:12

My Prayer for Today

Lord, I thank You for filling me with supernatural endurance to do the job You've given me to do. In the midst of all the problems, hassles, and challenges that have come against me, I am very aware that I wouldn't be able to do it without the divine gift of endurance You have placed in my life. Others may think I am strong, but I know that much of my strength and fortitude is due to what You have done inside me. So today I give You praise, and I thank You for continuing to strengthen me until I bring this assignment to a victorious end. I pray this in Jesus' name!

My Confession for Today

I confess that God is filling me with supernatural endurance to stay put until I have successfully done everything He has asked me to do. He gave me this assignment because He believed I could do it. He filled me with endurance to help me stay put and to be strong enough to finish it as I ought. I therefore declare that I am strong; I am filled with fortitude; and I will do precisely what God has asked me to do! I declare this by faith in Jesus' name!

The Helmet of Salvation

*And take the
helmet of
salvation....*

Ephesians 6:17

My Prayer for Today

Lord, I am so grateful for my salvation! It is the most wonderful gift You have ever given me. It changed my life and set me free; it brought healing to my body and deliverance to my mind. I want to wrap the knowledge of all that my salvation includes around my mind so tightly that the devil can never steal these benefits from my life. Holy Spirit, I ask You to help me study and to understand everything Jesus purchased for me at the Cross. Reveal it to me; convince me of its truth; and help me to wear that revelation knowledge on my head like a mighty, fortified, spiritual helmet! I pray this in Jesus' name!

My Confession for Today

I confess that I wear my salvation tightly around my mind like a helmet. When the enemy tries to attack my mind and to chop away at the benefits of my salvation, his attacks are completely ineffective! My mind is convinced of all that salvation means for me, and my mind is trained and taught to think correctly according to that knowledge. Therefore, the knowledge of my salvation becomes a helmet in my life. It doesn't matter how hard the devil tries to hack away at my mind, I still stand strong because I know what Jesus' death and resurrection purchased for me. I declare this by faith in Jesus' name!

A Partner To Help You

Likewise the Spirit also helpeth our infirmities: for we know not what we should pray for as we ought: but the Spirit itself maketh intercession for us with groanings which cannot be uttered.

Romans 8:26

My Prayer for Today

Lord, I need Your help! I am so frequently at a loss for words and don't seem to know what to say when I pray. Since You sent the Holy Spirit to help me, I am asking the Spirit of God to fall into my situation with me; to join me as my Partner; to collaborate with me in prayer; to become a part of my team; and to get me out of this mess I'm in, putting me on a right and stable path. I am obviously never going to get there without special assistance, so today I'm asking for HELP! I pray this in Jesus' name!

My Confession for Today

I confess that the Holy Spirit is my Partner! I call out to Him in my moment of need, and He quickly comes to my rescue. He enlightens my eyes; He shows me what I cannot see by myself; and He gives me the right words to say when I pray. Because I have the Holy Spirit, I am no longer speechless or helpless to know how I should pray. With Him as my Helper, I am getting better and better in prayer every day! I declare this by faith in Jesus' name!

Praying for Missionaries

My Prayer for Today

Lord, I ask You today to bless missionaries who are living and working in other parts of the world. Bless their families, their health, their finances, and everything that concerns them. Help them preach with little or no resistance. Empower them to run fiercely as they race to reach souls from being eternally lost. Protect them as they live, work, and dash back and forth through dangerous territory. I pray that the entrance of God's Word in their communities will break the powers of darkness and usher in a new triumphant day! Help me to remember to pray for them every day. I pray this in Jesus' name!

Finally, brethren, pray for us, that the word of the Lord may have free course, and be glorified, even as it is with you.

2 Thessalonians 3:1

My Confession for Today

I confess that I love missionaries and support them with my prayers and finances. I appreciate them for leaving their homes, their families, and their natural surroundings, and for uprooting their wives and children and moving to the other side of the world to take the Good News to those who do not have it. I will be faithful to remember them, to honor them, to pray for them, and to support them with my substance. The role I play to support them in prayer and with my finances is essential for their success, so I will fulfill my role faithfully. I declare this by faith in Jesus' name!

Make Time for God

But thou, when thou prayest, enter into thy closet, and when thou hast shut thy door, pray to thy Father which is in secret; and thy Father which seeth in secret shall reward thee openly.

Matthew 6:6

My Prayer for Today

Lord, I ask You to forgive me for making time for everything except You. The truth is, I haven't made my prayer time a priority in my life; therefore, I haven't been consistent in prayer. So often when I do start to pray, other things scream for my attention and distract me. So I am asking You to help me locate a time and place where I can be alone and uninterrupted with You. I know that this is essential for my spiritual life, so starting today, I am making this the highest priority in my life. I pray this in Jesus' name!

My Confession for Today

I confess that my daily time with God is the highest priority in my life. I treat my time with the Lord like it is the most important moment of my day and week. I am faithful to pray, to fellowship with the Father, to bare my heart before Him, and to listen to what His Spirit has to say to me. Because I make this time a priority in my life, I walk away from my prayer time energized and revitalized with the strength I need to face any situation that might come my way. I declare this by faith in Jesus' name!

Be Determined To Win

My Prayer for Today

Lord, help me have an attitude that is determined to win every struggle and fight that I face in life. You have given me spiritual power, spiritual weapons, and the wonderful Word of God. It is a fact that You have equipped me with everything I need to win. Now the victory depends on me and my attitude. Help me maintain the attitude that never gives in, never gives up, and never surrenders to defeat. As I make up my mind to take hold of Your power, Your spiritual weapons, and Your Word, it is guaranteed that I will push the devil clear out of my life. So please help me to make this decision and to do it quickly! I pray this in Jesus' name!

But thanks be to God, which giveth us the victory through our Lord Jesus Christ.

1 Corinthians 15:57

My Confession for Today

I confess that I am following the voice of my Commander-in-Chief. I will go where Jesus says to go, and I will do exactly what He tells me to do. I am committed to get in the fight and stay in it until the victory is won! I have an attitude that never gives in, never gives up, and never surrenders to defeat. God has given me spiritual power, spiritual weapons, and the promises of His Word on which I can stand. He has equipped me with everything I need to win—and now the victory depends on me! I declare this by faith in Jesus' name!

Refuse To Let Go

Now the just shall live by faith: but if any man draw back, my soul shall have no pleasure in him. But we are not of them who draw back unto perdition; but of them that believe to the saving of the soul.

Hebrews 10:38,39

My Prayer for Today

Lord, I am asking You to help me stay focused and to remain determined to stay in my race of faith until I reach the finish line and receive my long-awaited prize. When the devil tries to dissuade me from holding on to my faith, help me to rebuke him, to command him to be silent, and to order him to leave. With Your Spirit empowering me, I know I will be able to keep believing and walking by faith until I finally see the manifestation of my dreams. I pray this in Jesus' name!

My Confession for Today

I confess that regardless of how heavy the load or how long it takes, I am going to refuse to move from my faith position until I achieve the victory Jesus promises to me. I will remain steadfast in my commitment, and nothing can sway or move me to change my mind. I refuse to relinquish any of my God-promised territory! My faith is tough, resistant, persistent, obstinate, and stubborn. My spirit is so tenacious that it refuses to let go! It isn't a question of IF my victory will come—it's only a question of WHEN it will come! I declare this by faith in Jesus' name!

Prepare To Move Forward

My Prayer for Today

Lord, You know me better than anyone in the world, so I trust You to know exactly when I am ready for the next big promotion that You have designed for my life. Help me to quit being frustrated with my superiors for not promoting me more quickly, and help me instead to take a look at the deeper issues of my life that hold me back from being elevated. Holy Spirit, help me use this time in my life to clean up my act and to get my heart ready for the next upward step that Jesus has waiting for me. I pray this in Jesus' name!

Lay hands suddenly on no man, neither be partaker of other men's sins: keep thyself pure.

1 Timothy 5:22

My Confession for Today

I confess that my character, attitude, and actions are being refined by the fire of God in my life. The Holy Spirit is helping me discover any serious character flaws that would negatively affect my future. God is changing me, teaching me, and preparing me for greater responsibility. I am serious about my walk with God and about being greatly used by Him in this life. Therefore, I want Him to identify every part of my life that is out of order or that needs to be fixed. So today I yield to the Holy Spirit so He can delve deep into my soul and extract those traits that would keep me from the blessings and positions God would love to give me. I declare this by faith in Jesus' name!

Real Sword Power

*And take...the
sword of the
Spirit, which is
the word of God.*

Ephesians 6:17

My Prayer for Today

Lord, thank You for giving me the sword of the Spirit as part of my spiritual weaponry. When the devil attempts to attack me, please help me be sensitive to hear the exact rhema that the Holy Spirit desires to drop into my heart with which I can then deal the enemy a fatal blow. Starting right now, I open my heart and soul to listen so I can hear any scripture or word the Holy Spirit wishes to give me to use against the works of the devil in my life. I pray this in Jesus' name!

My Confession for Today

I confess that I have the sword of the Spirit, which is the Word of God, and that this spiritual weapon is working in my life. I have the exact word I need for every situation—a specific, quickened word from the Scriptures, placed in my heart by the Holy Spirit. Because this rhema from God is in my heart, I have real sword power to use against the enemy. I declare this by faith in Jesus' name!

Listening to the Voice of the Spirit

My Prayer for Today

Lord, I want to learn how to follow You more closely! I want to learn the sound of Your voice, to sense when You are speaking to me and trying to lead me, and to become so sensitive to You that I know when to act and when to wait. I am sorry for all the times I've acted before praying—and then assumed that You would bless what I was doing. I don't want to function this way anymore. I only want to initiate what I know You are leading me to do. So please help me become more sensitive. Give me the boldness to do what You say to do and to wait when I hear You tell me to wait. I pray this in Jesus' name!

And when Jesus departed thence, two blind men followed him, crying, and saying, Thou son of David, have mercy on us. And when he was come into the house, the blind men came to him: and Jesus saith unto them, Believe ye that I am able to do this? They said unto him, Yea, Lord. Then touched He their eyes, saying, According to your faith be it unto you. And their eyes were opened....

Matthew 9:27-30

My Confession for Today

I confess that I am completely dependent upon the Holy Spirit. Just as Jesus was constantly listening to the voice of the Spirit, waiting for that divine signal to act, to heal, to deliver, or to cleanse someone who was sick, I am also sensitive to the Holy Spirit's voice and wait for Him to speak to my heart. When He speaks, I hear; then I do exactly what He instructs me to do. Because I follow His voice, I make few mistakes and I see great results! I declare this by faith in Jesus' name!

Laboring With Others To Fulfill God's Plan

Let a man so account of us, as of the ministers of Christ, and stewards of the mysteries of God.

1 Corinthians 4:1

My Prayer for Today

Lord, I want to take my place in Your plan for my life—and I want to give 100 percent of my attention and strength to see it come to pass in my life. With all my heart, I tell You that I want to follow You and to do whatever is required to see that vision come to pass in my life. And thank You for calling others to come alongside to help me move this vision along a little faster. I pray this in Jesus' name!

My Confession for Today

I confess that I have taken my place in God's plan. I have grabbed hold of an oar, and I am rowing and rowing with all my strength and energy. The assignment God has given me probably won't be achieved quickly, so I have mentally prepared myself for a long-term stint at doing what God is calling me to do. It will take unbelievable strength and energy to move that vision from the realm of dreams to the realm of reality. But because of the power of the Holy Spirit in me, I have all the strength I need for this wonderful and awesome task. I declare this by faith in Jesus' name!

A Celebration of Victory

My Prayer for Today

Lord, I am stopping everything I'm doing right now to praise You for Your victory over Satan! Thank You for stripping him bare and for leaving him with nothing in his hands with which to retaliate. Thinking of what You did makes me want to shout—so right now I'm going to shout! Realizing what You did makes me want to jump with joy—so right now I'm going to leap up and down in praise to You! I'm excited about what You did, and I'm not ashamed to show how I feel about it. I praise and worship You for the great victory You gained! I pray this in Jesus' name!

And having spoiled principalities and powers, he made a shew of them openly, triumphing over them in it.

Colossians 2:15

My Confession for Today

I confess that I am free from Satan's grip on my life because Jesus stripped him bare and left nothing in his hands that he could use against me. Jesus defeated and disarmed Satan; then He gave me authority over the devil and all his works. Greater is He who is in me than he who is in the world. That means in Jesus Christ I am fully empowered to enforce Satan's defeat! I declare this by faith in Jesus' name!

Chosen by God

For ye see your calling, brethren, how that not many wise men after the flesh, not many mighty, not many noble, are called: But God hath chosen the foolish things of the world to confound the wise; and God hath chosen the weak things of the world to confound the things which are mighty, and base things of the world, and things which are despised, hath God chosen....

1 Corinthians 1:26-28

My Prayer for Today

Lord, I am so glad You don't choose only the intellectually brilliant. You are looking for anyone who has a heart to be used by You. Well, that's me, Lord. I want You to use me. I offer You everything I have—my good points, my weak points, my gifts, my talents, and everything else that I am. I want You to use me for Your glory! I've told You before, but today I'm telling You again that I want You to take my life and do something wonderful with me. I pray this in Jesus' name!

My Confession for Today

I confess that I am exactly the kind of person God can use! God is looking to carry out great victories through my life. His choice is not based on beauty or a lack of beauty, talent or lack of talent, education or lack of education, a diploma or lack of a diploma. No, God has chosen me because I have a heart that is right before Him. I declare this in Jesus' name!

Look at What You've Been Given

My Prayer for Today

Lord, forgive me for being so negative and for talking so badly about myself after You have given me so much. I have no excuse for accepting defeat or low self-esteem as a way of life, because You have made me totally new. Help me renew my mind to the truth about who You have made me to be, and help me guard the words of my mouth so that instead of speaking evil of myself, I affirm the truth about who I am in Christ. I pray this in Jesus' name!

But as many as received him, to them gave he power to become the sons of God, even to them that believe on his name.

John 1:12

My Confession for Today

I confess that the day I was born again, I received the dynamic, explosive power of God into my life. That power removed my old nature and made me a brand-new creature! Nothing from the old me continues to exist, for I am completely brand new. When God made me, He put forth His finest creative powers, and I now live on this earth as a masterpiece of His grace. God has made me into something quite spectacular! I declare this by faith in Jesus' name!

Resist Every Attack of the Devil

Submit yourselves therefore to God. Resist the devil, and he will flee from you.

James 4:7

My Prayer for Today

Lord, help me stay focused on my calling and remain determined to do what You've told me to do, even if I am assaulted by outside forces that seem to be beyond my control. I know the devil hopes to slow me down or even to stop me by orchestrating outside pressures to come against me. But I also know that Your Spirit works mightily in me, giving me all the power I need to resist every assault the devil tries to bring against me. Help me to be completely determined and committed to keep pushing ahead and to never let go until I've accomplished my God-given mission. I pray this in Jesus' name!

My Confession for Today

I boldly confess that I will not stop or give up until I have apprehended that for which Christ Jesus apprehended me. I will resist the devil's attacks and successfully achieve all God has called me to do, for I have determined that I will never stop until I have finished the task. I have the stamina, spunk, and doggedness it takes to get the job done. I have made the decision to stay in faith and slug it out with the power of God at my side. I can and will do exactly what God called me to do! I declare this by faith in Jesus' name!

Don't Give Place to the Devil

*Neither give place
to the devil.*

Ephesians 4:27

My Prayer for Today

Lord, I ask You to help me keep the doors to my heart and soul closed to the devil! I know he would like to slip into my relationships and ruin them, so I am asking You to help me stay free of offense, free of unforgiveness, and free of bitterness. I realize these wrong attitudes create "entry points" through which the devil tries to gain territory in my relationships. I don't want to give the devil a foothold in my affairs through a wrong attitude. So I'm asking You, Lord, to help me identify every wrong feeling or attitude in my life that the devil could use to ruin relationships with people I need and love. I pray this in Jesus' name!

My Confession for Today

I confess that I walk in forgiveness! Offense, bitterness, strife, and unforgiveness have no place in my life. The Spirit of God dwells in me, and He always convicts me of wrong attitudes that the devil could potentially use to bind me. I love Jesus, and I want to please Him; therefore, I refuse to allow these destructive attitudes to remain in me. I am full of mercy, longsuffering, and slow to anger. All of these qualities keep me safe and secure from the devil's attempts to invade me. I declare this by faith in Jesus' name!

Recognize and Respect Your Limitations

For I say, through the grace of God given unto me, to every man that is among you, not to think of himself more highly than he ought to think; but to think soberly, according as God hath dealt to every man the measure of faith.

Romans 12:3

My Prayer for Today

Lord, help me recognize and respect my gifts and limitations. Forgive me for the times I've been too prideful to admit I was in over my head and as a result did an inferior job. I'm so sorry I didn't step out of the way so someone else who was gifted for the job could take my place. Help me specialize in those areas where I feel confident that I will be a blessing. Teach me to embrace and appreciate those who are more gifted than I am in other areas. I pray this in Jesus' name!

My Confession for Today

I confess that I think soberly about myself and about my gifts and abilities. I thank God for the gifts and talents God has placed in my life, but I also recognize and respect my limitations. Just as I appreciate my own gifts and abilities, I am also grateful for those who are more gifted than I am in other areas. I need them, I embrace them, and I appreciate what they have to contribute. I can't achieve alone what can be accomplished in partnership with others. Therefore, I choose to partner my gifts and talents with the God-given gifts and talents in other people. I declare this by faith in Jesus' name!

Demonstrate Your Love for Jesus

My Prayer for Today

Lord, I ask You to help me be honest about what my finances reveal about me. I don't want anything else in my life to have a higher priority than You, so please teach me how to demonstrate my love for You with my finances. Help me to really worship You with my financial gifts and not to just casually throw them into an offering plate. Forgive me for the times I've said I didn't have enough money to give to the church or to missions, yet somehow I found a way to spend money on all kinds of material things. My priorities have obviously been wrong, so today I repent. I have made up my mind that I am going to honor You with my finances as I ought to do. I pray this in Jesus' name!

Then took Mary a pound of ointment of spikenard, very costly, and anointed the feet of Jesus, and wiped his feet with her hair: and the house was filled with the odour of the ointment.

John 12:3

My Confession for Today

I confess that I am growing more and more faithful in the giving of my tithes and offerings. Jesus Christ and the preaching of the Gospel are the greatest priorities in my life. Therefore, when I get paid, the first thing I do is set aside my tithe for the church and my offering for world missions and other worthy ministries. As I learn to love Jesus even more, my financial gifts are increasing as well. My treasure is in Jesus and the Gospel, because that is exactly where my heart is fixed. I declare this by faith in Jesus' name!

Serve With Excellence

And whosoever of you will be the chiefest, shall be servant of all. For even the Son of Man came not to be ministered unto, but to minister, and to give his life a ransom for many.

Mark 10:44,45

My Prayer for Today

Lord, I want to serve You with the highest level of excellence! Forgive me for times when I have tolerated a low standard in my life, my business, my ethics, my church, or my ministry. Nothing in the world is more serious than the services I render in Your name, so help me do it in a way that glorifies You. I pray this in Jesus' name!

My Confession for Today

I confess that I have a high standard of excellence in my life and that I am growing daily in my level of professionalism. As I serve God at work and at church, I demonstrate the excellence of Jesus' name. When people see me, they see the Kingdom of God. In fact, God is happy that I am His representative because my life shows forth an excellent image of who Jesus is and what He stands for in this world. I am His representative, and therefore I do everything with the highest level of excellence. I declare this by faith in Jesus' name!

You Can Flee From Temptation

My Prayer for Today

Lord, help me find the strength to say no to my flesh and to flee from temptation when it tries to wrap its long tentacles around my soul and drag me into some kind of sin. I know what it's like when sin calls out to my flesh, beckoning it to do something that is forbidden or wrong, but I don't want to cooperate with it anymore. I want to walk free—to flee from sin and break free of its vicious grip. Help me bring my mind under the control of the Holy Spirit so I can think rationally when Satan tries to attack me through my mind, my emotions, or my senses. I pray this in Jesus' name!

There hath no temptation taken you but such as is common to man: but God is faithful, who will not suffer you to be tempted above that ye are able; but will with the temptation also make a way to escape, that ye may be able to bear it.

1 Corinthians 10:13

My Confession for Today

I confess that God makes a way for me to escape temptation. I do not negotiate with sin! When it tries to call out to me, I get up and get out as quickly as I can. I flee, take flight, run away from, and escape as quickly as I can when I know the devil is attempting to lure me into his trap. That's when I put on my jacket, pick up my things, and let my feet fly! God always makes a way for me to escape—and I always make the right choice to jump through that escape hatch! I declare this by faith in Jesus' name!

Bringing Order to Your Life

Thus saith the Lord, Set thine house in order....

Isaiah 38:1

My Prayer for Today

Lord, help me bring order into my own personal life. Since what is happening in my private life is exactly what I will bring into my public life, I want to bring more order into my own personal affairs. Help me take an honest look at my life so I can see those areas that desperately need my attention. Once I acknowledge the areas that need fixing, please give me the courage to delve into those areas and to get things right. I want every area of my life to glorify You, so if there is a secret part of my life that doesn't bring honor to You, I'm looking to You to help me make the needed changes. I pray this in Jesus' name!

My Confession for Today

I confess that with God's help, I am putting my house in order. The way I handle my family life, my children, my physical home, and my finances brings glory to Jesus Christ. I am serious about my walk with God, and I therefore invite Him to invade every sphere of my life and to bring it under His Lordship. Jesus is Lord of my marriage, my children, my home, and my money. It all belongs to Him; therefore, I want to be a wise steward for His sake—and I will! I declare this by faith in Jesus' name!

Live Fearlessly in These Last Days

My Prayer for Today

Lord, I am so thankful that Your Word prepares us for every event that comes along in this life. I know that I am living in the last days and that these challenging times require a higher level of commitment from me if I am going to live free from fear. This is such a critical moment for me to be strong, free, and secure. When I am strong, I can be a tower of strength to others who are drowning in the world around me. Help me be that source of strength and power to the people who surround me, Lord. I want to be all that I need to be in this hour. I pray this in Jesus' name!

That ye be not soon shaken in mind, or be troubled, neither by spirit, nor by word, nor by letter as from us, as that the day of Christ is at hand.

2 Thessalonians 2:2

My Confession for Today

I confess that God's Word dominates my mind, my will, and my emotions! Because I have put God's Word into my heart, I am not shaken or easily moved by the things that occur in the world around me. I know who I am; I am secure in my Father's love; and I recognize that He destined me to live in these last days because He has a special plan for me. Regardless of what I see or hear, I take my stand on the promises of God's Word, and it provides me with safety and security. I declare this by faith in Jesus' name!

Press Forward Toward the Prize

Brethren, I count not myself to have apprehended: but this one thing I do, forgetting those things which are behind, and reaching forth unto those things which are before, I press toward the mark for the prize of the high calling of God in Christ Jesus.

Philippians 3:13,14

My Prayer for Today

Lord, I am so very thankful to You for all the progress I've already seen in my life. But today I am turning my eyes to the future because I know You have so much for me to do. I don't want to miss anything You have designed for me, so I am choosing to turn my attention to the vision and to run my race with all my might! Help me remove anything that would hinder my race so I can press forward toward the prize of the high calling of God for my life. I pray this in Jesus' name!

My Confession for Today

I boldly confess that I am focused, concentrated, and determined to run my race! God has called me and anointed me; therefore, I can do exactly what He has asked me to do. I have no excuse for failure or any reason to slow down or quit, for God's Spirit in me is ready to empower me to run this race all the way to the finish. Doing it halfway will never do, so I am committed to seeing this all the way through. I declare this by faith in Jesus' name!

Protection for Your Mind

Put on the whole armour of God, that ye may be able to stand against the wiles of the devil.

Ephesians 6:11

My Prayer for Today

Lord, I don't want the devil to fill my mind with insinuations and lies. My mind belongs to You, and the devil has no right to flood me with false perceptions, vain imaginations, or lies about who I am or what I will never be. I refuse to let him operate in me any longer! You have provided me with the helmet of salvation, and by faith I put it on to protect my mind against the devil's assaults. He can strike as hard as he wishes, but Your Spirit and Word protect me. I pray this in Jesus' name!

My Confession for Today

I confess that I bring every thought into the captivity of Christ. When the devil tries to invade my mind with lies, I capture those lies and drive them clear out of my brain! Rather than fall victim to the devil's attacks, I seize every thought that he tries to use to penetrate my mind and emotions. I grab each lie and force it into submission! Because I stand firm on the Word, the enemy's lies are not able to exert any power against me. I declare this by faith in Jesus' name!

Break Free From Compromise

No man can serve two masters: for either he will hate the one, and love the other; or else he will hold to the one, and despise the other. Ye cannot serve God and mammon.

Matthew 6:24

My Prayer for Today

Lord, I don't want to allow any spirit of compromise in my life. I don't want to live with one foot in the church and another foot in the world. I want to break free completely from the world and its influence so I can give myself completely to Your cause. I want to be holy, to live in a way that pleases You, and to experience Your power in my life. Today I am renewing my commitment to You all over again. I turn from the world, and I am running to You! I pray this in Jesus' name!

My Confession for Today

I confess that I am free from the world. I do not walk in compromise! I am determined to live a committed and holy life before the Lord. As a result of my firm determination to walk with God, I have power over sin, power over Satan, and power when I pray. God's Word promises that if I draw near to Him, He will draw near to me. I am drawing nearer and nearer to God every day, so I am confident that His Presence in my life is getting stronger too. I declare this by faith in Jesus' name!

Don't Jump Ship!

My Prayer for Today

Lord, help me today to keep a right perspective of what You have called me to do. When I get tired and the devil tries to convince me to quit, please help me remember that if everyone stops rowing the boat, it won't go anywhere. Even if no one else notices what I am doing, I know that You see every move I make. Whatever I do, Lord, I do for You! I pray this in Jesus' name!

...thy Father, which seeth in secret, shall reward thee openly.

Matthew 6:18

My Confession for Today

I confess that I have a job to do and that I'm going to do it! I will not jeopardize my destiny by succumbing to the discouraging voice of the enemy. If the boat is going to move, I must do my part to move it. Whether or not I ever hear the words "thank you" from anyone, I am the servant of God and I will do my service as unto Him. I declare this by faith in Jesus' name!

Free of Offense

*Looking diligently
lest any man fail
of the grace of
God; lest any root
of bitterness
springing up
trouble you,
and thereby
many be defiled.*

Hebrews 12:15

My Prayer for Today

Lord, help me keep my heart free of offense. You have given me authority over my own will, mind, and emotions, so I know I have the authority to tell offense that it has no right to dwell inside me. I refuse to blame everyone else for the mess I've allowed to grow inside my heart—and today I am asking You to help me, Holy Spirit, to quit making excuses for the wrong attitudes I've permitted to grow in my life. With Your supernatural help, I am making the choice to repent, to turn from these destructive thoughts, and to replace them with thoughts and words of kindness for those who have caused me hurt or grief in the past. I pray this in Jesus' name!

My Confession for Today

I confess that I deal diligently with my heart to keep my heart in good shape. I don't make excuses for rotten attitudes that try to fill my thoughts about people who have wronged me. Even if they really did commit a wrong, I refuse to let the devil use it to eat me up and ruin me. I am the bishop of my own heart, so I refuse to let wrong attitudes fester, take root, and begin to produce bad fruit in me. I declare this by faith in Jesus' name!

Investing in Good Fruit

My Prayer for Today

Lord, help me invest my life in people who will grow strong and who will bring forth good fruit. I want to give my life to people who are going to do something in this world. I want to know that I have made a difference in the life of someone who is going to make a difference in the lives of others. The last thing I want is to have lived this life and made no personal investment in anyone else, so please help me recognize those people You want me to pour myself into. Then give me the wisdom and grace to pull up alongside and share with them the treasure You have placed in me. I pray this in Jesus' name!

We are bound to thank God always for you, brethren, as it is meet, because that your faith groweth exceedingly, and the charity of every one of you all toward each other aboundeth; So that we ourselves glory in you in the churches of God for your patience and faith in all your persecutions and tribulations that ye endure.

2 Thessalonians 1:3,4

My Confession for Today

I confess that I bear good fruit in the lives of people whom God has called me to help. They are growing! They are prospering! They are learning to overcome the evil one! They are strong, stable, resilient, reliable, faithful, and committed to do whatever it takes for them to fulfill the assignment Jesus Christ has given them. My fruit is good fruit—fruit that remains! In this I know that my Father is glorified, because I am producing the kind of fruit that brings glory to His name. I declare this by faith in Jesus' name!

From Glory to Glory

But we all, with open face beholding as in a glass the glory of the Lord, are changed into the same image from glory to glory, even as by the Spirit of the Lord.

2 Corinthians 3:18

My Prayer for Today

Lord, I want to take the veil off my eyes and get honest about my situation. I can see that much of my present life is not glorious. I have wanted You to promote me from my mess to a new level of glory, but I see now that Your promotions always move from one level of glory to a higher level of glory. Show me every area in my life that needs to be changed, and help me give You complete liberty to transform those parts of my life. I want to go to a higher level of glory, Lord, so I am asking You to help me first make my present situation a glorious testimony of Your grace. I pray this in Jesus' name!

My Confession for Today

I confess that by God's grace, I am making my present situation more and more glorious! I have asked the Holy Spirit to open my eyes and to help me see those parts of my life that need to be transformed. As He shows me these areas, I will diligently pray about them and do everything I can to allow God to change me so this present season of my life can become glorious. Because the Holy Spirit sees my willingness to go through the necessary transformation process, He is preparing to move me upward into a more glorious phase in my life. I am going from glory to glory! I declare this by faith in Jesus' name!

The Holy Spirit: Your Guide in Life

My Prayer for Today

Lord, I thank You for the leadership of the Holy Spirit. I am so sorry that I've wasted time, energy, and money trying to find my way on my own when You have already sent me the Holy Spirit to be my Guide. Holy Spirit, please step into my life and take Your place as my Teacher, my Leader, and my Guide. I extend my heart and my hand to You today so You can begin to guide me through life. I thank You, Father, for providing the most wonderful Guide in the whole universe to help me make it successfully through life! I pray this in Jesus' name!

Howbeit, when he, the Spirit of truth, is come, he will guide you into all truth....

John 16:13

My Confession for Today

I confess that I am led by the Spirit of God. Because I cooperate with Him, I don't waste valuable time, energy, or money, and I don't shed a lot of unnecessary tears. I gladly let the Holy Spirit lead me, since He sees what I can't see; knows what I don't know; and understands the best routes, the most efficient shortcuts, and the safest paths to take. As a result, He leads me past every attack; He helps me avoid each strategy of the devil; and He safely guides me to the place where God wants me to be. I declare this by faith in Jesus' name!

Speak Only the Truth

Lie not one to another, seeing that ye have put off the old man with his deeds.

Colossians 3:9

My Prayer for Today

Lord, I admit that I've exaggerated the facts and embellished the truth on many occasions. I'm so sorry for doing this. I blamed it on my personality, but now I understand that You view this as dishonesty. I ask You to help me stop making excuses for this behavior and to accept responsibility for the words and messages I project to others. When I stand before You, I want a clear conscience that I have been honest, forthright, and balanced in the things I've said about myself or about others. Holy Spirit, I need Your help to bring correction to this part of my life, so today I yield myself to You. I pray this in Jesus' name!

My Confession for Today

I confess that I speak the truth and that I don't exaggerate the facts or speak lies. When people talk to me, they can count on the fact that I don't embellish the truth or twist the facts to my advantage. They can rest assured that I'm honest about myself and the situations in which I find myself. I keep my nose out of other people's business and concern myself instead with those issues that have to do with me and my areas of responsibility. Because God is my Helper and His grace is working mightily in me, I am becoming more and more honest every day. I declare this by faith in Jesus' name!

Take Authority Over the Devil

My Prayer for Today

Lord, I am asking You to help me take author-ity over the accusations that the devil has been speaking in my mind. He's been telling me all the reasons that I shouldn't have any hope and that I deserve to be in this mess. But Your grace is greater than any mistake I've made or sin I've committed in the past. I know that You have forgiven me and redeemed me from any mess I've created by my own actions. I thank You now for Your forgiveness and mercy, and today I lay claim to the power of restoration. Devil, right now I command you to leave me in Jesus' name! I refuse to listen to your accusa-tions any longer. I pray this in Jesus' name!

Be sober, be vigilant; because your adversary the devil, as a roaring lion, walketh about, seeking whom he may devour.

1 Peter 5:8

My Confession for Today

I declare that I have confessed all my past sins and mistakes. Therefore, I am forgiven, I am clean, and I am free in the sight of the Lord. He does not hold my past against me. He is my Redeemer, my Restorer, my Deliverer, and my Salvation. His Spirit is operating in me right now to get me out of every mess I have created, both intentionally or unintention-ally. My heart is repentant, and my desire is to do what is right. Therefore, God is helping me walk out of the problems that have tried to grip my mind and my life. I declare this by faith in Jesus' name!

Free of Wrong Attitudes

Looking diligently lest any man fail of the grace of God; lest any root of bitterness springing up trouble you, and thereby many be defiled.

Hebrews 12:15

My Prayer for Today

Lord, I ask You to please forgive me for allowing negative thoughts about others to consume me. Even though I don't like what they did to me, I have no right to be bitter and resentful. I realize now that I am acting just as ugly inwardly as they acted outwardly. In Your eyes, my sin is just as bad as theirs. I am truly sorry for allowing these attitudes to grow inside me, Lord. To the best of my ability, I turn right now from the wrong thoughts that have been consuming me, and I choose instead to speak well of those who have offended or hurt me. Holy Spirit, help me uproot those wrong feelings from my heart and replace them with love and forgiveness. I pray this in Jesus' name!

My Confession for Today

I confess that my heart is free of bitterness, resentment, strife, and unforgiveness. God's Spirit lives in me, and He doesn't allow me to keep living with wrong attitudes in my life. He speaks to me when I begin to think poorly of others; He convicts me of every wrong attitude; and He helps me bring my thoughts under His control. Because my mind and emotions are controlled by the Spirit of God, I think only positive thoughts about those who are near or around me. If any negative thoughts about someone else try to enter my mind, the Holy Spirit quickly helps me recognize them and bring correction to the way I am thinking. I declare this by faith in Jesus' name!

Thoroughly Furnished

My Prayer for Today

Lord, I thank You for loving me so much that You would give Your Word to equip me for life. I realize that all the answers I need are found in Your Word. I have often complained that I needed more power and wisdom. But the truth is, everything I need is in Your Word. Help me to diligently read my Bible, take it deeply into my heart and soul, and apply it to my life. As I do so, I ask that it would supernaturally release its divine power to transform me from being a simple, basic believer to becoming one who is super-equipped for life! I pray this in Jesus' name!

All scripture is given by inspiration of God, and is profitable for doctrine, for reproof, for correction, for instruction in righteousness: That the man of God may be perfect, thoroughly furnished unto all good works.

2 Timothy 3:16,17

My Confession for Today

I confess that God's Word has a central place in my life. I regularly read God's Word and meditate on its truths; therefore, my mind is being renewed with the Word day by day. As a result, that Word decks me out— equipping, outfitting, and furnishing me with all the spiritual gear I need to take the adventurous trip God has planned for my life. With God's Word fitted tightly in place, I am ready to set sail and follow wherever the Holy Spirit leads. I declare this by faith in Jesus' name!

Extinguish Every Fiery Dart of the Enemy

Above all, taking the shield of faith, wherewith ye shall be able to quench all the fiery darts of the wicked.

Ephesians 6:16

My Prayer for Today

Lord, thank You for giving me the shield of faith. Help me to be brave and bold and to hold my shield high in front of me to stop every attack of the enemy. I understand that I have a responsibility to soak my faith in Your Word so it can extinguish each and every flaming arrow the devil tries to shoot into my life. I ask You to help me be sincerely committed to making Your Word the top priority in my life—soaking my faith with that Word until it becomes an impenetrable wall of defense against the enemy's attacks! I pray this in Jesus' name!

My Confession for Today

I confess that my faith is saturated with the Word of God. The devil may try to attack me, but my faith is held out high in front of me, covering my life completely and extinguishing every flaming arrow the devil attempts to shoot in my direction. My faith is supernaturally energized, and I am empowered to stand against every assault the devil tries to make on my life. I declare this by faith in Jesus' name!

You Have the Mind of Christ

My Prayer for Today

Lord, I ask You to help me be wise, prudent, intelligent, discerning, and sensible in the way I think and act. You see everything and know exactly what is really happening, so I am leaning on You to lead me in every situation. Teach me when to sit still and when to act. You are my Leader, so I look to You to lead me and to help me do exactly what is right in each situation. I pray this in Jesus' name!

For who hath known the mind of the Lord, that he may instruct him? but we have the mind of Christ.

1 Corinthians 2:16

My Confession for Today

I confess that I have the mind of Jesus Christ. His mind makes me sensible, intelligent, prudent, discerning, and accurate in the way I think and behave. Because the Holy Spirit is producing the mind of Christ in my life, I make very few mistakes. In fact, I am getting better and better all the time at seeing things accurately and knowing what to do in different situations. I am careful to lay low when the Spirit says to wait, and I am bold to obey when the Spirit says to act. I declare this by faith in Jesus' name!

You Are the Kind of Person God Wants To Use

For ye see your calling, brethren, how that not many wise men after the flesh, not many mighty, not many noble, are called: But God hath chosen the foolish things of the world to confound the wise....

1 Corinthians 1:26,27

My Prayer for Today

Lord, I thank You for choosing to use people like me! I realize that I may not have the education, skills, culture, or high-level training that others may possess, but I do have a heart to be used by You. I want You to take me and use me for Your work in this earth. Today I surrender to You anew, asking You to take me and to use me mightily in this life. I pray this in Jesus' name!

My Confession for Today

I confess that I am exactly the kind of person God wants to use! My heart is right, my attitude is willing, and I deeply desire for God to use me in a special way in this life. I am willing to learn and ready to be corrected. I want God to shape me to become a mighty instrument in His hands. Because of my attitude and willing heart, God is going to use me mightily to further His Kingdom on this earth. I declare this by faith in Jesus' name!

Responding in Love

My Prayer for Today

Lord, please help me be patient with people who are inconsiderate of others and won't stop talking about themselves. When I am tempted to lose my patience and to become angry with them, give me the grace to moderate my emotions so that I can respond to them in the spirit of Jesus. I know that You have been patient with me so often, and now it is my turn to be patient with others. Help me to show them the same kindness You have shown me and to avoid falling into the trap of being judgmental and impatient. I pray this in Jesus' name!

Though I speak with the tongues of men and of angels, and have not charity [agape love], I am become as sounding brass, or a tinkling cymbal.

1 Corinthians 13:1

My Confession for Today

I confess that I am loving, patient, and kind, and I do not quickly lose my temper with people who are self-consumed. These "motormouths" are not my enemies. I am their friend. As God enables me, I will speak the truth to them in the spirit of Jesus Christ. I believe that in their hearts, they want to change. Therefore, I overlook their weaknesses and am patient with them as God works on transforming them day by day. I declare this by faith in Jesus' name!

Love Is Patient and Kind

Charity [agape love] suffereth long, and is kind; charity envieth not....

1 Corinthians 13:4

My Prayer for Today

Lord, I ask You to help me open my heart so that agape love can flow up from within me. I realize that I've allowed myself to get clogged up with my own self-interests far too often. I need to be more focused on the needs of others than I am on myself. I realize that the only way I can become this selfless is to yield to the Holy Spirit so He can do a deep work in my life. Holy Spirit, I am asking You today to do whatever is necessary to teach me how to regularly walk in this high-level, agape love of God. I pray this in Jesus' name!

My Confession for Today

I confess that I walk in the agape love of God. I am patient with other people. I am also very slow to anger or to get upset. I am so concerned about the welfare of others that one of my chief priorities in life is to become everything I need to be to meet their needs. Other people see me as a friend who wants to help them succeed. Although God has given me my own dreams and desires, I never neglect to help others achieve their dreams and aspirations as well. Because high-level love works in me, I am becoming more and more like Jesus Christ. I declare this by faith in Jesus' name!

Love Is Not Prideful

My Prayer for Today

Lord, I ask You to help me live my life in a way that glorifies You. You are my Lord, and I am Your servant and child. I don't want to do anything with my life that brings disrespect or dishonor to Your precious name. Help me to not exaggerate or embellish the truth. I ask You to correct me when I am lured into snobbery or pride and to lovingly rebuke me when I "act ugly" toward others. I want to be like You, Jesus, and I'm not going to stop pressing ahead until I demonstrate Your life and Your nature in my life. I pray this in Jesus' name!

Charity [agape love] suffereth long, and is kind; charity envieth not; charity vaunteth not itself, is not puffed up, doth not behave itself unseemly....

1 Corinthians 13:4,5

My Confession for Today

I confess that I am never going to stop until I have attained the high level of love Jesus wants me to have in my life. I don't go around talking about myself all the time, constantly exaggerating and embellishing the facts. I don't behave in a prideful, arrogant, haughty, superior, snooty, snobbish, or clannish manner. I'm not rude and discourteous. I'm not careless or thoughtless. As I spend time with Jesus, I am being changed into His image—and I demonstrate His life and His nature to other people. I declare this by faith in Jesus' name!

Love Considers Others

*Charity [agape
love] suffereth
long, and is kind;
charity envieth
not; charity
vaunteth not itself,
is not puffed up,
doth not behave
itself unseemly,
seeketh not her
own, is not
easily provoked,
thinketh no evil.*

*1 Corinthians
13:4,5*

My Prayer for Today

Lord, I ask You to help me put an end to any scheming or manipulating tendencies that still reside in my soul. I know that this is very grievous to You and damaging to my relationships. I repent for participating in this evil behavior, and I ask You to help me be honest in all my dealings with other people. Help me to curb my anger, hold my tongue, and refrain from speaking words that bring harm. Thank You for forgiving me for past sins. Today I am making a decision to wipe the slate clean regarding anyone who has ever acted unjustly or unfairly with me. I pray this in Jesus' name!

My Confession for Today

I confess that I don't try to manipulate situations or look for ways to scheme to get what I want. I don't deceptively twist situations to my advantage, nor do I deliberately engage in actions or speak words that cause an ugly or violent response. I have been forgiven much; therefore, I quickly forgive others, never keeping a record of others' wrongs, sins, or mistakes. God is doing a mighty work in me, and every day I am becoming more and more free! I declare this by faith in Jesus' name!

Love Rejoices When Others Are Blessed

My Prayer for Today

Lord, I ask You to help me overcome those fleshy moments when I am tempted to rejoice at someone else's hardships. I must admit that when I hear something has happened to a person who wronged me, something inside me secretly rejoices. I know that this is wrong and that it is not the way You behave. Please forgive me for responding in a way that is contrary to love. Help me to be concerned and prayerful for every person who is undergoing any kind of hardship in life—even those who have acted like they are my enemies. I pray this in Jesus' name!

Charity [agape love] suffereth long, and is kind; charity envieth not; charity vaunteth not itself, is not puffed up, doth not behave itself unseemly, seeketh not her own, is not easily provoked, thinketh no evil; Rejoiceth not in iniquity, but rejoiceth in the truth.

1 Corinthians 13:4-6

My Confession for Today

I confess that I am blessed when I see someone else receiving a blessing or special attention. It thrills me when I see other people moving upward in life. Even when someone steps into the blessing I've been believing for in my own life, I am elated for them! I declare this by faith in Jesus' name!

Love Endures All Things

Charity [agape love] suffereth long, and is kind; charity envieth not; charity vaunteth not itself, is not puffed up, doth not behave itself unseemly, seeketh not her own, is not easily provoked, thinketh no evil; Rejoiceth not in iniquity, but rejoiceth in the truth; Beareth all things, believeth all things, hopeth all things, endureth all things.

1 Corinthians 13:4-7

My Prayer for Today

Lord, I ask You to help me learn to operate in this supernatural, life-changing, high-level love. Please help me to quit judging others for the problems in their lives and to start thinking about how I can protect and cover them in times of difficulty. Holy Spirit, please help me believe the best about them. I also ask You for the strength to remain committed—to stick by their side until the victory has been won and they have become everything You intended for them to be! I am anticipating a new surge of Your power and strength right now to help me get started on this path, and I'll keep believing and confidently expecting until I see the results in my life that I know You want. I pray this in Jesus' name!

My Confession for Today

I confess that God's love operates mightily in my life. Because I walk in agape love, I protect, shield, guard, cover, conceal, and safeguard people from exposure. The love of God in my heart compels me to strain forward with all my might to believe the very best in every situation and the best about every person. This love of God that has been shed abroad in my heart never quits, never surrenders, and never gives up on other people. I bear all things, believe all things, hope all things, and endure all things! I declare this by faith in Jesus' name!

Love Never Fails

My Prayer for Today

Lord, I want to be the embodiment of Your love. I know that I fall very short of the agape love that You desire to see operating in my life. Therefore, I am asking You to help me move upward to the highest level of love so I can be a channel through which this love can be poured out to others whom I know and meet. Just as You have loved me, help me become a life-changing source of divine love to other people. I pray this in Jesus' name!

Charity [agape love] suffereth long, and is kind; charity envieth not; charity vaunteth not itself, is not puffed up, doth not behave itself unseemly, seeketh not her own, is not easily provoked, thinketh no evil; Rejoiceth not in iniquity, but rejoiceth in the truth; Beareth all things, believeth all things, hopeth all things, endureth all things. Charity never faileth....

1 Corinthians 13:4-8

My Confession for Today

I confess that God's love dwells in me. It flows from my heart to all those around me. People who are close to me are changed and transformed by this love that operates so mightily in me. When others see me, they think of the love of God, for it is demonstrated continually in my life. I declare this by faith in Jesus' name!

Choose Life

For I am in a strait betwixt two, having a desire to depart, and to be with Christ; which is far better: Nevertheless to abide in the flesh is more needful for you. And having this confidence, I know that I shall abide and continue with you all for your furtherance and joy of faith.

Philippians 1:23-25

My Prayer for Today

Lord, I want to run my race victoriously all the way to the finish line! I don't want to quit, give up, or die until I can say I've finished everything You have ever assigned for me to do. Forgive me for allowing thoughts of death to dominate me. I have too much living left to do to dwell on these kinds of self-defeating thoughts. Please help me shove aside my exhaustion, grab hold of Your power, and press forward to do what You have called me to do with my life. I pray this in Jesus' name!

My Confession for Today

I confess that I have a lot of living left to do before I die and go to Heaven. God has given me a huge assignment for my life, and I'm only getting started in fulfilling what He has asked me to do. Death is not an option right now. Life is my only choice. I am needed and wanted, and God is not calling me home yet. Therefore, I will live a long and prosperous life—and I will run my race with all my might so I can finish my race with joy and victory. I declare this by faith in Jesus' name!

Faithful To Keep Your Word

My Prayer for Today

Lord, please forgive me for the times I have been two-faced and double-tongued, speaking different things to different people. I realize it is wrong to act this way with those who are over me in authority. They need to be able to rest assured that I am being truthful with them, and now I see that I have given them a cause to doubt my word. Forgive me, and please help me conquer this serious character flaw in my life. Holy Spirit, help me today to uproot this double-tongued tendency from my life. Teach me how to habitually speak the truth! I pray this in Jesus' name!

> *Likewise must the deacons be grave, not doubletongued, not given to much wine, not greedy of filthy lucre.*
>
> *1 Timothy 3:8*

My Confession for Today

I confess that I am not two-faced or double-tongued. When I speak, people know that my word is as good as gold. I do not change my opinion based on the person I am with or what others think of me. What I say I mean, and I am faithful to keep my word. Every day I am growing in grace—and God is making me stronger, better, more dependable, and more truthful every day. I am exactly the kind of person my authorities can rely on. I declare this by faith in Jesus' name!

Never Forget the Goodness of God

Oh how great is thy goodness, which thou hast laid up for them that fear thee; which thou hast wrought for them that trust in thee before the sons of men!

Psalm 31:19

My Prayer for Today

Lord, I am thankful for Your goodness in my life. You have saved me, delivered me, redeemed me, and changed me. My entire life is marked by Your supernatural goodness and mercy! It is true that You have showered me with nonstop blessings—and today I want to take this opportunity to thank You for every good thing You've done in my life. The situations I have faced in my life have put You to the test, and You have jumped at every chance to prove how good You are. In fact, Your goodness to me has been constant and never-ending ! I pray this in Jesus' name!

My Confession for Today

I confess that I am grateful for and constantly aware of God's goodness in my life. I have every reason to trust Him, for He has proven Himself to me again and again and I know He will never let me down. He has shown His goodness and mercy to me, and I am a recipient of His grace. I choose to lift up my hands, open my mouth, and declare the goodness of the Lord. The Bible says, "Let the redeemed of the Lord say so," so I am saying so right now! Jesus, You are good, and Your mercy endures forever! Thank You for showering me with Your mercy and Your might. I declare this by faith in Jesus' name!

Live in Faith

My Prayer for Today

Lord, help me stick with the assignment You have given me for my life. I know that is where I am supposed to be—and I know that is what I am supposed to be doing. Forgive me for vacillating back and forth, in and out, backward and forward. I am asking You to help me become single-minded, concentrated, and focused in my determination never to move out of faith again. I want to live at the address of faith, for I know that is where I will please You the most. Holy Spirit, empower me to push aside every distraction of the devil and to remain fixed and focused on doing exactly what God has instructed me to do. I pray this in Jesus' name!

But without faith it is impossible to please him: for he that cometh to God must believe that he is, and that he is a rewarder of them that diligently seek him.

Hebrews 11:6

My Confession for Today

I confess that I live "in" faith. Although Satan tries to use situations to distract me and dissuade me from staying in faith, I have resolved that I am never moving from the place where God has called me to be. I will never relinquish the dream He has put in my heart. I will stay in this place; I will use my faith; I will be steadfast, unwavering, and committed to seeing His promises come to pass in my life. Because I have made this decision, I am a person who pleases God! I declare this by faith in Jesus' name!

Refuse To Be Taken Captive by the Devil

And that they may recover themselves out of the snare of the devil, who are taken captive by him at his will.

2 Timothy 2:26

My Prayer for Today

Lord, I never want the devil to take me captive to do his will in my church or place of employment. He is an accuser, so if I am tempted to accuse and slander, it means that the devil is trying to work through me. Give me the ability to recognize this strategy of the enemy as soon as it starts, and to put on the brakes before I get so embroiled in a conflict that I can't see or think correctly. Holy Spirit, You are the Spirit of Truth, so please enable me to both see and to hear the truth about myself, because I want to stay free. I pray this in Jesus' name!

My Confession for Today

I confess that I am free from the deception of the devil. My mind is renewed to the truth of God's Word. My mind thinks straight and clearly, and I am sound and balanced in my perspective of the situations I face in life. I am teachable when my friends tell me the truth, helping me see when I am getting too upset about things that aren't so important. Therefore, I'm able to walk free of the devil's snare and stay balanced in my emotions because of the Word that works mightily in me. I declare this by faith in Jesus' name!

You Can Be 'Fear-Free'

My Prayer for Today

Lord, I admit that I've allowed fear, worry, fretfulness, and anxiety to play a role in my life. When these negative emotions operate in me, I lose my peace and my joy. I am tired of living in this continual state of worry and fear about bad things that might happen. Jesus, today I am making the choice to turn all these destructive thoughts over to You. I don't want to live this way anymore. I know this isn't Your plan for my life, so by faith, I cast all my concerns on You. I release them into Your hands, Lord, and ask You to take them right now. I pray this in Jesus' name!

Be careful for nothing; but in every thing by prayer and supplication with thanksgiving let your requests be made known unto God.

Philippians 4:6

My Confession for Today

I confess that I am free from worry, fretfulness, and anxiety. These forces have no place in me. I have surrendered every care and concern to Jesus, and He has taken them from me. As a result, I am free of every burden, every weight, and every problem. Jesus is my great High Priest, and He is interceding for me right now. With God on my side, I can enjoy life as He intended for me to enjoy it. I boldly confess that I am fear-free and worry-free and that anxiety has no place in me. I declare this by faith in Jesus' name!

Reject the Temptation To Worry

Therefore take no thought, saying, What shall we eat? or, What shall we drink? or, Wherewithal shall we be clothed? ...for your heavenly Father knoweth that ye have need of all these things. But seek ye first the kingdom of God, and his righteousness; and all these things shall be added unto you.

Matthew 6:31-33

My Prayer for Today

Lord, I thank You for allowing me to come boldly before You in prayer. I know that You love me and want to richly meet the needs I am facing in my life today. My temptation is to worry and fear, but I know that if I will trust You, everything I am concerned about will turn out all right. Right now I reject the temptation to worry, and I choose to come before You to boldly make my requests known. By faith I thank You in advance for acting to answer my requests. I pray this in Jesus' name!

My Confession for Today

I confess that I am not ruled by worry, fear, or concerns. I go to God with those things that are on my heart, and I clearly articulate what I feel, what I need, and what I expect Heaven to do on my behalf. Because of the promises in God's Word, I know exactly how to boldly make my requests. I always match my requests with thanksgiving, letting God know how grateful I am for everything He does in my life. Heaven is on my side; therefore, I know I will survive and victoriously overcome each and every attack that ever tries to come against my family, my relationships, my business, my finances, and my life. I declare this by faith in Jesus' name!

Confess Good Things About Yourself

My Prayer for Today

Lord, I know I have been speaking badly about myself. When I hear my own words, even I can tell it's wrong for me to speak so lowly about myself. You have done a great work in me, and I have kept myself bound by the words of my mouth. Forgive me for speaking so wrongly and for allowing myself to remain imprisoned in self-defeat. I am truly repentant for these actions, and I ask You to forgive me and to give me the power to change my behavior. Holy Spirit, I can only do this by Your power, so I am asking and expecting You to empower me to make these changes in my life and in my mouth. I pray this in Jesus' name!

That the communication of thy faith may become effectual by the acknowledging of every good thing which is in you in Christ Jesus.

Philemon 1:6

My Confession for Today

I confess that I speak well of myself. I don't batter myself with wrong or negative words. I agree with all that God's Word declares me to be, and I speak these truths about myself. Every day I am getting more positive and more faith-filled, and my mouth is speaking what God says about me. As a result, I am getting better, freer, and I am stepping upward more boldly into the plan God has for me. I declare this by faith in Jesus' name!

Overcoming a Financial Attack

And let us not be weary in well doing: for in due season we shall reap, if we faint not.

Galatians 6:9

My Prayer for Today

Lord, thank You for showing me today how to respond to the financial attacks I am experiencing in my life. Please help me know where to sow an extra financial seed right now. Help me to sow it by faith, confidently expecting it to break the stranglehold that has been on my financial situation. Satan, I command you to take your hands off my finances! I am a giver and therefore a receiver of God's promised blessings. You have no right to exercise any control over my money and possessions. I tell you to go in Jesus' name! Father, I thank You for honoring Your Word and causing my situation to turn around. I thank You in advance for the abundance that is going to start flowing into my life. I pray this in Jesus' name!

My Confession for Today

I confess that I am an overcomer! Difficult circumstances do not control my life or my obedience. Instead of surrendering to the attacks that are assailing my finances, I am going to throw a knockout punch at the face of the devil! At this critical moment, I am going to sow an extra financial seed that will break the devil's stranglehold on my life. Once I obey what the Holy Spirit is telling me to do, I will boldly command the devil to take his foul hands off my finances! It won't be long before the seed I sow is multiplied back into my life. Then I'll stand in the manifestation of God's blessings. I declare this by faith in Jesus' name!

Walk in Mercy

My Prayer for Today

Lord, please forgive me for being so harsh and judgmental of other people when they make mistakes or behave in ways that shock me. I know I become judgmental when I forget the mercy and grace that has been extended to me through the years. Therefore, I ask You to help me walk in a constant awareness of all the times I've been loved, forgiven, and accepted in spite of my behavior. Holy Spirit, help me now to be an extension of this same mercy and grace to others who need it from me. I pray this in Jesus' name!

Wherefore, receive ye one another, as Christ also received us to the glory of God.

Romans 15:7

My Confession for Today

I confess that I walk in mercy and grace. I don't rush to judgment when others do things that are less than what I expected of them. I realize that everyone makes mistakes and that no one who truly loves Jesus would intentionally do the offensive and hurtful things I've seen some people do. These people don't realize how they are being perceived. I know they're making these mistakes because they need to grow and mature. So rather than judge others for what they have said, done, or failed to do, I will walk in mercy, grace, and forgiveness toward them just as I would want others to do for me. I declare this by faith in Jesus' name!

Esteeming Others

Let nothing be done through strife or vainglory; but in lowliness of mind let each esteem other better than themselves.

Philippians 2:3

My Prayer for Today

Lord, forgive me for the times I was so engrossed in my own ideas and convictions that I "hogged" entire conversations and didn't give others an opportunity to express what was on their hearts. I am truly repentant for giving people the impression that I thought I was the only one in the group with something worthy to say. Forgive me for being so self-absorbed and for not recognizing the other outstanding people with gifts, talents, and ideas that were just as valuable as my own. Please help me learn to think more highly of others, to keep my mouth shut more often, and to genuinely appreciate the gifts, talents, and ideas You have placed in other people. I pray this in Jesus' name!

My Confession for Today

I confess that I am very respectful of other people and that I recognize the gifts, talents, and ideas God has given them. I need the insights and gifts that God has put in other people. Because they are just as important as I am, I always give them time to express themselves and to let their gifts function as God intends. I am a part of a God-gifted group, and every member is filled with gifts and ideas that I need. Therefore, I make room for them to let those gifts and ideas flow. I declare this by faith in Jesus' name!

Confess Your Faults One to Another

My Prayer for Today

Lord, I thank You for speaking to my heart today about confessing the things that are secretly bothering me. It is no secret to You that I have been struggling with fear, insecurity, and temptation. You know that I desperately need someone to stand with me in faith and to assure me that everything is going to be all right. Help me to know exactly to whom I should go to discuss what is disturbing me—someone who will be faithful to hold what I say in confidence. Once I confess this burden and get it off my heart, please let this be the very act that sets in motion the power to liberate me. I pray this in Jesus' name!

Confess your faults one to another, and pray one for another, that ye may be healed....

James 5:16

My Confession for Today

I confess that I have friends who are trustworthy and in whom I can confide when Satan is trying to pound my mind with his lies. I do not fear that friends will laugh at me or repeat what I tell them. They will stand with me, speak the truth to me, and help me step out of the darkness and into the light. My confession will break Satan's vice grip on my mind and bring wholeness and soundness of thinking to my soul. I declare this by faith in Jesus' name!

Listen to the Holy Spirit

After they were come to Mysia, they assayed to go into Bithynia: but the Spirit suffered them not.

Acts 16:7

My Prayer for Today

Lord, help me follow the Holy Spirit's leading whenever He impresses me to do something. I know there have been moments in my life when the Spirit was leading me to do something. But because I didn't understand it, I didn't obey—and later I was always sorry. Please help me become more sensitive to the Holy Spirit and to trust Him when He speaks to my heart. I want to be obedient and to experience the supernatural life that He wants to give me. I pray this in Jesus' name!

My Confession for Today

I confess that I listen to the leading of the Holy Spirit. Because I follow His leading, I am able to circumvent traps that the devil tries to set for me. If the Holy Spirit impresses me to stay home, I stay home. If He tells me not to get on an airplane, I don't get on that airplane. If He nudges me to give a special offering, I sow that offering. Whatever the Spirit impresses me to do is exactly what I do! I declare this by faith in Jesus' name!

Focus on God's Plan

My Prayer for Today

Lord, I am asking You to help me to really know my calling so I can ardently follow after it with all my might. Help me push all distractions out of my way and to put my sights on fulfilling the assignment You have designed for me. I know this is going to take the greatest concentration, so please help me to focus on Your plan and to refuse to allow anything to pull me away from reaching Your goal for my life. I pray this in Jesus' name!

Not as though I had already attained, either were already perfect: but I follow after, if that I may apprehend that for which also I am apprehended of Christ Jesus.

Philippians 3:12

My Confession for Today

I confess that I will achieve what God has planned for my life. I am fiercely determined to keep pressing ahead, and I will never stop until every part of my God-given assignment has been fulfilled. I have set my sights on reaching God's plan—and I will not stop until I can confidently say, "I've done exactly what Jesus wanted me to do!" I declare this by faith in Jesus' name!

Rip Out the Root of Bitterness

Looking diligently lest any man fail of the grace of God; lest any root of bitterness springing up trouble you, and thereby many be defiled.

Hebrews 12:15

My Prayer for Today

Lord, I don't want any bitterness to sprout inside me, so I am asking You to turn on the spotlight of the Holy Spirit and reveal any unforgiveness or resentment that might be lurking inside my heart. I know that the fruit of bitterness is very sour, and I don't want that fruit to be a part of my life. So, Holy Spirit, I ask You to please show me every root of bitterness, and then help me rip it clear out of my soul! I pray this in Jesus' name!

My Confession for Today

I confess that I refuse to allow a root of bitterness to grow deep into the soil of my heart. The instant I recognize that a seed of bitterness is trying to sprout in me, I will grab hold of that root, and through the act of repentance, rip those destructive roots out of my soul. I choose to walk in forgiveness and to stay free. I declare this by faith in Jesus' name!

Ask God for Wisdom

My Prayer for Today

Lord, help me to come to You when I find myself lacking answers about situations that need to be changed in my life. When I have done all I know to do and don't know what else to do, remind me that every answer I need resides with You. Your wisdom holds the answers I am looking for; therefore, I am making the decision to come to You now so You can start speaking to me. I pray this in Jesus' name!

If any of you lack wisdom, let him ask of God, that giveth to all men liberally, and upbraideth not; and it shall be given him.

James 1:5

My Confession for Today

I boldly confess that I go to the Father when I need wisdom from above. He has the answers to all my problems, and He is standing before me, ready to help. God is on my side. He wants to help me. He is waiting for me to come into His Presence so He can give me the wisdom I need to confront and overcome every situation I am facing right now. God wants me to succeed, and His wisdom is what I need to achieve what is in my heart. So rather than try to figure it all out on my own, I run to the Father and ask Him for wisdom—and He is swift to give me the wisdom I need. I declare this by faith in Jesus' name!

Spend Time in His Presence

*...times of
refreshing shall
come from the
presence of
the Lord.*

Acts 3:19

My Prayer for Today

Lord, I know that You are a giving God who wants to meet my needs and answer my questions. But I understand now that I have a condition to meet first: You require me to come close to You so You can reveal to me those things I need to know. Please forgive me for rushing in and out of your Presence so quickly in the past—making my demands and insisting on those things I need, but not taking enough time to fellowship with You and meet Your need to be with me. I am so sorry for the times I've been in such a hurry that I neglected spending time with You. Starting today, I want to change my daily schedule so I can spend time in Your Presence and come closer to You than ever before. I pray this in Jesus' name!

My Confession for Today

I confess that spending time with God is the highest priority in my life. This time with Him is not an option in my life. He wants to give me all the wisdom and answers I need, but first I must meet His requirement to come close to Him. When I get right next to God, He is obliged to open His hand and show me everything I need to see. I live continually in His Presence; therefore, no form of darkness or ignorance nor any defect in my character can remain in my life. I declare this by faith in Jesus' name!

Be Supportive of Your Husband

Likewise, ye wives, be in subjection to your own husbands; that, if any obey not the word, they also may without the word be won by the conversation of the wives.

1 Peter 3:1

My Prayer for Today

Lord, I ask You to please forgive me for complaining to my husband about everything he does that I don't like. He needs me to be his friend and supporter, and I now realize how often he must perceive me as another enemy he has to fight. Please help me to come to You with all my complaints while maintaining a helpful and supportive attitude toward my husband. I am sorry for the damage I've done, and I now ask You to help me turn things around in my marriage relationship. Teach me how to respond in every situation with a respectful and supportive attitude toward my husband. I know I need Your help, Lord, so I am looking to You for the grace and the strength I need to do this right. I pray this in Jesus' name!

My Confession for Today

I confess that I am a supportive wife who demonstrates love in the way I approach my husband. He doesn't see me as a nagging and complaining wife but as a friend to confide in and to look to for strength. God is able to speak to my husband without my interference. I trust God to speak to him, and I trust God to deal with my heart and to help me take on a supportive role in our home. I declare this by faith in Jesus' name!

Knowing When To Speak

While they behold your chaste conversation coupled with fear.

1 Peter 3:2

My Prayer for Today

Lord, I ask You to help me learn when to speak and when to be silent. I don't want my husband to perceive me as a nagging wife. Please forgive me for preaching at him when I should have been praying for him. Help me to stop focusing on all the things I don't like about him and to start working on all the things that need to change inside me. I want to be a blessing to my husband. Please help me live a life so godly and powerful that it becomes my pulpit in our marriage. I pray this in Jesus' name!

My Confession for Today

I confess that I live a powerful, godly, and chaste life before my husband and am therefore a constant encouragement to him. He seeks my advice; he wants my help; and he desires to know what I believe is right regarding decisions that affect our family and relationship. God's Spirit is changing me and making me to be the kind of wife He wants me to be. I declare this by faith in Jesus' name!

Beautiful Inside and Out

My Prayer for Today

Lord, thank You for wanting me to look beautiful, both inside and outside, both for myself and for my spouse. I take this word to my heart today, and I make the decision that from this day forward, I will spend at least the same amount of time beautifying my spirit as I spend looking nice in my outward appearance. Forgive me, Lord, for those days when I have found time to dress properly and look outwardly attractive, but I didn't take the time to pray or read my Bible. Help me get my priorities in order as I make the development of my spirit a higher priority than fixing my hair or putting on makeup. I pray this in Jesus' name!

Whose adorning let it not be that outward adorning of plaiting the hair, and of wearing of gold, or of putting on of apparel; but let it be the hidden man of the heart, in that which is not corruptible, even the ornament of a meek and quiet spirit, which is in the sight of God of great price.

1 Peter 3:3,4

My Confession for Today

I confess that the beautifying of my spirit is a high priority in my life. I don't make the mistake of putting all my time and effort into improving my outward appearance while forgetting to invest time in the development of my spirit. I read my Bible, I pray, and I let God deal with my heart. Because I have made the choice to make my spirit beautiful, I am becoming more godly and beautiful all the time. I have an inward beauty that far outshines anything I could ever do to improve the appearance of my outward man. I declare this by faith in Jesus' name!

Adorned With Godliness and Grace

Whose adorning let it not be that outward adorning of plaiting the hair, and of wearing of gold, or of putting on of apparel; But let it be the hidden man of the heart, in that which is not corruptible, even the ornament of a meek and quiet spirit, which is in the sight of God of great price.

1 Peter 3:3,4

My Prayer for Today

Lord, help me give adequate attention to my heart so I can develop my spirit and become more godly in how I live my life. I pray that the strength and godliness that resides in my spirit will manifest in my life, emanating from within me and making me more gracious and more beautiful the older I get. I look to You, Lord, for help in growing old gracefully and emanating power in my older years. I pray this in Jesus' name!

My Confession for Today

I confess that my spirit is getting stronger and stronger as I get older. My inner man is adorned with godliness and grace. The older I get, the more visible my inward man becomes—and what is seen coming from within me makes me attractive, even though I am getting a little wrinkled and gravity is having its effects on my physical form. I am inwardly strong and beautiful, and this inner beauty is what attracts people to me. I declare this by faith in Jesus' name!

A Meek and Quiet Spirit

My Prayer for Today

Lord, help me learn how to keep a rein on my tongue and how to submit my attitude to the Cross of Jesus Christ. Help me also to perceive how I can become a contributor to peace and tranquility instead of strife and conflict. I want to be one of those rare and special women You consider of such great value and worth. Holy Spirit, it's going to take a deep work of Your grace in my life for me to become this kind of person. So today I ask You to initiate this vital work deep inside my soul. Please transform me and make me into the person You want me to be. I pray this in Jesus' name!

But let it be the hidden man of the heart, in that which is not corruptible, even the ornament of a meek and quiet spirit, which is in the sight of God of great price.

1 Peter 3:4

My Confession for Today

I confess that I am a source of stability and peace in my home. I don't give in to anger or fly into a rage and say things I later regret. My husband and my children can depend on me to be a tower of strength even in the midst of turmoil and difficult situations. Because I am so stable, I help bring stability to my husband, to my children, and to the general atmosphere in my home. Instead of being a contributor to strife, conflict, and turmoil, God uses me to bring peace and tranquility to all those who are near me. I declare this by faith in Jesus' name!

Giving Time to Your Wife

Likewise, ye husbands, dwell with them according to knowledge, giving honour unto the wife, as unto the weaker vessel, and as being heirs together of the grace of life....

1 Peter 3:7

My Prayer for Today

Lord, I ask You to forgive me for not spending enough time with my wife. I know that she needs me and that I haven't done what I should do to show her the love and attention she deserves. She does so much for me. She loves me and our children and serves us with her whole heart. I am so sorry I've been so selfish and haven't been the husband I need to be for my wife. I repent for my self-centeredness, and I make the decision today to reverse my actions. I want to love her as I should and to do everything I can to communicate that love. Please help me, Lord, to become all I need to be for my wife. I pray this in Jesus' name!

My Confession for Today

I boldly confess that I am a loving, caring, attentive husband. As God's Spirit works in me and transforms me more and more into the image of Jesus Christ, I am becoming a better husband to my wife. Because I love her deeply and regularly show my love to her, she feels secure and confident in our relationship. As a result, she is willing to follow me wherever God leads and is supportive of my decisions. Investing in my life partner is the best investment I can make in my own life. Therefore, I choose this day to invest love and attentive care into my wife—the most important person in my life! I declare this by faith in Jesus' name!

A Loving and Caring Husband

Husbands, love your wives, even as Christ also loved the church, and gave himself for it;

Ephesians 5:25

My Prayer for Today

Lord, I am asking You to please forgive me for being so selfish, self-centered, and neglectful of my wife and her needs. I expect her to faithfully serve me, but I have given her so little in return. I am truly sorry that I've ignored her and, as a result, hurt her. I accept responsibility for the role I have played in wounding her and making her feel unimportant. Please help me become more sensitive to my wife. Teach me to speak words that build her up, not words that put her down. As I follow Your leading in this area, please heal my wife's heart and bring tenderness back into our relationship once more. I accept Your challenge to purposefully show the honor, attention, respect, and tenderness she deserves. Thank You for helping me change in this vital area of my life. I pray this in Jesus' name!

My Confession for Today

I confess that I am a loving and caring husband. My wife feels loved, respected, esteemed, and special because I do the things that communicate value to her. The Holy Spirit is helping me become more considerate, more tender, and more thoughtful. Every day I am dying to the flesh and becoming less selfish and self-centered. I am a godly example of what a husband ought to be, and my actions give a great sense of worth to the wife whom Jesus has given to me. I declare this by faith in Jesus' name!

OCTOBER 10

Partners in Life

For this cause shall a man leave his father and mother, and shall be joined unto his wife, and they two shall be one flesh.

Ephesians 5:31

My Prayer for Today

Lord, help me treat my wife like the partner You intended for her to be in my life. You gave her to me to be a co-ruler and co-inheritor of the grace of life. You placed her at my side to be my helper, my companion, and my partner. You called us together to achieve Your will for our family. I am sorry for the times I have ignored her or unintentionally forgotten to treat her like the partner she is in my life. Starting today, please help me reverse any of my behavior patterns that my wife perceives to be unkind or insensitive. Show me ways to demonstrate to her that she is truly my partner and my co-ruler in this life! I pray this in Jesus' name!

My Confession for Today

I confess that my wife is my co-ruler in life. She is my helper, my companion, and my partner. God called us together to make an impact in this world. Without her, I am incomplete, lacking all that is necessary to do this job. I acknowledge that I need my wife. I treat her as my equal partner whom God has joined to my life. She and I together make a powerful team, and together we are achieving great things! I declare this by faith in Jesus' name!

Having Compassion for Each Other

My Prayer for Today

Lord, help me to put aside my fleshly pride and to do everything I can to understand my precious spouse. I confess that there are times when I just don't understand what my spouse is trying to say or do. I often get frustrated and allow myself to get upset. Therefore, Holy Spirit, I am telling You right now that I need Your assistance to remain calm, to be at peace, and to let sympathy flow from my heart in place of the aggravation I have allowed to pester me. Today I want to turn a new page in my life. I want to be the best friend my spouse has ever had. Help me recognize where I need to change in order to be what I need to be in this marriage relationship. I pray this in Jesus' name!

Finally, be ye all of one mind, having compassion one of another, love as brethren, be pitiful, be courteous.

1 Peter 3:8

My Confession for Today

I confess that I am an understanding and compassionate spouse. My mate feels no judgment or rejection from me. We are working on our relationship. We are becoming more understanding of one another. We are achieving more unity than we've ever known in our relationship. As a result, we are on our way to being happier than we've ever been at any other time in our marriage. The worst days are behind us, and the best days are before us. Because the Holy Spirit is helping us, we are overcoming every struggle and experiencing new realms of victory in our lives. I declare this by faith in Jesus' name!

Respect Your Spouse

Not rendering evil for evil, or railing for railing: but contrariwise blessing; knowing that ye are thereunto called, that ye should inherit a blessing.

1 Peter 3:9

My Prayer for Today

Lord, please forgive me for the times I have spoken wrongly to my spouse. Help me to never take my spouse for granted again, but to always remember that if for no other reason, I should speak kindly to my mate out of respect for his (or her) position in Christ. I admit I've done wrong in the way I've spoken to my mate in the past. I know I wouldn't speak that way to anyone else in the church. Please help me to love my spouse as one of my brethren in the Lord and to reverence the Holy Spirit who lives in him (or her). I pray this in Jesus' name!

My Confession for Today

I confess that I treat my spouse as a brother (or sister) in Christ. I speak to my spouse with respect; I reverence the Spirit of God who lives inside him (or her); and I honor my mate as a part of the Body of Christ. As God works in me and transforms me day by day, I am becoming more controlled and more temperate in the way I relate to my spouse. I don't fly off the handle with him (or her) and say things that are unacceptable to say to a brother or sister in Christ. I declare this by faith in Jesus' name!

Give Encouragement to Your Spouse

My Prayer for Today

Lord, I want to be moved with compassion toward my spouse! Help me to truly feel compassion for what my spouse is going through, and teach me how to let mercy flow from my spirit to strengthen him (or her). I know that my spirit is filled with everything my spouse needs in moments of difficulty, so I want to know how to release those good things from my spirit to strengthen and edify him (or her). Holy Spirit, please help me be moved with compassion toward my spouse. Teach me how to esteem and to treat him (or her) as more important than myself. I pray this in Jesus' name!

For he that will love life, and see good days, let him refrain his tongue from evil, and his lips that they speak no guile: Let him eschew evil, and do good; let him seek peace, and ensue it.

1 Peter 3:10,11

My Confession for Today

I confess that I am filled with compassion and that I let that force of compassion flow from my heart to my spouse. I am the strongest source of blessing and encouragement in my spouse's life. I deliberately think of ways I can be a blessing to him (or her), and I speak words of blessing that will bring the strength and encouragement my spouse needs from me. I declare this by faith in Jesus' name!

Speak Blessings Into Your Marriage

Finally, be ye all of one mind, having compassion one of another, love as brethren, be pitiful, be courteous: Not rendering evil for evil, or railing for railing: but contrariwise blessing; knowing that ye are thereunto called, that ye should inherit a blessing.

1 Peter 3:8,9

My Prayer for Today

Lord, forgive me for allowing myself to get so upset in the past that I have acted unkindly toward my mate and made ugly remarks in moments of rage. I'm wrong for permitting my flesh to control me in such an ungodly way. Even though my spouse has been wrong as well, he (or she) couldn't have been any uglier or more hurtful than I was when I spoke those harsh, retaliatory words. Please help me to become more like Jesus—to release blessing after blessing as I speak only words of kindness to my spouse. I know that my words have the power of life and death, so help me turn around every difficult situation as I start speaking blessings into my marital relationship. I pray this in Jesus' name!

My Confession for Today

I confess that I speak blessings into my relationship with my spouse. I don't speak curses, nor do I pay back abuse with abuse or insult with insult. I am called to be a blessing; therefore, I AM a blessing, and my mouth speaks good things even when I am tempted to say words that are not so edifying. I refuse to get into the retaliation business, for I am called to be in the blessing business! I take every opportunity—both pleasurable times as well as moments of conflict—to speak blessings over myself, over my spouse, and over our relationship together. I declare this by faith in Jesus' name!

If You Want To See Good Days

My Prayer for Today

Lord, help me to become more committed to my marriage. Forgive me for being a contributor to strife and conflict, and teach me how to refrain my tongue from speaking evil so I can bring benefit and blessing to my spouse. Open my heart and my eyes, Lord. Show me things I can do to encourage my mate. No one has more influence in my spouse's life than I do, so I am asking You to help me to be the right kind of influence he (or she) needs. I pray this in Jesus' name!

For he that will love life, and see good days, let him refrain his tongue from evil, and his lips that they speak no guile: Let him eschew evil, and do good; let him seek peace, and ensue it.

1 Peter 3:10,11

My Confession for Today

I confess that I am a great encouragement to my spouse. I work hard on my marriage. I find ways to be a blessing. The Spirit of God is showing me the steps I need to take to obtain peace with my spouse. I am not a source of conflict, and I refuse to let the devil use me any longer. From this day forward, the enemy will not use my lips as his entryway into my marriage. I will do everything needed to make my marriage strong and healthy, just the way Jesus wants it to be! I declare this by faith in Jesus' name!

Believe the Impossible

*...If thou canst
believe, all things
are possible to him
that believeth.*

Mark 9:23

My Prayer for Today

Lord, since Your Word says all things are possible to the one who believes, I am asking You to help me renew my mind to believe I can do anything You ever ask me to do with my life. Help me to truly understand that there is absolutely nothing impossible to me when I believe. I so regret the times I've listened to voices of doubt and unbelief who talked me out of the great victories You had in store for me. With the assistance of the Holy Spirit, I will shut my ears to the voices of unbelief from this moment forward. I release my faith today to believe that ANYTHING is possible for me to do, as long as You are the One asking me to do it! I pray this in Jesus' name!

My Confession for Today

I confess that I can do anything God puts in my heart to do. Nothing is impossible to me, because everything is possible to him who believes. I believe God's Word. I believe I can do what He tells me to do. I believe the vision He put in my heart is achievable. Because I believe, I will receive the impossible! I declare this by faith in Jesus' name!

Stay Fiercely Committed

My Prayer for Today

Lord, I ask You to help me stay fiercely committed to fulfilling the assignment You have given to me. Forgive me for the times I've given in to weakness and allowed myself to complain when I should have grabbed hold of Your strength and pressed full steam ahead. I repent for allowing my flesh to talk me into moments of defeat. Today I choose to push forward to do exactly what You've told me to do. Holy Spirit, if the devil creates an impasse for me, please show me a better route to take so I can fulfill my divine assignment. I pray this in Jesus' name!

Wherefore we would have come unto you, even I Paul, once and again; but Satan hindered us.

1 Thessalonians 2:18

My Confession for Today

I confess that I am led by the Holy Spirit and that He shows me how to get around every obstacle the devil tries to put in my path. No impasse the devil puts before me is sufficient to prevent me from achieving what Jesus has asked me to do and to be. I refuse to accept no for an answer, and I reject any temptation to quit. I am empowered by the Spirit of the Almighty God, and I can do anything He will ever ask me to do! I declare this by faith in Jesus' name!

Keeping a Good Attitude at Work

Always give yourselves fully to the work of the Lord, because you know that your labor in the Lord is not in vain.

1 Corinthians 15:58

My Prayer for Today

Lord, I want You to help me become a worker who pleases You. Help me also to please my employer and direct supervisor with the quality of my work. Forgive me for wanting to take it easy and for complaining when I am asked to do something extra or to fulfill a task that isn't in my job description. I want to be the kind of Christian worker who brings joy and pleasure to those who are over me and who presents a good testimony to the name of Jesus. This is really my desire, so I am asking You to help me to do more, to be more, and to demonstrate an attitude of excellence regarding my work. I pray this in Jesus' name!

My Confession for Today

I confess that I am a Christian who brings glory to the name of Jesus by the way I work and the attitude I demonstrate on the job. When people think of me, they think of how willing and cooperative I am to do anything that needs to be done and what a pleasure it is to work with me. When my attitude is wrong, I quickly repent and let the Holy Spirit make me what I should be. My supreme desire is to please God and to do a good job for those who pay me. I declare this by faith in Jesus' name!

Persistent Against Every Attack

My Prayer for Today

Lord, I thank You that because Your Spirit lives in me, I have everything I need to overcome any attack the devil would try to orchestrate against me. Because Your resurrection power resides in me, I am stronger than the devil; I am tougher than any problem; and I can outlast any time of difficulty. It is not a question of IF I will win, but of WHEN I will win the victory! I thank You for giving me the power of the Holy Spirit to outlast every attack and to persist until I have accomplished what You have asked me to do. I pray this in Jesus' name!

Are they ministers of Christ? (I speak as a fool) I am more; in labours more abundant, in stripes above measure, in prisons more frequent, in deaths oft.

2 Corinthians 11:23

My Confession for Today

I confess that I am totally focused on finishing the assignment Heaven has given to me. I will successfully push beyond each attack of the enemy because the Holy Spirit is empowering me. I don't have to be a defeated victim. I choose to take advantage of the power that is available to me. Therefore, the Spirit of God will energize and lift me to a place of victory over any obstacle the devil tries to throw in my way. I have resurrection power residing inside me, and it supernaturally quickens me to overcome every demonic attack that tries to assault me and my purpose in life. I declare this by faith in Jesus' name!

Power To Overcome

These things I have spoken unto you, that in me ye might have peace. In the world ye shall have tribulation: but be of good cheer; I have overcome the world.

John 16:33

My Prayer for Today

Lord, I am so thankful that You have overcome the world and given me the power to overcome it! I am so sorry for the times I've allowed my flesh to whine and complain when I should have been digging in my heels and latching on to the power of the Holy Spirit. I know that even though victory is mine, I must take it and make it my own. Please help me take charge of my whining, complaining flesh so I can reach out by faith to seize the power of the Holy Spirit— the very thing I need to make me a winner in my situation today. I thank You in advance for this inflow of power. I pray this in Jesus' name!

My Confession for Today

I confess that Jesus Christ has given me the power to be an overcomer in every situation in life. I am not a victim who has fallen to defeat. I don't have to take what the devil tries to send my way. In the power of the Spirit and in Jesus' name, I am well able to stand against each attack, to resist every devilish scheme that comes against me, and to maintain the victory of Jesus Christ in every part of my life. Jesus purchased victory for me, and I will not budge from my decision to have, to hold, to possess, and to enjoy His victory in my life. I declare this by faith in Jesus' name!

Conquering Circumstances

My Prayer for Today

Lord, I want to be the kind of person who never allows the circumstances of life to stop me from accomplishing Your plan for my life. I am sorry for the times I've acted weak and complained that the circumstances I faced were too hard to deal with. The truth is, You have given me Your Spirit and Your power. That means there is no problem, no challenge, and no hardship I cannot conquer and overcome. If I take the power You make available to me, I can do anything You tell me to do. So today I am making my choice. I am reaching out by faith to grab hold of Your Spirit's power so I can be supernaturally quickened to complete every assignment Heaven ever asks me to do. I pray this in Jesus' name!

By thee I have run through a troop; and by my God have I leaped over a wall. It is God that girdeth me with strength, and maketh my way perfect. I have pursued mine enemies, and overtaken them: neither did I turn again till they were consumed.

Psalm 18:29,32,37

My Confession for Today

I confess that I am the kind of person God can count on to get something done. God knows I will never surrender to any attack of the devil. I regularly demonstrate that I am going to keep forging ahead to finish my assignment and that I will never quit until I can say the job is done. Jesus overcame the world, and today He gives me the power to overcome it too. Like Jesus and other strong men and women of God before me, I will overcome the world and every form of opposition the devil puts in my way. I declare this by faith in Jesus' name!

Turn Your Memories Around

Brethren, I count not myself to have apprehended: but this one thing I do, forgetting those things which are behind, and reaching forth unto those things which are before.

Philippians 3:13

My Prayer for Today

Lord, I admit that I've allowed some bad memories to paralyze me and keep me from taking the step of faith I need to be taking right now. I forgot to consider how You saved me, delivered me, and rescued me from the events that caused those painful memories. I only reflected on the bad part, failing to recognize how faithful You were to help me in that situation. Today I am making the choice to turn my memories around. Holy Spirit, help me see my past bad experiences in the light of God's goodness and faithfulness. Fill my mind with the good things God has done for me and the knowledge that He will continue to be faithful to deliver me, no matter what opposition comes my way. I pray this in Jesus' name!

My Confession for Today

I confess that God is good! He has been faithful to me. He has never failed me. He will never fail me in the future. Even when bad things tried to come against me, God saved me, delivered me, and brought me out with no permanent harm. It is a miracle I survived everything that happened to me in the past. But from this moment on, I choose to turn my memories around and to reflect only on how good God has been to me through all of life's events. I will trust in Him to show me how to get around every impasse so I can finish the job He's given me to do. I declare this by faith in Jesus' name!

Forge Ahead to the Finish

I press toward the mark for the prize of the high calling of God in Christ Jesus.

Philippians 3:14

My Prayer for Today

Lord, help me to stay absolutely committed to the assignment You've given me, ready to do whatever is necessary to finish the job. Forgive me for giving up so easily in the past when I ran into barriers. Help me to get more creative the next time I hit an impasse so I can find a way to do what You've called me to do. I know that by the power of Your Spirit, I can show much more fortitude in the face of obstacles than I've done in the past. Forgive me for being so easy on myself. I ask You now to teach me how to operate in Your strength and wisdom when I encounter impasses so that I can forge ahead to finish the job You've given me to do. I pray this in Jesus' name!

My Confession for Today

I confess that regardless of what I face or what I cross through to fulfill God's plan, nothing takes God by surprise! When He called me, He equipped me with all the power, wisdom, and insight I will ever need to get across the hurdles Satan tries to put in my path. There is no impasse I cannot get through on my way to achieve God's will for my life. I declare this by faith in Jesus' name!

The Holy Spirit Will Lead You

...he [God] leadeth me in the paths of righteousness for his name's sake. Yea, though I walk through the valley of the shadow of death, I will fear no evil: for thou art with me....

Psalm 23:2,4

My Prayer for Today

Lord, I ask You to help me put aside fear and to believe that You will protect me as I follow Your call on my life. I know that You would never give me an assignment that You didn't think I could do. The fact that You've asked me to take this path means You are confident that I am capable of succeeding. Naturally speaking, I would feel fear at the prospect of taking such a step of faith. So please help me to permanently put away that fear and to trust that the Holy Spirit will carefully lead me past every danger and risk that lies along the way. I pray this in Jesus' name!

My Confession for Today

I confess that I am fear-free and ready to follow the Lord wherever He calls me. Even though there are dangers and risks along the way, the Holy Spirit will carefully lead me so I can circumvent every area of danger and move forward safely toward my goal. The Holy Spirit sees everything; He knows everything; and He has my best in mind. Therefore, He supernaturally leads me down the right path, alerting me along the way when there is something that could hurt or hinder me. Because I am led by Him, I dodge every attack the enemy has planned for my life. I declare this by faith in Jesus' name!

Avoid the Spirit of Religion

My Prayer for Today

Lord, help me to demonstrate the love of Jesus Christ and to never allow the unkind, cruel spirit of religion to operate in me. Help me also to love those who operate in this mean spirit and to counter their attitude with the love of Jesus Christ. And, Lord, when I am confronted by godless unbelievers, give me the wisdom to demonstrate the love of Jesus to them in a way that will touch their hearts. Both the religious and the irreligious need Jesus, so show me how to be an instrument of life to both types of people when I encounter them along the way. I pray this in Jesus' name!

If any man among you seem to be religious, and bridleth not his tongue, but deceiveth his own heart, this man's religion is vain. Pure religion and undefiled before God and the Father is this, To visit the fatherless and widows in their affliction, and to keep himself unspotted from the world.

James 1:26,27

My Confession for Today

I confess that I will take the Gospel anywhere God tells me to take it. That means I am willing to go to every country, every city, and every village in the world. Nothing—no force, no group, no religion, and no godless, pagan influence—can stop me from going where God has called me. No danger is so terrifying that I can't conquer it by the power of God. I am mighty in the Spirit and can push my way through the most wicked, spiritually dark conditions using the power and the love of God. I declare this by faith in Jesus' name!

Strengthen Your Spiritual Foundation

*Be strong in
the Lord, and
in the power
of his might.*

Ephesians 6:10

My Prayer for Today

Lord, I know I need to deepen the level of my commitment if I am going to accomplish the vision You have placed in my heart. To complete the task You've given me is going to require much of me, for I'm sure that Satan will try to resist Your plan for my life. I will have to stand strong and firm in order to obtain my goal; therefore, Holy Spirit, I am asking You today to show me every place in my spiritual foundation that needs to be fixed, strengthened, or repaired. I want to be completely fit and fully equipped to finish my race and win my prize. I pray this in Jesus' name!

My Confession for Today

I confess that I am strong in the Lord. I am strong enough to do anything God will ever tell me to do. The Word of God abides in me, and the power of the Spirit works through me. Therefore, I am well able to overcome the strategies of the enemy. The future is mine because I have the promises of God's Word and the power of the Spirit on which I can rely. I declare this by faith in Jesus' name!

Developing a Keen Discernment

My Prayer for Today

Lord, I admit that I've been misled by certain people on several occasions. It has shown me that I need a better sense of discernment about those I allow to get close to me. Yet at the same time, I don't want to become hard-hearted or callous because of what I've been through. So today I choose to turn from bitterness against those who have misled me. I make the decision to forgive them, to release them from the wrong they have done, and to turn my attention toward my future. Holy Spirit, I can only do this with Your help, so I am looking to You to empower me. I pray this in Jesus' name!

In journeyings often, in perils of waters, in perils of robbers, in perils by mine own countrymen, in perils by the heathen, in perils in the city, in perils in the wilderness, in perils in the sea, in perils among false brethren.

2 Corinthians 11:26

My Confession for Today

I confess that the Holy Spirit is helping me to develop a keener discernment about people. I am able to recognize those who are genuine, and I can detect those who have ulterior, undeclared motives for getting close to me. Because the Holy Spirit sees and knows everything, I rely entirely on Him to lead and direct me in my relationships. As a result of being Spirit-led, I am making fewer mistakes in whom I choose to be my friends and close associates. I declare this by faith in Jesus' name!

A Reputation for Excellence on the Job

They were astonished beyond measure, saying, "He has done all things well."

Mark 7:37

My Prayer for Today

Lord, help me to be a good employee. I know I can do more than I've done and perform at a much higher level. And if I give 100 percent of myself to my place of employment, I know I can help my employer make a better profit and become more efficient. Please forgive me for taking a salary for work that hasn't been done with a full commitment to excellence. Jesus, I want to change in this area of my life. I ask You to help me become conscientious about the way I perform at my job. I pray this in Jesus' name!

My Confession for Today

I confess that I am a good employee. I am so faithful at the tasks given to me that my employer or supervisor trusts me completely when I am assigned a new task. Because I work with all my heart, I bring blessing to my place of employment and to my employer. Every day the Spirit of God is showing me how I can improve in my work skills. Because I am a blessing at my place of employment, I give a good testimony of Jesus Christ to everyone I work with. I declare this by faith in Jesus' name!

Be a Team Player

*These all
continued with
one accord....*

Acts 1:11

My Prayer for Today

Lord, help me to have the attitude of a team player. I want to be of benefit to my organization or place of employment and my church. I ask You to help me recognize opportunities where I can serve; then help me serve in these positions with all my heart. Help me to have the initiative to pitch in and become a helper to the rest of the team rather than to sit on the sidelines and watch everyone else work. I never want to think I'm so high and mighty that I can't do a menial, mundane task. Holy Spirit, help me to have the attitude of Jesus and to be willing to stoop low and do whatever is necessary in order to get the job done. I pray this in Jesus' name!

My Confession for Today

I boldly confess that I am willing to do whatever is required to finish the task that has been assigned to me. If there is no one else to do a job, no matter how menial, I am willing to do it—and I'll do it with a happy heart. I don't think of myself as so high and mighty that I can't do a mundane, boring, time-consuming, or undesirable job along the way. I am valuable to my organization and church because I demonstrate a willingness to do whatever is needed. Since what I sow is what I will reap, I am going to give of myself and become a team player—and as a result, a day will come when I reap other team players to help me fulfill my own dream or vision. I declare this by faith in Jesus' name!

Make an Attitude Adjustment

In every thing give thanks: for this is the will of God in Christ Jesus concerning you.

1 Thessalonians 5:18

My Prayer for Today

Lord, please forgive me for the times I've been a whiner and a complainer. I am so sorry that I've made life miserable for the people who work with me at my job or at church. I recognize that I complain more than I should, and I admit that I have been wrong. I repent for my wrong behavior, and I'm asking You today to help me make a mental adjustment. Help me learn to be thankful for the blessings I have and for the salary my employer pays me. Help me to serve with a happy heart and to be a continual source of blessing instead of a continual source of complaint. I pray this in Jesus' name!

My Confession for Today

I confess that I am a blessing to my employer, my boss, my director, my supervisor, and to my pastor. They see me as a team player and a fine example of a Christian worker. My attitude is positive. I am willing to do what I am asked to do. I am never a source of contention; instead, I am a constant source of blessing to those who are over me. They are glad I work under them because I exhibit such a cooperative spirit of joy and thankfulness. I declare this by faith in Jesus' name!

Staying Qualified

My Prayer for Today

Lord, I never want to become a castaway who was once used mightily by You but who has now become disqualified for further use. I know of other people to whom this has happened. They were once mightily used, but they have since become discredited and disqualified because of their lack of passion or the immoral mistakes they have made in their lives. Help me to maintain Your fire in my soul and to walk a straight and narrow path that leads to life and abundance. I don't want to stray from the path You have set before me or to knock myself out of the race. Holy Spirit, I am asking You today to help me do everything I need to do to remain a viable, useful vessel in the hands of God. I pray this in Jesus' name!

But I keep under my body, and bring it unto subjection: lest that by any means, when I have preached to others, I myself should be a castaway.

1 Corinthians 9:27

My Confession for Today

I confess that I walk with God and make it my aim to be an upright, moral, and godly example. I refuse to allow sin to have a place in my life. When evil thoughts try to invade my mind, I take those thoughts captive and command them to leave. I am the temple of the Holy Spirit, and these thoughts and ideas have no place inside me. I have invested too much of myself into the work of God to allow such low-level thoughts to pull me down and take me out. Because I am committed, determined, and serious about my walk with God, my future is bright and the anointing of God will grow ever stronger on my life. I declare this by faith in Jesus' name!

Be Faithful and Dependable

And the Lord was with Joseph, and he was a prosperous man; and he was in the house of his master the Egyptian. And his master saw that the Lord was with him, and that the Lord made all that he did to prosper in his hand. And Joseph found grace in his sight, and he served him: and he made him overseer over his house, and all that he had he put into his hand.

Genesis 39:2-4

My Prayer for Today

Lord, I ask You to help me become faithful and dependable. I want to be the kind of person others can rely on. I ask You to forgive me for those times when I got so lazy and complacent that I didn't follow through on commitments and, in the end, let other people down. I thank You for the gifts and talents You have placed in my life, but please help me bring my character to such a high level that You and others will know I can be trusted. I pray this in Jesus' name!

My Confession for Today

I confess that God's Word and God's Spirit are turning me into a tower of strength. When people think of me, they think of reliability. I do what I'm asked to do, and I do it with excellence. People find me faithful and trustworthy, and they want me to be a part of their team. I am exactly the kind of person who helps bring success—and as a result, both God and man are excited to have me on their team. I declare this by faith in Jesus' name!

Stir Up Your Desire

My Prayer for Today

Lord, please help me stir up my desire to make significant changes in my life. I am so sorry for the times I've allowed complacency to keep me stuck in the same ol' place for such a long time. I want to change. I want to grow. I want to be different. I am asking You to supernaturally fill me with so much desire that no power on earth and no force in hell can stop me from becoming everything You want me to be! I pray this in Jesus' name!

The desire of the righteous shall be granted.

Proverbs 10:24

My Confession for Today

I confess that I am filled with enough desire to make significant leaps forward in my life. I am not going to stay the same as I have been in the past. I am getting up and moving forward. I'm stretched out to the goal and completely committed to achieving the dream God has for me. I will not stop, nor will I allow anything to distract me from reaching out to become ALL that God has planned for me to be. I declare this by faith in Jesus' name!

The Peaceable Fruit of Righteousness

Now no chastening for the present seemeth to be joyous, but grievous: nevertheless afterward it yieldeth the peaceable fruit of righteousness unto them which are exercised thereby.

Hebrews 12:11

My Prayer for Today

Lord, I admit that I need help in bringing discipline to my flesh and my emotions. Forgive me for being too easy on myself, and help me to be fiercely committed to bringing my body and my flesh under the control of the Holy Spirit. I want to be Your instrument so Your power can flow freely through me. So please help me today to submit to Your Word and to the control of Your Spirit. From this day forward, I purpose to no longer give my flesh the freedom to have its way in my life. I pray this in Jesus' name!

My Confession for Today

I declare that the Word of God and the Spirit of God are working inside me. Every day my flesh is being rendered inoperative and my body is responding less and less to sin as I reckon myself alive unto God. I am God's instrument. His power flows through me. Because I am allowing God to bring discipline into my life on a daily basis, I have become a mighty weapon He can use to set people free and to make a significant difference in the world around me. I declare this by faith in Jesus' name!

Embrace God's Call on Your Life

My Prayer for Today

Lord, help me to stay focused on what You have called me to do and to embrace everything that comes with Your call on my life. Forgive me for the times I've tried to find a shortcut to avoid responsibility. I want to put my whole heart into the race You have set before me—to fulfill my assigned task fervently, passionately, and with the highest level of excellence. I pray this in Jesus' name!

[God] Who hath saved us, and called us with an holy calling, not according to our works, but according to his own purpose and grace, which was given us in Christ Jesus before the world began.

2 Timothy 1:9

My Confession for Today

I confess that I am both faith-filled and realistic about what God has called me to do. I realize that it's going to take hard work and commitment to take this assignment to the high level that God expects of me. I refuse to shrink from my responsibilities, and I choose to put my whole heart and soul into the task Jesus has given to me. I declare this by faith in Jesus' name!

Remove Anger From Your Life

Let not the sun go down upon your wrath: Neither give place to the devil.

Ephesians 4:26,27

My Prayer for Today

Lord, I am sorry for the times I've allowed my anger to rise up and take control of me. I realize that I have no excuse, for the Spirit of God inside me is present to restrain me and to produce the fruit of the Spirit in me. I now see that I have opened the door to the devil in the past by allowing wrong attitudes to be pervasive in my life. I want to shut the door to the devil so he can no longer find access to me, to my family, to my business, to my church, or to any part of my life. To shut that door tight, I am asking You to help me remove uncontrolled anger from my life. I pray this in Jesus' name!

My Confession for Today

I confess that the Holy Spirit is producing His fruit in me and my character. I am filled with the mind of Christ; therefore, anger and temperamental outbursts have no place in me. I am self-controlled, patient, and kind. When others do or say something to me that is wrong or unjust, I respond in the spirit of Jesus Christ. I refuse to allow offense to gain a foothold in my mind. I am determined to keep the door shut so the devil can no longer gain access to my life. I declare this by faith in Jesus' name!

Confront, Forgive, and Forget

My Prayer for Today

Lord, please help me have the courage to lovingly speak to those who have sinned against me. Help me know how to tell them what they did wrong and kindly ask them not to do it again. If they repent and say they are sorry, please help me forgive them for what they did and then release them completely from that grievance, never to bring it up again. Help me put that offense out of my mind forever, just as You have done so many times for me. I pray this in Jesus' name!

...If thy brother trespass against thee, rebuke him; and if he repent, forgive him.

Luke 17:3

My Confession for Today

I confess that I am courageous, bold, and loving in the way I confront people who have sinned against me. I do not hold bitterness inside my heart; instead, I politely speak to those who have wronged me so my heart can stay free and they can learn from the experience. God's Spirit is changing me and helping me to speak to my offenders from a gracious, helpful spirit, rather than from a spirit that is bitter and critical. Therefore, the end result of each difficult situation is reconciliation and peace instead of division and discord. I declare this by faith in Jesus' name!

Partners in the Gospel of Jesus Christ

Always in every prayer of mine for you all making request with joy, for your fellowship in the gospel from the first day until now.

Philippians 1:4,5

My Prayer for Today

Lord, I thank You for allowing me to be a participant in the Gospel by sowing my finances every month into ministries that are touching the world. Help me to always be aware of the great impact my gifts have and to never let the devil make me think that what I do is unimportant. My gifts and prayers help "put gas in the tanks" of these ministries so they can take the Gospel forward. I want to give faithfully to these works, Lord. Therefore, I ask You to increase me financially so I can give even more! I want to partner with them to take the Gospel to the ends of the earth and to help fill Heaven with the souls of those for whom Jesus died. I pray this in Jesus' name!

My Confession for Today

I confess that I am a faithful supporter of the work of God. I give regularly, consistently, and passionately to see the Gospel go forward around the world. My gifts are important. What I sow really does make a difference. Because of this, I am faithful to do my part, and God will reward me both here and in eternity for the financial seed I've sown to help further His Kingdom around the world. I declare this by faith in Jesus' name!

God's Mercy Works in You

My Prayer for Today

Lord, I thank You for making special mercy available to help me in times of struggle and hardship. I admit that I often try to handle all my challenges on my own, but I know it is impossible for me to overcome my obstacles without the help of Your mercy. So today I am opening my heart and asking You to extend a special measure of mercy to assist me through this challenging time in my life. I thank You in advance for pouring this mercy upon me, and by faith, I receive it right now. I pray this in Jesus' name!

Many sorrows shall be to the wicked: but he that trusteth in the Lord, mercy shall compass him about.

Psalm 32:10

My Confession for Today

I confess that God's mercy is working in me! God promises mercy to me, and I receive it by faith. That mercy empowers me to overcome my negative emotions, my struggles, and all the obstacles the devil has tried to set before me. Because God's mercy is working in me, I am well able to rise above the struggles I face and to overcome them victoriously. I declare this by faith in Jesus' name!

Full Steam Ahead

But none of these things move me, neither count I my life dear unto myself, so that I might finish my course with joy....

Acts 20:24

My Prayer for Today

Lord, I ask You to help me remain focused on my goals, even when the devil tries to use people to steal my focus and distract me. Knowing that the devil tries to use people, I ask You to help me equip myself spiritually and mentally so I will be able to keep my eyes on the goal You have given for my life. I choose to forgive those whom the devil uses. I will pray for them to change and to repent for their actions; I will keep my heart free of offense; and I will continue to march full steam ahead to achieve what God has told me to do. Holy Spirit, please help me stay on track and keep my heart free from all strife. I pray this in Jesus' name!

My Confession for Today

I confess that Satan is unable to distract me from what God has told me to do. Although the enemy tries very hard to knock me off track, I will not take my eyes off the goals God has given me, nor will I ever stop pursuing those goals until I know they have been achieved. The power of God resides in me. The power of Christ's resurrection operates in my life. I have all the power I need to shove aside every distraction and to keep pressing toward the mark for the prize of the high calling of God in Christ Jesus. I declare this by faith in Jesus' name!

God's Grace Is Sufficient for You

My Prayer for Today

Lord, I realize today that I've been praying the wrong prayer. I've been asking You to remove all the problem people from my life; meanwhile, You've been wanting to reinforce me with sufficient strength to live with these people victoriously. Forgive me for wanting to run from my challenges. Help me face them bravely and confidently in the power of the Holy Spirit from this day forward. I know You want to give me this power, so I open my heart to receive it right now. I pray this in Jesus' name!

For this thing I besought the Lord thrice, that it might depart from me. And he said unto me, My grace is sufficient for thee: for my strength is made perfect in weakness...."

2 Corinthians 12:8,9

My Confession for Today

I confess that God's grace is sufficient for me! When I feel distressed because of what people do to me, I turn to the grace of God and allow the Holy Spirit to fill me with sufficient power to love the unlovely, to be patient with those who act ugly, and to walk in kindness and longsuffering with everyone I encounter throughout the day. My weakness in dealing with people disappears when I yield to the power of the Holy Spirit that dwells inside me. I declare this by faith in Jesus' name!

Choose Godly Friends

Now we command you, brethren, in the name of our Lord Jesus Christ, that ye withdraw yourselves from every brother that walketh disorderly, and not after the tradition which he received of us.

2 Thessalonians 3:6

My Prayer for Today

Lord, I ask You to help me truthfully examine my relationships to determine which of them are helping me and which are hindering me. If any of my relationships are with people who are disorderly or rebellious and unwilling to change, please give me the courage to follow the instructions of Your Word. Holy Spirit, I am depending on You to lead and guide me and to help me do exactly what Jesus wants me to do. I pray this in Jesus' name!

My Confession for Today

I confess that I carefully guard my life by closely affiliating with people who love God's Word, respect God-established authority, and act as positive influences in my life. I do not allow myself to be dragged into relationships with people who refuse to seriously walk with God. Those who could negatively influence me are not the people I choose to be my closest friends. Nothing in the world is more important than my walk with God. Since those who are close to me have a tremendous influence on my life, I choose friends who, like me, make their walk with God their greatest priority. I declare this by faith in Jesus' name!

God's Door of Opportunity

My Prayer for Today

Lord, I ask You to set a great and effectual door of opportunity before me. Please help me recognize when that door opens, for I desire to truly appreciate what You are doing in my life. At the same time, I need You to help me be spiritually discerning so I can differentiate my true friends from opportunists who might come to take advantage of me and steal this victory from my life. Give me spiritually discerning eyes to help me see who is and isn't with me whenever a great and effectual door is uniquely opened to me for Your purposes. I pray this in Jesus' name!

For a great door and effectual is opened unto me, and there are many adversaries.

1 Corinthians 16:9

My Confession for Today

I confess that God is setting a great and effectual door before me. I have prayed and waited for this day to come, and now is the time when God is opening that door to me. I don't take this unique time lightly. Rather, I am grateful to God for counting me faithful to receive such a rare and special opportunity. Because God's Spirit works in me, I am able to recognize those whom God has sent to help and those whom Satan has sent to hinder. I declare this by faith in Jesus' name!

Surrender to God's Purpose

I beseech you therefore, brethren, by the mercies of God, that ye present your bodies a living sacrifice, holy, acceptable unto God, which is your reasonable service.

Romans 12:1

My Prayer for Today

Lord, today I am surrendering myself as a living sacrifice to be used in whatever way You choose. I know You are beckoning me to come higher and closer than ever before, so right now I approach You with great reverence and surrender myself more fully to You. With all my heart I vow to give You my soul, my emotions, my spirit, my body, and everything else that I am and that I possess. I want to live for You and to serve You for the rest of my life. Starting today, I yield to You completely. When You speak, I will do exactly what You tell me to do. I pray this in Jesus' name!

My Confession for Today

I confess that I am surrendered to the purposes of God. I daily consecrate myself to God—to what He wants and to live a life that is pleasing to Him. My flesh may try to wage war against this consecration, but I take authority over my flesh and I tell it what to do. My body does not control me. Instead, I control it, using it as my instrument to do whatever God asks me to do. Every day when I awake, I renew my consecration and personal commitment to serve God with all my heart. I am His completely, and I will obey whatever His Spirit prompts me to do. I declare this by faith in Jesus' name!

Nothing Can Separate You From the Love of God

My Prayer for Today

Lord, I am so thankful for Your love that never fails me and never deserts me. I am filled with gratitude that nothing in this world has the power to disconnect me from Your awesome, powerful, life-changing love. In moments when I feel overwhelmed by circumstances or problems, I ask that You give me a special awareness of Your unfailing love in my life. I pray this in Jesus' name!

For I am persuaded, that neither death, nor life, nor angels, nor principalities, nor powers, nor things present, nor things to come, nor height, nor depth, nor any other creature, shall be able to separate us from the love of God, which is in Christ Jesus our Lord.

Romans 8:38,39

My Confession for Today

I confess that God's love is with me and never leaves me. There is nothing that can happen in this world or in my life to disconnect me from His awesome, powerful, wonder-working, life-transforming love. I walk through each day in peace because I know that the Lord loves me. I have been persuaded, and I remained absolutely convinced, that nothing can separate me from the love of God, which is in Jesus Christ, my Lord! I declare this by faith in Jesus' name!

Keep Your Words Seasoned With Grace

Follow peace with all men, and holiness, without which no man shall see the Lord: Looking diligently lest any man fail of the grace of God; lest any root of bitterness springing up trouble you, and thereby many be defiled.

Hebrews 12:14,15

My Prayer for Today

Lord, please help me refrain from speaking words today that will negatively affect other people. I am so sorry for the times I've "run at the mouth" and said things I shouldn't have said. I realize how wrong this is and how I've stained other people's opinions because I didn't control my mouth and emotions. I am turning to You for help, and I'm asking You to help me control my tongue as I deal with these issues that have festered inside me. Holy Spirit, please help me overcome the flesh and to allow You to have Your way in me. I pray this in Jesus' name!

My Confession for Today

I confess that I carefully monitor the condition of my heart and regulate what comes out of my mouth. Because my words are seasoned with grace, those who are near me today will be positively impacted. I speak words of kindness, and I refrain from speaking ugly words that I would later regret. My heart is clean toward others, and my mouth speaks only words that build up and edify those who are listening. I declare this by faith in Jesus' name!

Spiritual Exercise

*...Exercise thyself
rather unto
godliness.*

1 Timothy 4:7

My Prayer for Today

Lord, I ask You to help me change the way I've been looking at the hardships and challenges in my life. Yes, it's true that I don't enjoy them, but since I'm in this time of my life, help me use my time to the maximum by strengthening my faith and exercising myself spiritually. Rather than be broken by this difficult season, I want to come out of it stronger than ever. Holy Spirit, please help me today to change the way I am looking at life. I want to make a firm commitment to exercise myself unto godliness until I am so strong spiritually that nothing in life can stop me from fulfilling the dreams God has put in my heart. I pray this in Jesus' name!

My Confession for Today

I confess that I am getting stronger and stronger in the Lord. I have made the choice to use everything that comes into my life as an opportunity to exercise my faith and develop myself spiritually. This is not a one-shot reaction, for I am making this my lifetime passion and devotion. I will exercise, train, and do everything I can to become stronger and stronger in the Lord. I declare this by faith in Jesus' name!

Planting Seed for the Harvest

Say not ye, There are yet four months, and then cometh harvest? Behold, I say unto you, Lift up your eyes, and look on the fields; for they are white already to harvest.

John 4:35

My Prayer for Today

Lord, I never realized the power that one single seed could make on such a large group of people. I have mistakenly thought that witnessing to one person was not as important as preaching to multitudes. Please forgive me for overlooking the power of a single seed sown into the human heart. Holy Spirit, I want to be ready when the harvest comes in—and that includes having enough friends and coworkers on hand to pitch in and help. So I ask You to dispatch a group of ready and willing workers who can step into the harvest field and assist me in bringing in the sheaves. I pray this in Jesus' name!

My Confession for Today

I confess that the seed I sow into people's hearts has the power to bring great change to entire groups of people. Every time I share the Word of God with people who don't know the Lord, a seed is planted in their hearts and minds that has the power to revolutionize their lives, their families, their friends, and even their entire cities. Every person I touch has the potential of taking the Gospel message further, thus creating a larger harvest for the Kingdom of God. Therefore, I am bold to speak to anyone whenever I see an open door of opportunity to tell the Good News of Jesus Christ. I declare this by faith in Jesus' name!

Serve God by Giving

My Prayer for Today

Lord, I am so grateful for the opportunity to serve You with my income and assets. I only want to give more and more with each passing year. Please give me wisdom to know how to increase my personal wealth so I can become an even bigger giver to the Kingdom of God. It isn't important to me that other people know what I've done, for I know that You see the seed I've sown and will reward me for what I have done. Help me to never use funds designated for Your work on anything else, Lord, but rather to make the advancement of Your Kingdom the highest priority in my life. I pray this in Jesus' name!

And certain women, which had been healed of evil spirits and infirmities, Mary called Magdalene, out of whom went seven devils, And Joanna the wife of Chuza Herod's steward, and Susanna, and many others, which ministered unto him of their substance.

Luke 8:2,3

My Confession for Today

I confess that I am a significant giver to the Kingdom of God. God's Word promises financial blessings to His children. Since I am God's child, I have a right to be financially blessed. From the financial resources that God entrusts to me, I purpose to be a major giver and a source of great blessing to the work of the ministry. Souls are waiting to hear the Gospel message, and I am going to use the resources God gives me to make sure the life-changing message of Jesus Christ reaches as many people as possible! I declare this by faith in Jesus' name!

Fight Like a Soldier

Thou therefore endure hardness, as a good soldier of Jesus Christ.

2 Timothy 2:3

My Prayer for Today

Lord, please forgive me for being so soft and wimpy about my faith and my commitment to Your call on my life. Please help me to become tough in the Spirit so I can deal with any attack the devil might try to bring against my life. I am so sorry that I've bent under pressure, whining and complaining that things were too hard, despite the fact that the power of Your resurrection lives inside me. I don't want to waste one more minute feeling sorry for myself. Therefore, I ask You to help me brace myself, grab hold of Your power, and bravely overcome every situation in the power of the Holy Spirit. I pray this in Jesus' name!

My Confession for Today

I boldly confess that I am filled with faith, courage, and confidence. I am able to face and overcome every situation in life with the promise of God's Word and the power of the Holy Spirit. I refuse to let fear rule me, and I choose to believe that I can do all things through Christ who strengthens me. With God's power working in me, I am more than enough for every challenge that will ever come up in my life. I declare this by faith in Jesus' name!

Staying Spiritually Fit

My Prayer for Today

Lord, I want to be strong enough to overcome any situation I'll ever face in life. Forgive me for sitting around and wasting valuable time that I could have used to train and prepare myself to be spiritually fit. I'm sorry I've allowed myself to be lazy at times, and today I am making the decision to throw myself into spiritual preparation. I have decided to strive for the masteries and make my life count! Holy Spirit, please help me become everything Jesus intends for me to be and to make the changes in my mental outlook that are required for me to become a winner in life. I pray this in Jesus' name!

And if a man also strive for masteries, yet is he not crowned, except he strive lawfully.

2 Timothy 2:5

My Confession for Today

I confess that I am serious about staying fit spiritually. I refuse to let laziness be a part of my life. I reject any temptation to moan, groan, and complain about how hard life is. I choose instead to see every event in life as an opportunity to flex my spiritual muscles and to become stronger in the Lord. I declare this by faith in Jesus' name!

Reap the Harvest of Your Dreams

The husbandman that laboureth must be first partaker of the fruits.

2 Timothy 2:6

My Prayer for Today

Lord, I am so blessed to know that You want me to eat the sweet fruit of victory. That knowledge makes me want to work my ground even harder to produce a great harvest for Your Kingdom. I know that in my own flesh, I will never be able to fulfill the dream You've given me. But by Your Spirit, I can do all things! So I ask You to fill me with so much strength and motivation that I'll never stop until I finally reap the harvest of my dreams. I pray this in Jesus' name!

My Confession for Today

I confess that I will never stop until I see the harvest of my dream. It's going to take hard work and some time, but I am going to keep plowing and cultivating my ground until I see my crops mature. A day is coming in my future when I will pull up to the table, take out my knife and fork, and dive into the sweet victory for which I've worked so hard. I declare this by faith in Jesus' name!

Managing God's Funds

My Prayer for Today

Lord, thank You for the blessings You have given to my family and me. You have abundantly blessed me, and I am so grateful for everything You have done. I ask You to help me keep the right attitude toward others who have less than I do; to refrain from a false attitude of pride or haughtiness; and to see myself as the manager of divinely assigned funds. I want to trust in You, Lord—not in the things You have placed at my disposal. Possessions and material things are fleeting, but You are always the same. Therefore, I choose to fix my hope on You and not on the financial increase with which You have blessed me. I pray this in Jesus' name!

Charge them that are rich in this world, that they be not highminded, nor trust in uncertain riches, but in the living God, who giveth us richly all things to enjoy.

1 Timothy 6:17

My Confession for Today

I confess that because my trust is the Lord, I am never shaken. My identity is not in what I own but in who I am in Jesus Christ! Even though I am financially blessed, I keep WHO I AM separate from WHAT I OWN. Who I am is much more important than what I own, and my relationships are much more important than the material things I possess! I will not let my prosperity go to my head and make me think that I am better than others. God has blessed me so I can be a blessing. Therefore, I see myself as the servant of God, called to manage and distribute the funds at my disposal as He desires. I declare this by faith in Jesus' name!

Enjoy God's Blessings

Charge them that are rich in this world, that they be not highminded, nor trust in uncertain riches, but in the living God, who giveth us richly all things to enjoy. That they do good, that they be rich in good works, ready to distribute, willing to communicate;

1 Timothy 6:17,18

My Prayer for Today

Lord, I have asked You to bless me financially. So when increased finances begin to come, please help me have the grace both to enjoy them and to use them for the advancement of Your Kingdom. I don't want to flaunt the money I possess or to frivolously spend it. Instead, I want to use it to do something positive and eternal in this life. At the same time, please teach me how to enjoy the financial increase You have blessed me with and to know that it is all right for me to personally derive some benefit from it as well. Help me to truly understand that You give us ALL things richly to enjoy. I pray this in Jesus' name!

My Confession for Today

I confess that I am blessed of the Lord. My personal finances are growing, and I am being positioned to become a source of huge financial blessing to other people. I have worked hard for the blessings that are coming my way, and I have every right to enjoy a part of them personally. The Holy Spirit is giving me wisdom to know how to administrate my finances—to whom I should give funds, as well as how I should spend and invest my money. I have the mind of Christ to deal appropriately with the financial blessings that God is sending into my life. I declare this by faith in Jesus' name!

Excited About Giving

My Prayer for Today

Lord, I ask You to help me see exactly where I should sow my finances. Please help me to see those people and organizations that will wisely handle the money I sow; then give me the ability to sow into those places with elation and joy! I want to be excited about my giving! I want to give, knowing that my gift is truly going to make a huge difference. And as I give to benefit others, I ask You to honor Your Word and multiply it back to me again so I can continue to give and be a blessing to the Christian community. I pray this in Jesus' name!

Charge them that are rich in this world, that they be not highminded, nor trust in uncertain riches, but in the living God, who giveth us richly all things to enjoy; That they do good, that they be rich in good works, ready to distribute, willing to communicate.

1 Timothy 6:17,18

My Confession for Today

I confess that God's Spirit speaks to me and helps me know exactly where I am supposed to sow my finances. I am serious about my giving; therefore, I sow carefully and thoughtfully. My money is not to be spent selfishly only on myself, for God has richly blessed me so I can be a rich blessing to others for the sake of the Gospel. I therefore use my resources to do good works that will leave people in better condition than they were before I gave. I am excited about living my life as a liberal, generous, open-handed giver. Therefore, God continues to richly bless me, for He knows I will be a channel through which His blessings can keep flowing out to those who need it. I declare this by faith in Jesus' name!

Investing in Your Eternity

Laying up in store for themselves a good foundation against the time to come, that they may lay hold on eternal life.

1 Timothy 6:19

My Prayer for Today

Lord, help me to always keep in mind that eternity lies before me. Too often I get so consumed in the affairs of this life that I forget to think about my eternal existence. I don't want to be so focused on making myself comfortable in this life that I forget to do what I must to make myself comfortable in the next life. Help me lay up a good foundation for the eternity that lies in my future. Holy Spirit, I ask You to teach me not only how to cause my personal wealth to grow here and now, but also how to sow financial seed into the Gospel that will benefit many and cause me to reap great rewards when I pass into the life yet to come! I pray this in Jesus' name!

My Confession for Today

I boldly declare that I am investing in my future. All of eternity lies before me, so I am sowing seed into the Kingdom of God, believing that it will be multiplied back to me now as it is also laid up for me in my eternal future. I am a wise investor, so I sow regularly and faithfully into the work of God's Kingdom—and my faith investments are reaping for me a great harvest in the days to come. I declare this by faith in Jesus' name!

Prepared for Jesus' Return

My Prayer for Today

Lord, help me to be sensitive to Your Presence so I can be aware of that moment when Your coming is near to us. Help me close my ears to those mockers who say You will never come. By Your grace, I will hold tightly to Your promise that You will come one day to collect Your people for Yourself. Help me live a life that is holy—one that pleases You and for which I will not be ashamed when You suddenly appear to gather the Church to Yourself. I pray this in Jesus' name!

Now we beseech you, brethren, by the coming of our Lord Jesus Christ, and by our gathering together unto him, That ye be not soon shaken in mind, or be troubled, neither by spirit, nor by word, nor by letter as from us, as that the day of Christ is at hand.

2 Thessalonians 2:1,2

My Confession for Today

I confess that I am living a holy life that pleases God, a life for which I am not ashamed. I say no to sin; I crucify my flesh; and I do my very best to yield to and walk in the Spirit. I am sensitive to the Presence of God. And when the moment draws near for Jesus to come and collect His people for Himself, I will sense the growing strength of His Presence in the Church and will recognize it as a signal that God's people will soon be leaving planet earth! I believe in Jesus' coming; I expect it in my lifetime; and I am doing all I can to preach the Gospel to the lost so they won't be left out when Jesus gathers the Church to Himself. I declare this by faith in Jesus' name!

Boldness To Speak Truth

Let no man deceive you by any means: for that day shall not come, except there come a falling away first, and that man of sin be revealed, the son of perdition; Who opposeth and exalteth himself above all that is called God, or that is worshipped; so that he as God sitteth in the temple of God, shewing himself that he is God.

2 Thessalonians 2:3,4

My Prayer for Today

Lord, I ask You to give me the boldness I need to present the Gospel to my friends and family members who are unsaved. I know that if they don't receive Jesus, they will be lost in sin and caught in the delusion that is coming upon the world in the days to come. I don't want to stand before You knowing that they are lost because I was too afraid to open my mouth and tell them of Your saving blood. Holy Spirit, please give me the boldness I need and the right words to speak to those who are near and dear to my heart. When I stand before You, I want to be assured in my heart that I did everything I could to rescue those who are lost and perishing. Please help me to do this and to start today! I pray this in Jesus' name!

My Confession for Today

I confess that I am not afraid to testify of Jesus Christ to others. In fact, the love of God compels me to reach out to those who are lost. I know I will give account for those I could have reached but didn't, so I will do everything I can to speak to them, to reach them, and to make sure they have an opportunity to hear the Good News of Jesus Christ. If they refuse to listen or to receive, I will be freed from my responsibility. My part is just to make sure they had a chance to hear and to believe. The Holy Spirit is empowering me to testify, so starting today, I will follow His leading and speak to unbelievers about Jesus as God provides opportunities for me to do so. I declare this by faith in Jesus' name!

The Great Restrainer

My Prayer for Today

Lord, I thank You for holding back the evil forces that want to manifest in the world today. It's hard to imagine what the world would be like if Your Spirit no longer suppressed the evil in the hearts of men. I thank You for working in the world today, and I thank You for giving my friends, family, associates, and acquaintances one last chance to come to You. Please help me recognize divinely appointed moments when I can present the Gospel to those who are near me. And I ask You to help me formulate my words so they can understand what I am communicating to them. Holy Spirit, as I speak to people, I ask You to do the work of conviction in their hearts so they will have a desire to believe and to repent. I pray this in Jesus' name!

And now ye know what withholdeth that he might be revealed in his time. For the mystery of iniquity doth already work: only he who now letteth will let, until he be taken out of the way. And then shall that Wicked be revealed....

2 Thessalonians 2:6-8

My Confession for Today

I confess that I am sensitive to opportunities that God gives me to share the Gospel of Jesus Christ. I don't have a spirit of fear about witnessing. Because the power of the Holy Spirit lives inside me, I am brave, bold, and courageous when it comes to telling the Good News of Jesus Christ. People need the Gospel—and that means they need to hear what I have to tell them. When I speak, God's Spirit anoints me and people listen. As a result of my obedience, I am being used by God to bring many people to salvation in these last days. I declare this by faith in Jesus' name!

Obliterate the Enemy's Attack

And then shall that Wicked be revealed, whom the Lord shall consume with the spirit of his mouth, and shall destroy with the brightness of his coming.

2 Thessalonians 2:8

My Prayer for Today

Lord, I thank You for Your awesome power that You have chosen to share with Your children. I don't ever have to let the devil run freely in my life. By opening my mouth and speaking the Word of God to my situation, Your power can be released to obliterate the enemy's work in my life. Thank You for making me Your joint heir and for investing Your great power in my life. I pray this in Jesus' name!

My Confession for Today

I boldly declare that God's power resides in me. There is enough power inside me to obliterate any attack the devil would attempt to bring against my life. Rather than sit in fear and fret about what is happening to me, I will open my mouth, speak the Word of truth, and watch the power of God attack, overwhelm, and overcome the strategies that the devil has tried to use against me. I declare this by faith in Jesus' name!

Living for Eternity

My Prayer for Today

Lord, please help me to live soberly and to invest not only in the present, but also in the eternity that is to come. I don't want to be among those who lived only for the present and therefore suffered loss because they forgot to invest in Heaven. Teach me how to manage and increase the material possessions You have given me so that I can use them to increase my wealth in Heaven. I am grateful for the things I own, but I am more thankful for the souls who are in Heaven because I used my resources to invest in eternity. Help me to use my life wisely and to live as I ought to live in light of eternity. I pray this in Jesus' name!

Seeing then that all these things shall be dissolved, what manner of persons ought ye to be in all holy conversation and godliness?

2 Peter 3:11

My Confession for Today

I confess that I am living for eternity. Although I thank God for all the possessions He has given me, I realize that all of these are temporary blessings. The greatest investment I can make is in my spiritual future, so in addition to managing the physical blessings God has given me, I am a wise investor in my eternal destiny. I spend the bulk of my time, my money, my talents, and my energies on things that will further God's Kingdom and outlast this world. I declare this by faith in Jesus' name!

Permanently Set Free

(For the weapons of our warfare are not carnal, but mighty through God to the pulling down of strong holds;) Casting down imaginations, and every high thing that exalteth itself against the knowledge of God, and bringing into captivity every thought to the obedience of Christ;

2 Corinthians 10:4,5

My Prayer for Today

Lord, I realize that the enemy has been attempting to control my self-worth and my self-image through lies that have been operating in my mind and emotions for a very long time. Because I allowed the devil access to my thought life in times past, I have been like a hostage held captive in an inner prison. I can see now how others have tried to help me, but they haven't been able to break through the strong walls of these mental lies that have surrounded my thinking. So today I am turning to You, Holy Spirit. I ask You for help as I learn to utilize the weapons of my warfare that You have supplied. Please help me uproot, tear down, and permanently walk free of every mental lie of the enemy for the rest of my life! I pray this in Jesus' name!

My Confession for Today

I confess that I will no longer permit the devil to have a foothold in my mind and emotions. I am employing the use of the power of God, the weapons of the Holy Spirit, and the name of Jesus Christ, and I command the devil to withdraw his lies from my mind and emotions and to flee from me! The enemy has no right to operate inside my mind, and I refuse to allow his operation in my soul to continue. I will believe right, think right, and renew my mind daily with the Word of God. I am now permanently set free from lies that have controlled me for such a long time. From this moment forward, I am dominated by the truth of God's Word. Lies that have held me captive for so long have no more power over me! I declare this by faith in Jesus' name!

Using Your Lance of Prayer

My Prayer for Today

Lord, I thank You for entrusting me with all the weapons I need to keep the devil defeated in my life. Forgive me for not always taking advantage of the full weaponry You have provided. Prayer is powerful—yet I admit that I have neglected this piece of weaponry in my life. Forgive me for allowing myself to get too busy to make time for prayer. Instead of ignoring this vital piece of weaponry, I want to learn how to use every form of prayer that is available to me so I can stop the devil from making up-close attacks in my life. Thank You for this vital weapon of warfare. Please teach me to use it powerfully, forcefully, and effectively against the works of the devil. I pray this in Jesus' name!

Praying always with all prayer and supplication in the Spirit, and watching thereunto with all perseverance and supplication for all saints.

Ephesians 6:18

My Confession for Today

I confess that prayer is a vital piece of my spiritual weaponry. Because I use this strategic piece of weaponry, I am able to stop the enemy from attacking me from up close. I pray with authority, and that authority gives me the ability to strike the enemy from a distance while maintaining a victorious position in my life. With the lance of prayer at my disposal, I can be sure of absolute and total victory. Although the devil tries to attack me, I overcome each of his attacks by striking him from a distance as I thrust the lance of prayer and supplication into the realm of the spirit. I commit myself to using the lance of prayer and supplication in all its various forms. As I do, I will continually reinforce Jesus Christ's triumphant victory over Satan and gloriously demonstrate Satan's miserable defeat in every area of my life! I declare this by faith in Jesus' name!

Leading Others as a Servant of the Lord

And the servant of the Lord must not strive; but be gentle unto a ll men, apt to teach, patient.

2 Timothy 2:24

My Prayer for Today

First of all, Lord, I thank You for loving me enough to put people over me who were willing to bring correction into my life in the past. Although that correction was difficult to receive, I needed it and it ultimately benefited my life. For this, I am so thankful. Second, I ask You to help me now to be a blessing to those You have placed under my sphere of authority. When I see attitudes in them that need to be corrected, help me know how to approach them in a way that is positive and uplifting. I ask You to give me the wisdom I need to challenge those under my authority to a higher level in every area of their lives. I pray this in Jesus' name!

My Confession for Today

I confess that those under my authority listen to me and submit to my spiritual authority; therefore, I am able to help them grow and mature in the Lord. I accept the fact that bringing correction to people under my sphere of authority is part of my responsibility. As I pray and seek the mind of the Lord, the Holy Spirit shows me how to correct people in love. He teaches me how to help them see what they need to change in their lives and attitudes so they can move up higher in God. I willingly make it my goal to bring the people under my care to a higher level in every area of their lives. I declare this by faith in Jesus' name!

Jesus Is Your Helper

My Prayer for Today

Lord, I admit that I've been feeling pretty lonely in the situation I am facing right now. Even though my friends try to understand, they simply can't comprehend the emotional ordeal I am going through. But I know that You understand everything, Lord, so today I am asking You to step forward and assist me in my hour of need. Please stand at my side to help me, support me, and fill me with a fresh dose of the Holy Spirit's mighty power so I can victoriously overcome in the midst of this challenging trial. I know that with Your Presence and power at my side, I will win this fight of faith that I'm engaged in right now. I pray this in Jesus' name!

At my first answer no man stood with me, but all men forsook me: I pray God that it may not be laid to their charge. Notwithstanding the Lord stood with me, and strengthened me; that by me the preaching might be fully known, and that all the Gentiles might hear: and I was delivered out of the mouth of the lion.

2 Timothy 4:16,17

My Confession for Today

I confess that Jesus loves me and understands me. Even though friends may desert me or fail to understand the dilemma I am facing in my life, Jesus completely comprehends the entire situation. Not only does He understand, but He is also my biggest Helper in my time of need. When I cry out to Jesus in faith, He responds by manifesting His strong Presence at my side. His Presence is with me to assist me, support me, and give me the strength I need to conquer all the attacks that come against my life. With Jesus, I can and will endure everything I face in life! I declare this by faith in Jesus' name!

Testing Your Faith Level

When Jesus then lifted up his eyes, and saw a great company come unto him, he saith unto Philip, Whence shall we buy bread, that these may eat? And this he said to prove him: for he himself knew what he would do.

John 6:5,6

My Prayer for Today

Lord, I thank You for loving me so much that You help me discover the genuine level of my faith before I get into a situation where I seriously need it. To realize my need for improvement now is so much better than to find out when a difficult situation arises that my faith isn't sufficient for the challenge. So I thank You for the tender, loving care You have shown me by placing me in this challenging situation that reveals the true level of my faith. Help me to press forward and to grow in this area of my life. I pray this in Jesus' name!

My Confession for Today

I confess that my faith is growing and getting stronger every day. I am thankful for the situations that have exposed my true faith level, for now I can work on improving the capacity of my faith. I know that faith comes by hearing the Word of God, so I purpose to baptize my spirit and soul in the truth of God's Word until my faith grows to a higher level than I've ever attained before! I want to possess mountain-moving faith, so I determine to press forward with my whole heart and soul toward the goal of increasing the capacity of my faith. I declare this by faith in Jesus' name!

Completely Covered by Your Shield of Faith

My Prayer for Today

Lord, I thank You for giving me a shield of faith that completely covers me from head to toe. I don't have to constantly succumb to the devil's attacks. By holding my shield of faith above all and out in front so that it covers me completely as You intended it to do, I can be protected from the attacks that the enemy would like to wage against me. Forgive me for the times I've let my shield lay at my side while I stayed busy complaining about the devil giving me fits. I realize now that it's up to me to pick up my shield of faith and put it where it belongs. So with Your help, Lord, I am reaching out right now to pick it up, to hold it out front, and to do my part to make sure the enemy has no access to me. I pray this in Jesus' name!

Above all, taking the shield of faith, wherewith ye shall be able to quench all the fiery darts of the wicked.

Ephesians 6:16

My Confession for Today

I confess that God has given me a shield of faith that protects me against the works of the enemy. If I will hold my faith out front—and today I commit myself to doing just that—God's Word guarantees that this mighty shield will thwart the fiery darts that the enemy wants so desperately to throw at me. My shield will cause those darts to bounce off, thereby protecting me from being struck. I will walk with my shield of faith out in front so that it covers me as God intended for it to do. As long as I do that, I can be confident that I will move forward in life without the enemy winning any full-scale attack against me. I declare this by faith in Jesus' name!

Seeking Real Help From God

Is any among you afflicted? let him pray....

James 5:13

My Prayer for Today

Lord, today I am asking You to forgive me for the times I've talked to people about my problems more than I've talked to You. I confess that I have leaned on people more heavily than I have leaned on You when facing difficult situations that required solutions. Now that I realize what I have done, I am making the decision to change the way I respond to challenges. I thank You, Lord, for the friends You have given me whom I can trust and confide in, but I know I will only find my real help and most permanent solutions as a result of being in Your Presence. Therefore, today I purpose to run to You first whenever the problems of life try to assault me. Only after I have received comfort and direction from You, my primary Source of help, will I consider turning to others whom You have given me for support. I pray this in Jesus' name!

My Confession for Today

I confess that I run to the Lord whenever problems try to overwhelm me. He is my High Tower, my Strength, my Hiding Place, and the One in whom I trust. He has never failed me or forsaken me, and I know I can trust in Him. I thank God for the friends He has given me, but they can never take the place that only He has in my life. From this moment forward, I make the decision that before I pour out my heart to people, I will first pour out my heart to Him. I am willing to do whatever He asks and to give up anything He requires so that I may obtain the victory I need in my life. I declare this by faith in Jesus' name!

Overflowing With Joy

*...Is any merry? let
him sing psalms.*

James 5:13

My Prayer for Today

Lord, I needed this encouragement today, and I thank You for speaking to me through Your Word. I do have something to shout about, so I make the decision today to go ahead and let out the joy that is in my heart! I thank You for being a part of my rejoicing and for the great and awesome things You are doing in my life. I pray this in Jesus' name!

My Confession for Today

I confess that I don't need other people with me in order to truly rejoice in the Lord. When I feel the strings of my heart being plucked with joy, I am going to open my mouth and sing it out. When I feel so full of joy that I can't sit still, I am going to throw off my shoes and start dancing before the Lord. When I think I'm going to explode if I can't scream and yell with joy, I'm going to go somewhere where I can yell my head off without worrying about people who might be listening. God gave me emotions so I could rejoice—so I intend to rejoice with all my being whenever I am overflowing with the joy of the Lord! I declare this by faith in Jesus' name!

Praying for the Sick

Is any sick among you? let him call for the elders of the church; and let them pray over him, anointing him with oil in the name of the Lord: And the prayer of faith shall save the sick, and the Lord shall raise him up....

James 5:14,15

My Prayer for Today

Lord, thank You for giving such clear instruction about how the critically ill are to call for the elders of the church to come pray for them. Please help me be an instrument of help to those who are gravely ill. Please alert me to the seriousness of their physical condition. Remind me to urge them to call for the local elders to come pray for them so that they might be restored to health. Help me to urgently press upon them the importance of exercising this God-given right. And, Lord, I ask You to raise them up by Your power so they can live a healthy life. I pray this in Jesus' name!

My Confession for Today

I confess that I am quick to help the gravely ill remember that they have a right to call on the elders of their local church to come anoint them with oil and pray the prayer of faith for their recovery. The moment that the prayer of faith is prayed, God's power will be released—and that power will literally raise up the sick from the bed of affliction and out of the sickness that has disabled them. Jesus purchased healing for all believers. All they have to do is exercise their right to receive their healing by faith, and they will walk free of physical sickness and disease. I declare this by faith in Jesus' name!

The Devil Must Flee

*...Resist the devil,
and he will flee
from you.*

James 4:7

My Prayer for Today

Lord, because You have given me the promises of Your Word and the right to use Your name, I refuse to let the devil bombard my mind any longer. Right now I stand up to resist him, oppose him, and put him on the run. Devil, you will no longer have free access to my mind and emotions, for I am standing up to resist you. You better put on your running shoes, because if you stick around me, I intend to prosecute you with the full authority of God's Word! I tell you to GO in Jesus' name! And, Heavenly Father, I thank You so much for giving me the great privilege of using Your Word and the authority of Jesus' name. I pray this in Jesus' name!

My Confession for Today

I confess that I am not a weakling! I have the power of God, the Word of God, and the name of Jesus Christ at my disposal. When I step into the full authority God has given me, the devil knows that he must flee. I will not submit to the devil's lies. If he tries to stick around and harass me, I will enforce God's authority upon him! That's why I know he will start to flee when I stand up to resist him in Jesus' name. So right now, I am taking charge over my mind and commanding the devil to take flight! I declare this by faith in Jesus' name!

Empowered To Say No to Sin

Dearly beloved, I beseech you as strangers and pilgrims, abstain from fleshly lusts, which war against the soul.

1 Peter 2:11

My Prayer for Today

Lord, I ask You to help me say no to the temptations that are constantly assailing my mind and emotions. There are moments when my flesh screams to participate in sinful behavior. But I know that with the power of Your Spirit working inside me, I can resist and refuse to give in to these sinful impulses. Holy Spirit, I am leaning heavily on You to strengthen me so I can continue to abstain from fleshly lusts that wish to war against my soul and take me captive. I pray this in Jesus' name!

My Confession for Today

I confess that I live like a stranger who is simply passing through this world. God has blessed me and made my journey comfortable, but I never forget that this is only a brief journey in my eternal destiny. When sin cries out for me to participate in its activities, I remind sin and the flesh that I am not a resident of this world and that I therefore do not have the right to enter into its activities. Because the Spirit of God lives in me, I am fully empowered to say no to sin and to remain free from its detrimental effects. I declare this by faith in Jesus' name!

The Genuine Love of a True Friend

My Prayer for Today

Lord, I ask You to please forgive me for the times I've been an unfaithful friend. I know there have been times in my life when I gossiped and talked about people who were supposed to be my close friends. And I didn't stop there. Rather than confess what I did and ask for forgiveness, I tried to cover it up by acting like I hadn't done anything wrong. I am so sorry for what I have done. Please forgive me for lying. Please forgive me for being a phony in my relationships. I don't ever want to do this again, so I ask You to help me walk in truthfulness, integrity, and in genuine agape love. I pray this in Jesus' name!

Let love be without dissimulation....

Romans 12:9

My Confession for Today

I confess that I walk in the agape love of God. I am a sincere, truthful, and dedicated friend. When I say that I love, I genuinely love. I don't talk behind people's backs. I don't gossip. I don't betray the friends God has brought into my life. If I do accidentally say something that is out of order, I quickly go to my friend to confess it and to ask for forgiveness. This truthfulness causes my friends to trust me and to know that I am truly a friend indeed. I declare this by faith in Jesus' name!

Guard Against Evil Influences

*...Abhor that
which is evil;
cleave to that
which is good.*

Romans 12:9

My Prayer for Today

Lord, I ask You to help me be sensitive to the influences I allow in my home and life. I realize that You have given me the responsibility to watch over my life and that I need to be careful about the information and images I allow to pass into my spirit and mind. Please help me recognize the influences that are acceptable and those that are not. When I am quickened in my spirit that what I am watching, reading, or hearing is unprofitable, give me the strength of will to turn it off, lay it down, or walk away from it. I pray this in Jesus' name!

My Confession for Today

I confess that I carefully guard what goes into my spirit and my mind because God has given me the responsibility to do so. Therefore, I will not permit any evil garbage into the domain of my life. By keeping my mind free of evil influences, I will protect my life and stop the devil from many of the attacks he would like to launch against me. I refuse to open the door and invite the enemy in by watching or listening to the wrong things. Instead, I will turn my attention to those influences that are good and profitable for me. I am going to put my whole heart and soul into meditating on that which will enrich my life and take me to a higher level. I declare this by faith in Jesus' name!

Be Affectionate to One Another

My Prayer for Today

Lord, I thank You for the incredible friendships You have placed in my life. I am immeasurably blessed to have such loving, faithful, and true relationships. When I think of all the people who live such lonely lives, it makes me want to stop and express my gratefulness to You for placing such precious people in my life. Lord, I also ask You to please help me see those who need to be loved so I can include them as a part of my life. I want to give to others the love and support that I have received. Holy Spirit, help me to start doing this today. I pray this in Jesus' name!

Be kindly affectioned one to another with brotherly love; in honour preferring one another.

Romans 12:10

My Confession for Today

I confess that God has given me a host of godly relationships. I am blessed with genuine friends who love me like family; who treat me like a brother (or sister); and who will walk in covenant with me for many years to come. This is God's will for my life. I will not be isolated or live in a way that is disconnected from God's family; rather, I will continually look for ways to grow closer and closer to His family. Also, just as God is blessing me with precious friends, I believe He is teaching me how to be a better friend to those who are near me. I declare this by faith in Jesus' name!

Enthusiastic About Jesus

That ye be not slothful, but followers of them who through faith and patience inherit the promises.

Hebrews 6:12

My Prayer for Today

Lord, I am very convicted by Your Word. I don't want to allow any area of my life to be a bad testimony of who Jesus is. Therefore, I am asking You to open my eyes and show me those areas of my life that need to come up to a higher level. Please forgive me for being tolerant of low standards that are not compatible with the excellence of Jesus' wonderful name. Starting today, I want to move up higher. Holy Spirit, please help me as I start taking steps toward making serious changes in my life, my attitude, and my actions. I pray this in Jesus' name!

My Confession for Today

I confess that I will no longer be satisfied with living a low-level existence. God has something great planned for me, and I have made the decision to abandon the negligent attitudes that have dominated my life. Jesus has called me to be a servant who brings Him pleasure, so that is what I am going to do. I will not allow laziness or apathy to be a part of me any longer. I intend to start projecting continual enthusiasm and excitement about what Jesus has asked me to do. I declare this by faith in Jesus' name!

Meeting the Needs of Other Believers

*Distributing to
the necessity
of saints....*

Romans 12:13

My Prayer for Today

Lord, especially at this time of the year, I want to look beyond my own challenges and problems to see what I can do to meet the needs of brothers and sisters whose situations are more serious than mine. I don't want to be so self-focused on my own needs that I forget that there are others who are struggling more seriously than I am. In fact, even though I have been facing difficult times, I know that my life is much more blessed than some of my brothers and sisters who live in other parts of the world. Lord, please help me to always be grateful for what I have. Guide me as I seek to distribute a portion of my finances and make a difference in someone else's life. And please, Lord, multiply this seed that I am sowing by faith so that it comes back to meet the needs I am facing in my own life. I pray this in Jesus' name!

My Confession for Today

I boldly declare that I am a giver! I refuse to allow the devil to make me focus so intensely on my own problems that I forget about the needs others are facing. Instead of taking care of only my own needs, I declare that I am going to give a portion of my finances to meet the needs of other believers who are in a more serious condition than I am right now. To the best of my ability, I will give from my resources to make a difference in someone else's life, especially during this holiday season. I also claim the promise of God that what I sow will be multiplied back to me again. I declare this by faith in Jesus' name!

Learning To Be Hospitable

...Given to hospitality.

Romans 12:13

My Prayer for Today

Lord, I ask You to please forgive me for only seeing the needs of my own social circle. The fact is, there are so many people who are in serious need, and I could be doing something to help at least one of them. I am asking You to help me take my eyes off myself and my little circle of friends and to start seeing the needs that are all around me. I don't want to be guilty of helping only those who bring a blessing to my life. I want to be a blessing even to those I don't know and who will never be able to return the favor to me themselves. I pray this in Jesus' name!

My Confession for Today

I confess that I am a blessing to fellow believers who are in need. My heart is open; my home is open; my pocketbook is open; and I am willing and ready for the Lord to use me to help others. I thank God that He can use me to make an impact in other people's lives. I believe that He will bless me for stepping out of my limited little social circle to do a good deed for a fellow believer who really needs a helping hand. And I declare that I won't casually carry out an occasional act of mercy. Instead, I will aggressively pursue the attitude of hospitality until I catch it and become a genuinely hospitable person. I declare this by faith in Jesus' name!

Bless People Who Wrong You

My Prayer for Today

Bless them which persecute you: bless, and curse not.

Romans 12:14

Lord, I want to forgive those who have done so much wrong by speaking lies and nonsense about me. I don't understand why they have spoken those lies, but now people are listening to the garbage they have told about me. Rather than respond in anger and speak a bunch of negative words that won't help anyone, I choose today to speak words of kindness and blessing over those who have tried to hurt me. Lord, I ask You to bless them, change them, help them, and lead them into a higher way of life. In the meantime, I am asking You to use this hurtful situation to bring about needed changes in me. I pray this in Jesus' name!

My Confession for Today

I confess that I don't speak evil words about anyone—not even against those who seek to hurt me and to do harm to my life. My words are powerful, so I select the words I speak very carefully. I choose to bless and to curse not, and I declare that because I have taken this course of action, the strategies that the enemy is trying to use against me will be frustrated and stopped. I declare this by faith in Jesus' name!

Sensitive to What Others Are Going Through

Rejoice with them that do rejoice, and weep with them that weep.

Romans 12:15

My Prayer for Today

Lord, I ask You to help me know how to respond appropriately to those who are around me. When they rejoice, help me put aside my own struggles and problems and enter into rejoicing with them. When people weep and I'm not feeling the pain they feel, help me set aside my own lighthearted mood so I can be the kind of friend they need in that vulnerable moment. Holy Spirit, I know You can teach me how to appropriately respond to the different situations I face in life. So I ask You to start teaching me how to be what I need to be in every type of circumstance. I pray this in Jesus' name!

My Confession for Today

I confess that I am sensitive to the emotional climate around me. When people are rejoicing, I join in and rejoice with them. When people are weeping and feeling brokenhearted, I am careful to show love and compassion to them. Because the Holy Spirit is teaching me how to appropriately respond to the various situations that arise in life, I am becoming more fit to minister to people in any given circumstance. I declare this by faith in Jesus' name!

Keep a Right Attitude Toward People

My Prayer for Today

Lord, thank You for speaking to me today. Forgive me for the times I've acted like I was better than other people. I am sorry for that behavior, and I don't ever want to do it again. I ask You to convict me when I start to act this way and to show me how to quickly change my behavior. I really want to be an example that will make people want to know Jesus, so help me to change any part of my behavior that does not give a proper impression of Your holy character. I pray this in Jesus' name!

Be of the same mind one toward another. Mind not high things, but condescend to men of low estate. Be not wise in your own conceits.

Romans 12:16

My Confession for Today

I confess that I do not have a superior attitude about myself. I have the mind of Christ, and I demonstrate an attitude of love and acceptance to everyone I meet. When people walk away from me, they feel like they have been accepted, embraced, and treated with respect. Every day the Holy Spirit is teaching me more about how to give others a sense of value about themselves. I thank God that an attitude of superiority has no place in me and that each day I am getting better at reaching out to others to benefit and bless their lives. I declare this by faith in Jesus' name!

Let God's Peace Rule in Your Life

*Recompense to no
man evil for evil....*

Romans 12:17

My Prayer for Today

Lord, I thank You for encouraging me to keep my heart free of strife during this extremely busy time of the year. There is so much to do, so many places I have to be, and so many people I need to see. I admit that the demands of this time of year put a lot of stress and strain on me. In the middle of all these activities, I don't want the devil to get the best of me, so I am asking You to fill me with Your peace. Let that divine peace rule me and my emotions so I don't let Satan get the upper hand in any of my relationships during this special time of year. I pray this in Jesus' name!

My Confession for Today

I confess that I am free of strain and stress. My heart is filled with the peace of God, and that wonderful peace is ruling my heart, my mind, and my emotions. I am not quickly angered or offended. I walk in patience and kindness, and I am quick to forgive and to overlook the inappropriate actions of other people. Because God's peace is ruling in my heart, I will remain calm, peaceful, and undisturbed by anything that happens around me during this very busy holiday season. I declare this by faith in Jesus' name!

You Have Jesus as Your High Priest

My Prayer for Today

Lord, I am so thankful that You beckon me to come boldly to Your throne of grace. It is so reassuring to know that You want me to not only come to You, but to speak up and boldly make my needs known. According to Your Word, there is no better time for me to be bold than when I am facing a need, so today I am going to be very bold and tell You what is on my heart and what I need. I thank You that Jesus is my High Priest and that He understands me and everything that affects my life. I pray this in Jesus' name!

Seeing then that we have a great high priest, that is passed into the Heavens, Jesus the Son of God, let us hold fast our profession.

Hebrews 4:14

My Confession for Today

I confess that no one wants me to succeed more than Jesus Himself. He knows the challenges I face as I pursue what He has put in my heart. He knows I will face moments when I am physically tired and mentally exhausted. Jesus understands every single emotion and temptation I will ever face, and He is always right there to provide grace to help me in my time of need. God wants me to be very direct about telling Him when I need help, so today I come boldly before His throne to tell Him about the needs I am facing in my life. I never have to be timid or fearful about telling the Lord exactly what I need because He encourages me to speak up and be bold. I declare this by faith in Jesus' name!

Thank You, Jesus, for Loving Us

Who, being in the form of God, thought it not robbery to be equal with God: But made himself of no reputation, and took upon him the form of a servant, and was made in the likeness of men.

Philippians 2:6,7

My Prayer for Today

Lord, I thank You for loving me so much that You would leave Your realms of majestic glory to come dwell among men. If it had not been for Your great love that compelled You to come and redeem me, today I would still be lost in sin. Because You loved me so much, You were willing to come to this earth and purchase my salvation. You were born as a baby in Bethlehem, yet You always existed, and You came here with a definite plan to save me from an eternity separated from You. Thank You so much for coming, Lord. Thank You for loving me enough to temporarily shed Your glory and become a man so You could pay for my sin and save me to the uttermost! I pray this in Jesus' name!

My Confession for Today

I confess that Jesus Christ is God come in the flesh! Before He was ever born as a baby in Bethlehem, Jesus always existed, for He is God Almighty. His birth in Bethlehem proves how vast His love is for me. He so desired to have me as His child that He was willing to make the ultimate sacrifice. And because He dressed Himself in flesh and lived as a man for thirty-three years, He understands everything I face and every temptation that comes my way. Oh, how wonderful it is to know that Jesus loves me! I declare this by faith in Jesus' name!

The Real Reason for Christmas

My Prayer for Today

Lord, I thank You for coming to earth so You could redeem me. When I think of the extent to which You were willing to go in order to save me, it makes me want to shout, to celebrate, and to cry with thankfulness. You love me so much, and I am so grateful for that love. Without You, I would still be lost and in sin. But because of everything You have done for me, today I am free; my life is blessed; Jesus is my Lord; Heaven is my home; and Satan has no right to control me. I will be eternally thankful to You for everything You did to save me! I pray this in Jesus' name!

And being found in fashion as a man, he humbled himself, and became obedient unto death, even the death of the cross.

Philippians 2:8

My Confession for Today

I confess that Jesus Christ loves me! He demonstrated His love to me by leaving behind Heaven's glory and taking upon Himself human flesh. And He did it for one purpose: so that one day He could go to the Cross and die for me and thus reconcile me unto God. There is no need for me to ever feel unloved or unwanted, because Jesus went the ultimate distance to prove that He loves me! I declare this by faith in Jesus' name!

Giving the Eternal Gift

Wherefore God also hath highly exalted him, and given him a name which is above every name: That at the name of Jesus every knee should bow of things in Heaven, and things in earth, and things under the earth; And that every tongue should confess that Jesus Christ is Lord, to the glory of God the Father.

Philippians 2:9-11

My Prayer for Today

Lord, I ask You to help me to be bold today when I see my family and friends. If I see people who I know are not saved, please give me the boldness I need to speak up and ask them to pray with me to make Jesus the Lord of their lives. I don't want this day to end without taking advantage of any opportunity that arises to present Jesus to someone who needs You and to lead that person in a prayer of salvation. Holy Spirit, I look to You for the wisdom and the boldness I need to be Your instrument in someone else's life on this special day. I pray this in Jesus' name!

My Confession for Today

I confess that I am filled with the Holy Spirit. Right now He is giving me the boldness I need to tell my family and friends about Jesus Christ and His death on the Cross for them. There is no better gift I could give to anyone today than the message of the Gospel, so I am choosing to give an eternal gift in addition to all the other gifts that will be exchanged. The Holy Spirit is helping me recognize opportunities to witness and to pray with people who need to confess Jesus Christ as the Lord of their lives. I declare this by faith in Jesus' name!

The Power of Teamwork

My Prayer for Today

Lord, I want to thank You in advance for bringing me the team members I need to fulfill the vision You have put in my heart. I don't want to run this race by myself. I realize that even though I can do part of my assigned task alone, the greatest results can only be achieved with a team. Help me adjust my thinking so that I can think like a team member. Lead my team and me into a true sense of unity so that maximum power can be released through us to a world that desperately needs Jesus. I pray this in Jesus' name!

For as the body is one, and hath many members, and all the members of that one body, being many, are one body: so also is Christ.

1 Corinthians 12:12

My Confession for Today

I confess that God has made me a part of an awesome team. Every day we are becoming better and better, and as a result of the unity that exists between us, we are achieving more than we ever dreamed. So much power is released as we strive together to reach the common purpose God has given us. In fact, the impossible is possible, and the supernatural seems natural! With the help of the Holy Spirit, strife is removed and harmony is at work as we all reach toward our common, God-given goal. I declare this by faith in Jesus' name!

Faith To Forgive

Take heed to yourselves: If thy brother trespass against thee, rebuke him; and if he repent, forgive him. And if he trespass against thee seven times in a day, and seven times in a day turn again to thee, saying, I repent; thou shalt forgive him. And the apostles said unto the Lord, Increase our faith.

Luke 17:3-5

My Prayer for Today

Lord, thank You for speaking to my heart about getting rid of bitterness, unforgiveness, and offense. I know from experience that these attitudes are a killer to my spiritual life. When I am filled with bitterness and unforgiveness, I become a sour hostage to my memories. When I am consumed with offense, I lose my joy and peace and my relationships with other people are horribly affected. I thank You for giving me all the faith I need to deal with this issue, Lord. Today I am asking You to help me start the process of ripping those foul roots out of the soil of my heart and soul. I pray this in Jesus' name!

My Confession for Today

I confess that I genuinely wish to be set free from bitterness, unforgiveness, and offense. I am weary of the way these poisonous roots have produced their deadly fruit in my life for so long. I am ready to do whatever is required to rip those roots clear out of my heart so they won't be able to resurface in my life again. By the power of the Holy Spirit and the authority God has given me, I repent of these detrimental attitudes that have been killing my joy, stealing my peace, and nullifying my spiritual life. By faith I am walking free from these enemies of my soul. I declare this by faith in Jesus' name!

Faith To Change Your Attitude

My Prayer for Today

Lord, I intend to exercise my God-given authority and to raise my voice to tell these attitudes that they will no longer hound and dominate me! Bitterness, I command you to leave me in Jesus' name! Unforgiveness, I refuse to be bound by you any longer, and I tell you to leave me right now! Offense, I will not be held hostage by you any longer, and I am telling you to flee from me in the name of Jesus! The Lord has redeemed me, and I refuse to allow you to operate in me any longer. I command you to go RIGHT NOW in Jesus' powerful name! I pray this in Jesus' name!

...If ye had faith as a grain of mustard seed, ye might say unto this sycamine tree, Be thou plucked up by the root, and be thou planted in the sea; and it should obey you.

Luke 17:6

My Confession for Today

I confess that I will not tolerate attitudes of bitterness and unforgiveness in my life anymore. I'm not going to just think about how bad these attitudes are and how I need to change. I'm going to lift my voice and speak to them like enemies of my soul that have come to destroy my life and ruin my relationships. I simply will not allow myself to be subjected to these hounding thoughts any longer. I proclaim that I am free of the memories of those who did wrong to me. I forgive them. I choose to let it all go. I am walking completely free from these attitudes and will not be controlled by them from this day forward! I declare this by faith in Jesus' name!

Take Authority Over Your Soul

These things speak, and exhort, and rebuke with all authority.

Titus 2:15

My Prayer for Today

Lord, I thank You that I don't ever have to be stalked and hounded by bitter attitudes and wrong thinking for the rest of my life. With the authority You have given me, I can speak to those attitudes and command them to go! I can speak to my flesh, and it will obey me. Rather than be conquered by my flesh, my negative emotions, and my wrong attitudes, I am asking You to help me rise up to take authority over my soul and clean up the mess that has been made inside my head. I know that with Your help, my whole perspective can change! I pray this in Jesus' name!

My Confession for Today

I confess that it is time for me to rise up and take charge of the situation in my soul. It is my soul, so I am responsible for what happens there. Even if others did wrong to me, I choose to forgive, forget, and permanently walk free. Right now it doesn't matter who is right or wrong. What matters is that I uproot the tree of bitterness before it produces any more deadly fruit in my life. So by faith, I am reaching out to grab hold of the base of that ugly growth. I am gripping it tightly and pulling with all my might to rip those roots right out of my heart! Those old thoughts no longer have a right to operate inside me. They are now dead issues—cast once and for all into the sea where they can't hound me anymore! I declare this by faith in Jesus' name!

Spiritual Rest

My Prayer for Today

Lord, I know that You have been calling out to me, beckoning me to spend time with You. But I've been so busy that I haven't made time in my schedule to come to You. Today I am making the choice to put everything else aside and to make my time with You the top priority in my day. I need Your strength; I need Your fellowship; I need Your tender touch; and I need to hear Your voice. Spirit of God, my schedule is very full, and I need special strength to make it through this busy time. So I am coming to You today to be refreshed so I can carry on! I pray this in Jesus' name!

Come unto me, all ye that labour and are heavy laden, and I will give you rest.

Matthew 11:28

My Confession for Today

I confess that the only way I can remain continually effective is to spend time with the Lord. I will therefore quiet myself from the commotion of life and get into the Presence of Jesus. I will settle down and plan to stay there long enough to get everything I need from Him. Staying in His Presence is not an option! It is my key to remaining steadfast and strong enough to keep on schedule and to stay on track with everything I need to do. The Holy Spirit will release His resurrection power in me, and I will be strengthened, refreshed, recharged, and empowered by God. Then I can get back out there with a fresh perspective and new energy to finish what I've started. I declare this by faith in Jesus' name!

Living by Faith in the Last Days

God hath not given us the spirit of fear; but of power, and of love, and of a sound mind.

2 Timothy 1:7

My Prayer for Today

Lord, as an end-time believer, I need to be filled with faith and not with fear. Help me to fill my heart with Your Word, to stand on Your promises, to follow the leading of the Holy Spirit, and to exercise my faith more than ever before! I know that fear has blurred my thinking in times past, but it will NOT have any place in my life from this day forward! Instead, I release my faith and confidently expect to be a partaker in the last and greatest harvest of souls ever to be reaped for the Kingdom of God. Holy Spirit, help me rise to the occasion as I become an instrument God can use in these last days. I pray this in Jesus' name!

My Confession for Today

I confess that I am filled with faith and not fear, and that I am excited to live in these last days. God has chosen for me to live in some of the most challenging days the world has ever seen, but I will face these times victoriously. He has given me a sound mind, the promises of His Word, and the leadership of His Spirit. Therefore, I will NOT retreat in fear or panic; instead, I am believing to be a part of the mightiest harvest of souls that history has ever seen! I declare this by faith in Jesus' name!

Prayer of Salvation

God loves you—no matter who you are, no matter what your past. God loves you so much that He gave His one and only begotten Son for you. The Bible tells us that "...whoever believes in him shall not perish but have eternal life" (John 3:16 NIV). Jesus laid down His life and rose again so that we could spend eternity with Him in heaven and experience His absolute best on earth. If you would like to receive Jesus into your life, say the following prayer out loud and mean it from your heart.

Heavenly Father, I come to You now, admitting that I am a sinner. Right now I choose to turn away from sin, and I ask You to cleanse me of all unrighteousness. I believe that Your Son, Jesus, died on the cross to take away my sins. I also believe that He rose again from the dead so that I might be forgiven of my sins and made righteous through faith in Him. I call upon the name of Jesus Christ to be the Savior and Lord of my life. Jesus, I choose to follow You and ask that You fill me with the power of the Holy Spirit. I declare that right now, I am a child of God. I am free from sin and full of the righteousness of God. I am saved in Jesus' name. Amen.

If you prayed this prayer to receive Jesus Christ as your Savior for the first time, please contact us on the Web at **www.harrisonhouse.com** to receive a free book.

Or you may write to us at

Harrison House

P.O. Box 35035

Tulsa, Oklahoma 74153

About the Author

Rick Renner is a highly respected leader and teacher within the global Christian community. He ministered widely throughout the United States for many years before answering God's call in 1991 to move his family to the former Soviet Union and plunge into the heart of its newly emerging Church. Following an apostolic call on his life, Rick works alongside his wife Denise to see the Gospel preached, leadership trained, and the Church established throughout the world. Today Rick's broadcast "Good News With Rick Renner" can be seen across the entire former USSR, reaching a potential audience of more than 100 million viewers.

He has distributed hundreds of thousands of teaching audio and videotapes, and his best-selling books have been translated into five major languages—Spanish, Portuguese, French, Russian, and German—as well as multiple other languages that are spoken throughout the former Soviet Union.

Rick is the founder of the Good News Association of Churches and Ministries, through which he assists and strengthens almost 700 churches in the territory of the former Soviet Union. He also pastors the fast-growing Moscow Good News Church, located in the very heart of Moscow, Russia.

Rick Renner Ministries has offices in England, Latvia, Russia, Ukraine, and the United States. Rick, Denise, and their family live in Moscow, Russia.

To contact Rick Renner, please write to:

Rick Renner Ministries
P.O. Box 702040
Tulsa, OK 74170-2040
(918) 496-3213
Or 1-800-RICK-593
E-mail: renner@renner.org
Website: www.renner.org

Please include your prayer requests
and comments when you write.

Other Books by Rick Renner

Seducing Spirits and Doctrines of Demons

Living in the Combat Zone

Merchandising the Anointing

Dressed To Kill

Spiritual Weapons To Defeat the Enemy

Dream Thieves

The Point of No Return

The Dynamic Duo

If You Were God, Would You Choose You?

Ten Guidelines To Help You Achieve Your Long-Awaited PROMOTION!

It's Time for You To Fulfill Your Secret Dreams

Isn't It Time for You To Get Over It?

Sparkling Gems From the Greek Daily Devotional

Additional copies of this book
are available from your local bookstore.

Fast. Easy.
Convenient.

For the latest Harrison House product information and author news, look no further than your computer. All the details on our powerful, life-changing products are just a click away. New releases, E-mail subscriptions, Podcasts, testimonies, monthly specials—find it all in one place. Visit harrisonhouse.com today!

harrisonhouse